Artists Handbooks
Across Europe

The artist's personal guide to travel and work

edited by
David Butler

AN
PUBLICATIONS

AN Publications

AN Publications exists to produce an information service for artists, craftspeople, photographers and those involved in art administration or education. It publishes the monthly magazine Artists Newsletter, Artists Handbooks, directories and Fact Packs. See back of book for details.

Grant aid	This book has been grant aided by the Arts Council and supported by Projects UK through grant-aiding from Northern Arts
Editor	David Butler
Sub-Editor	Sharon McKee
Editorial assistance	Tracey Musgrove
Information research	Emma Lister
Translation	Sandra Davison, Violette Heger, Camilla Kappel, Louise Thayne (Interlingua)
Cover Design	Neil Southern
Design & Layout	Richard Padwick & Neil Southern
Printed	Mayfair Printers, Print House, William Street, Sunderland, SR1 1UI
Copyright	The writers, photographers and AN Publications (Artic Producers Publishing Co Ltd) © 1992
ISBN	0 907730 15 9

**AN Publications is an imprint of
Artic Producers Publishing Co Ltd,
PO Box 23, Sunderland SR4 6DG tel 091 567 3589**

Acknowledgements

With thanks to Michael Collins, John Davis, Anna Engel, Peter Fryer, Helen Ganly, Beryl Graham, David Gross, Paul Ilegens, Susan Jones, Lucien Kayser, Emma Lister, Jan-Erik Lundström, Jill Morgan, Vladimir Muzhesky, Deborah Nash, Joseph Pletsch, Monica Ross, David Solomon, Caroline Taylor, Transmissions Gallery, Sara Worral, Lispeth Wouters.

Cover illustration

The Bridge, felt tapestry by **Michele Angelo Petrone**, who was one of twelve artists at an international artists' symposium, 'Bridge to the East', held in Frankfurt-am-Oder in October 1991. The artists used an industrial carpet-making technique new to them, that was widely used in what was East Germany, but is disappearing as part of the economic effect of German unification. The tapestries form an installation 'A House for Europe' which is touring Europe. The other artists were Serge Borobjow (Russia); Alla Tpofimenkowa (Ukraine); Andrez Owczarek and Leszek Polinewicz (Poland); Esther Sellner, the symposium organiser, and Brittan Steinmanns (Germany); Guido Dobbelaere (Belgium); DonTitchnor (USA); Malcolm Dow, Janet Ludlow and John Edwards (UK). Michele Angelo Petrone is English/Italian.

Contents

About this book

Frontiers are opening, trade barriers are coming down – Europe beckons. *Across Europe* responds to that challenge by asking artists who have already travelled through Europe to talk about their experiences. The message that comes through strongly from all writers is – go and see/come and see.

Across Europe describes travel and work done on a shoestring and often in the face of great adversity. What these artists have had to support them is other artists. What they have gained and given is real cultural exchange. This is not a book celebrating official 'internationalism'. It is a book that heralds the opening of frontiers, demonstrating that artists were there first and offering a welcoming hand for the future.

We tried to represent every country in Europe. Political developments, particularly in 1991, have made this impossible. Byelorussia, Ukraine and Russia are represented as the Commonwealth of Independent States (the former Soviet Union). Latvia, Lithuania and Estonia are not represented at all. Yugoslavia is represented as one country but with reference to the situation current at the beginning of 1992. Albania proved impossible to make any contact in. Turkey and Cyprus are not covered. We will correct all this in future editions and readers of *Artists Newsletter* will also be able to update the book with articles in the magazine from all these countries.

The book is written primarily from a UK perspective, but it can be used by all artists throughout Europe. *Across Europe* deals with 24 countries and has 47 contributors representing a wide range of practice in art, craft and photography. For each country we asked an artist from the UK and an artist from that country to describe what it is like to live and work there. This is backed up with information and contacts.

Specific information on a country is found at the beginning of that chapter and in the chapter. General information is found under 'Contacts and Further Reading' at the end of the book. This is where most of the information on the UK will also be found More detailed information is available as Fact Packs (eg 'Travelling, Working and Selling in the EC') from AN Information (tel 091 567 3589).

All phone numbers have been listed without international or area codes. These codes can be found at the front of any telephone directory – you just need to know the number you are calling and the town and country (for international directory enquiries dial 153).

The European Community (EC), whatever the attitudes of individual states, will be the dominant force in Europe for economic, and therefore political planning, in the near future. Non-member states are eager to join. Member states are uneasy about this, and so are non-European states, particularly the USA. Black artists have justifiable worries about the further marginalisation of non-European cultures in the EC as arts bodies of all kinds, and indeed artists, embrace pan-Europeanism with open arms. The growth of nationalism in Eastern Europe and racism throughout the continent adds to this confusion as to whether Europe offers free cultural exchange for all or only some.

So Europe beckons us but towards a state of flux. And in that flux culture and the arts are fragile elements. The 1957 Treaty of Rome didn't include culture. The Maastricht Treaty, in 1991, for the first time requires the EC to take account of culture. There is a commissioner with specific responsibilities in this field, but they head a department of only 25 staff with a budget of £10m. They are not looking to develop an EC cultural policy but towards encouraging and supporting national and, maybe more importantly for artists, regional development of cultural policies. The grounding of a cultural policy regionally could allow artists to actually participate in policy development, and hence support for their own work, and may provide one means of dealing with 'Eurocentrism'. Direct EC financial support for the arts will probably still come through other areas (eg Regional Development) and often rely heavily on the support of individual commissioners, MEPs or good relations between interested civil servants in local and national and EC government bodies.

The other main pan-European body is the Council of Europe. This has a wider membership than the EC, with signatories from Eastern Europe. It has a greater interest in culture but no political power. The introduction to each chapter identifies whether that country is a member of the EC or the Council of Europe. What that means for individual artists depends very much on the politics of individual states but it will become increasingly important. More important though has to be what artists do for themselves. That is essentially the message of *Across Europe*. What is important about these accounts of Europe is that they are seen through the eyes of artists, describing what it really means for them and their art to be in one particular country.

Austria

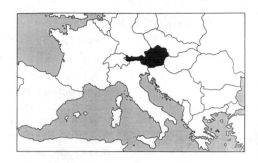

Member of the Council of Europe

LANGUAGE
Official: German
Others spoken: Croat and Slovene speaking minorities
English spoken: extensively, especially centres

CURRENCY
Official: 100 groschen = 1 Austrian Schilling
Convertible or not: yes
Travellers cheques/Eurocheques/credit cards: widely accepted

DOCUMENTS YOU NEED
Holders of full British passport can enter and stay for up to six months (3 months with visitors passport). For information on visas, registration, work permit, residence permit contact: Austrian Embassy, 18 Belgrave Mews West, London SW1X 8HU tel 071 235 3731

AUSTRIAN DTI DESK
OT 3/3c Room 373 tel 071 215 4798/4349

BANKS
Open 7.45-12.30 and 14.15-16.00 Monday to Friday, with variations

POST OFFICES
Open 8.00-12.00 and 14.00-18.00 Monday to Friday, longer hours & some Saturday mornings in centres

BUSINESS HOURS
Monday to Friday 9.00-18.00, Saturday 9.00-12.00 (Saturday afternoon closing and long lunch outside main centres)

ART GALLERIES/MUSEUMS
Often closed on Mondays

PUBLIC HOLIDAYS
Jan 1, Jan 6, Easter weekend, May 1, Aug 15, Oct 26, Nov 1, Dec 8, Dec 25/26

CONTACT IN THE UK
Austrian Institute, 28 Rutland Gate, London SW7 1PQ 071-584-8653
Austrian National Tourist Office, 30 St. George Street, London W1R 0AL tel 071 629 0461

CONTACT ABROAD
British Council, Schenkenstrasse 4, A-1010, Vienna tel 5332626
Ministry of Education, the Arts and Sport, Minoritenplatz 5, 1014 Vienna tel 53120
Embassy/Consulate:
British Embassy, Jauregasse 12, 1030 Vienna tel 7131575. Consulates in Graz, Innsbruck, Salzburg and Bregenz
Chamber of Commerce:
Federal Economic Chamber, Wiedner Hauptstr. 63, 1045 Vienna tel 50105
Artists Associations:
Gewerkshaft Kunst, Medien freie Berufe (artists, musicians, etc) Maria Theresien Str. 11, 1090 Vienna IX tel 343600
Berufsverband Bildender Kunstler Oesterreiches (BVO), obere Donaustr 97/1/63, 1620 Vienna tel 261322
Copyright/moral rights:
DACS initially, tel 071 247 1650. In Austria: VBK Tivoligasse 67/8, A-1120 Vienna tel 8152691

Gerhild Tschachler-Nagy

Writing about what it is like to live and work as an artist in Austria is like trying to find an answer to the question 'where is here?' For some, 'here' is the academy for fine arts in Vienna, the academies for applied arts in Vienna and Linz, and a host of other art schools. For others, 'here' is any place in the world where they find artists who are willing to, and capable of, helping them find their own way. It is also the various organisations, private or public, which provide some kind of networking and promotion – the *Kunstverein* (Artists' Conference), membership of which gives prestige and status, the *Berufsvereinigung bildender Künstler Österreichs,* a kind of trade union which provides a minimum of social security for artists, or the *Initiative Kunsthandwerk* (Crafts Initiative), which essentially provides opportunities for marketing. Beyond that, 'here' is often 'elsewhere'. For reasons cultural and linguistic, it is often Germany. Take, for instance, publishing. With no arts journal published in Austria, you turn to *Neue Keramik (New Ceramic), Kunst und Handwerk (Art and Craft),* or *ART,* all coming out of Germany. But then, 'here' is also the niche individual artists carve out for themselves in their endless struggle to prove their worth.

When I started doing ceramics, 15 years ago, I was too innocent to think much about how I was going to make a living. I soon found out there were neither art galleries nor craft shops which would take ceramic work, so I could sell only through my studio. It provided some solace to think this was what other ceramic artists were also facing. They, like me, had to promote themselves, but there were not very many ceramic artists in Austria at the time. There had always been a handful or so studio potters but the crafts movement of the sixties and seventies never became as widespread here as it did in Britain or the United States. On the other hand, graduates from art schools and academies were mostly trained to become designers and would go into industry rather than compete in the art market, while those who would go independent had mostly been made over in the image of their master teacher.

Not having attended an academy or art school myself has not made it any easier for me to make a living from my work. For a start, I was not trained to follow the current trend of abstraction and formal reduction, nor the revival of art nouveau or the Bauhaus. Secondly, ceramics was not yet fully acknowledged as an art form. To what extent this attitude still prevails was brought home to me when a fine art gallery politely asked me not to put any ceramic vessels on show but rather to do installation work (they had heard I was also known for this). While I do not myself care too much for such philosophical subtleties, I concurred at the time.

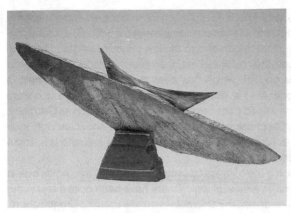

Boat Shape, Gerhild Tschachler-Nagy, **from a cycle of works titled 'La Nave Va'.**

Since then, I have learned not to include functional work in personal shows hosted by fine art galleries, while I see no reason for a gallery not to have functional work as part of its regular program. This also seems to be the policy of Austria's one and only ceramic gallery, Vienna-based Ceramic Art. But can a gallery which specialises in contemporary clay work survive here? Who are the buyers? As the gallery's owner has said, the number of individuals collecting ceramic art has been going up over recent years even if it is still about as small as the number of ceramic artists here. However, smallness cannot sufficiently explain the fact there is no collection of ceramic art in Austria as yet, neither a private nor a public one.

Which brings me back to the fact ceramics has not been fully acknowledged as an art form here. As a consequence, trying to find a gallery willing to take in ceramic works may be a harrowing experience, particularly since there simply are not that many fine art galleries in Austria in the first place.

And once a suitable gallery has been found, who says they will like what they see? Hence the aspiring artist might want to consider teaching. Art is taught in Austrian schools at many levels. Unlike other countries, however, the Austrian school system does not know the concept of the artist-in-residence. What they require is some formal training as a teacher. Left with a choice between a university degree or a degree from a teacher training college, this will cost you from three to five years of your life. There is also teaching outside the national education system. Courses in the arts are offered by community colleges or as extension classes. With the growth of the tourist industry, there is a chance to offer summer classes and workshops, which means reaching mostly people who have at best an amateurish interest in the arts or who think of it as a way to spend a rainy day. I have taught summer courses for many years, and I am happy to say in the case of the summer courses offered in Moosburg, Carinthia, I have been able to instil a certain degree of seriousness and professionalism.

If it is merely a matter of financial survival, selling at craft fairs is an option, particularly since their numbers have gone up dramatically. There is, however, no jurying at these fairs, which rather discourages

Austria

Galerie Ceramic Arts,
Nussdorfer Strasse 53,
1090 Vienna
tel 343396

**Initiative
Kunsthandwerk**
(Crafts Initiative),
Färberplatz, 8010 Graz

**Hochschule für
Industrielle
Gestaltung** (School of
Industrial Design),
Hauptplatz 8, 4020 Linz
tel 785173

Neue Galerie (New
Gallery), Sackstrasse
16, 8010 Graz

**Berufsvereinigung
Bildender Künstler
Österreichs** (Austrian
Association of Careers
Advisers in Art), 13
Schloss Schönbrunn,
Ostseite, 1030 Vienna;
Kaigasse 6, 5020
Salzburg and
Feldkirchnerstrasse,
9020 Klagenfurt;
Landstrasse
(Ursulinenbau), 4020
Linz

**Kunstverein für
Kärnten** (Association
of Art for Carinthia),
Goethepark 1, 9020
Klagenfurt tel 55338

Kunst Gewerbeverein
(Association of
Applied Arts),
Landhaus G 7, 8010
Graz tel 830605

professional artists. This is not so much for reasons of artistic snobbery (although I would not rule this out completely) but because professional artists cannot afford to conform to the low prices of amateur artists in case it ruins both their business and their good reputation. For ceramic artists there is one fair which has been doing well, which is held in Gmunden, Upper Austria, every July. Professional and amateur potters from Austria, as well as from neighbouring countries such as Germany, Hungary and Czechoslovakia, come together to show and sell their wares. As far as I can tell, the fair has sustained the precarious balance between art and craft.

Sustaining the balance between art and craft also holds true in equal opportunities affairs, of which there have been quite a few in the past. I myself was invited to participate in a show titled 'Konfrontationen', organised by the women's section of the student union at the University of Vienna *(Österreichische Hochschülerschaft)* and sponsored by various organisations, both private and public. While I do see the merits of attempts to promote equal opportunities, the experience also taught me that being marked 'woman artist' can be a liability.

There are equally paradoxes and dilemmas in being married and having a daughter. Even if some of the worst existential fears are removed, guilt and moral scruples remain. How much time spent doing art is acceptable? How much of the family income can you use to build your business? Undoubtedly it is an asset not to have to conform to mainstream art, not to have to peddle your wares to the galleries, all of which means you have to live up to someone else's expectations. To a certain extent, I can afford to be asked to show my work. I can also afford to develop 'unsaleable' work, such as installations, which if you are lucky may be purchased by a museum or a public gallery. But then, I also take in commissioned work to make ends meet. This is absolutely essential since there is a heavy mortgage on the studio I built for myself some five years ago. Despite this, I infinitely prefer the present arrangement to the time when I was renting a run-down shed in a backyard. Being self-employed and often having to sell from the studio, even the look of the place matters. Consequently, I divided the studio building (which totals about 80 square metres, ie some 900 square feet) into a work space and a gallery space. I also have a work area, partly covered, around the studio building, which I use as a storage area and firing place. I like the set up but I do feel running a studio in Austria has many disadvantages. For instance, most of the raw materials I use have to be imported. There is no stoneware from Austrian pits. Technical equipment, machinery, glazes, and other materials are not manufactured in Austria. Even if membership in the European Community does away with tariffs and customs duties, the high cost of transportation will remain.

Dave Miller

I lived in Austria between December 1989 and December 1991. I had just graduated from MA Graphic Design in the UK and wanted to move to somewhere more exotic. My girlfriend was Austrian, living in Vienna, so that was the obvious choice. Vienna is a large capital city (about one million inhabitants) with a rich and varied cultural past.

At the time, going to Vienna felt an irresponsible thing to do. I was turning my back on my education and taking a risk to try to live and work in a culture I had little knowledge of. But I also felt a sense of freedom in that I didn't have to step into a predefined role (which I would have done in the UK) and I knew there was a positive side to having little control over my fate, in that it can bring unexpected opportunities.

I aimed to split my time: to work as a graphic designer and artist, concentrating in both activities on multimedia and the electronic arts. The graphic design work would be my immediate means of survival – the idea of trying to exist just as an artist, in a foreign land, with no previous experience or reputation was too much for me to consider.

Before leaving the UK I wrote many letters to Viennese computer/ video companies and organisations. The overseas business department of Liverpool City Library was very useful for addresses.

The official side of life in Austria was complicated and bureaucratic. I was never told how to make my stay in Austria official, I learned mostly by word of mouth; there was no information on what to do, and no organisations to give advice. It was ironic and frustrating that the least helpful people were the police, with whom I was trying to make myself official. The British Consulate in Vienna even didn't know how to help me (but maybe it's worth talking to the Austrian Embassy in London).

The first thing I did was register with the local police. This is standard practice in Austria – when anyone moves to a new address they must do this. This entitled me to stay as a visitor for three months. To stay longer, I needed a visa. This meant applying to the *Fremdenpolizei* (special police for foreigners). My understanding is that to get a visa you need either to have a work permit, a tax number, or be able to show enough savings to support yourself for a long time. With membership of the EC getting closer for Austria it's getting easier for British citizens to get visas.

After a couple of months I found freelance graphic design work. I hired a tax advisor (Austrian tax law is complicated and it's best to do this) who got me a tax number, which I presented to the police. They gave me a visa for six months; it cost me about £40. Later I took a permanent job, and this entitled me to a work permit; then when I got my next visa, it was valid for a year. Each time, a visa costs about £40.

Decide, Dave Miller**, computer generated video.**

Finding work in Vienna was difficult at first. I must have contacted 500 companies and organisations without success. My main source of addresses were the local Yellow Pages and adverts in the local daily papers. Eventually I found an essential book *Creative Productions* published by Falter Press, which lists all the commercial creative people, companies and organisations in Austria.

Probably my biggest obstacle to finding work was my minimal knowledge of German: I spoke no German when I first arrived, and as most people spoke good English (or wanted to practice their English) I only learned slowly. Certainly being English often worked to my advantage, as I was a novelty and people were interested in meeting me. Austrians generally like the British and they have a good opinion of British art and culture. Creatively I know I missed a lot by not learning the language earlier.

I used part of my flat as a studio. I couldn't afford to rent a separate studio, they are hard to find in Vienna and often expensive. Flat rents are generally the same as in London, but often you have to pay money for the 'key'. This is an illegal system where you pay the previous tenant in order that you can have the flat. You get it back when you leave, as the next tenant pays you, but it's often as much as £5,000.

Medienwerkstatt (Media Workshop), Neubaugasse 40a, 1070 Vienna, tel 963667. This is a non profit centre for alternative video. It has a video library, regular screenings, training courses and seminars, rental equipment, and full editing facilities.

Hochschule fur Angewandte Kunst (The Art School), Oskar Kokoschka Platz 2, 1010 Vienna, tel 711110.

Vienna has an international image of being very expensive, but this is only the tourist view. I found the cost of daily living the same as the UK, though special items such as art materials were expensive. Salaries and pay are slightly lower than in the UK. I looked for part-time work in the art school, but had no success. Tracking down the staff at the Art School *(Hochschule fur Angewandte Kunst)* proved very difficult. I wrote many times, but got no reply. In the end I gave up trying.

The higher education system is quite different to the UK. Anyone with a *Matura* (the equivalent of 'A' levels) can study over a much longer time than here, and courses are much less structured. Students must finance themselves, there are few grants, though all fees are paid by the state. Many students complain the standard of education is low and they lack facilities and staff.

To produce my own artistic work, I dealt mostly with my own commercial contacts. Through my work I came across many people who

Galerie Grita Insam, Koellnerhofgasse 6, 1010 Vienna, tel 525330. Gallery which exhibits art and advanced technology works video, multimedia installations.

Austrian Computer Graphics Association (ACGA), Karlsplatz 13/180, 1040 Vienna.

Ars Electronica Brucknerhaus, Untere Donaulaende 7, 4010 Linz, tel 275225 International annual electronic arts festival.

Falter Weekly what's-on in the art scene magazine for Austria. Published by the Falter Press, Marc Aurel Strasse, 1010 Vienna.

were interested in the electronic arts and in working with me. We shared equipment and helped each other on various projects – commercial and artistic. Working in the electronic arts is expensive in Austria (equipment is about 30% more expensive than in the UK) and so sharing resources was essential. At times we felt as though we were working in the worst place in Europe for this subject; technology and technological culture seemed to come from the West. With the borders between Austria and Eastern Europe being removed, I expected a strong cultural influence to come into Vienna, particularly from Budapest and Prague but it hasn't happened so far – perhaps the Austrian people aren't ready yet?

We worked independently of any arts scene in Vienna; somehow we felt excluded and were forced into this role. I found the computer arts scene dominated by those who have been through, and work at, the art school. If you don't get in with them, you're excluded from most of the activity. This may sound cynical, but I think if you come to Vienna as an already established artist, with a name, then many doors will be opened for you.

I contacted a number of galleries, which were friendly and interested in my work. At least one gallery specialises in electronic art. There are about forty galleries in Vienna, and good opportunities for international artists to show their work.

We entered work for two electronic arts festivals in Austria, and though we won no prizes, it was good to participate. There is definitely a growing interest in Austria in the electronic arts, as can be seen from the popularity of these types of festivals. The *Ars Electronica,* held in Linz each year, is one of the major international electronic art festivals.

Certainly I enjoyed the experience of living and working as an artist in Vienna. I learned a lot from such a different and interesting culture, and I'm glad that I did it. However I often felt excluded, and discriminated against as a foreigner, without the rights and opportunities of an Austrian. Just a quick scan of the Vienna evening papers for the classified ads tells the story – many advertisements for flats stipulate that foreigners need not apply!

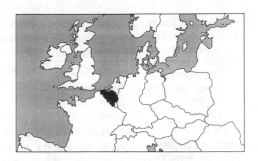

Belgium

Member of the Council of Europe and the EC

LANGUAGE
Official: French, Dutch (Flemish) and German
English spoken: extensively

CURRENCY
Official: 100 centimes = 1 Belgian Franc
Convertible or not: yes
Travellers cheques/Eurocheques/credit cards:
widely accepted

DOCUMENTS YOU NEED
For information contact: Belgian Embassy, 103-105
Eaton Square, London SW1W 9AB tel 071 235
5422

BELGIAN DTI DESK
OT 3/3a Room 369 tel 071 215 4709/5486/4794

BANKS
Open 9.00-12.00 to 14.00-16.00 Monday to Friday
(open lunchtime and Saturday morning in main
centres)

POST OFFICES
Monday to Friday 9.00-17.00; Saturday 9.00-12.00
in some main centres

BUSINESS HOURS
9.00-18.00; some close for two hours at midday
but stay open until 20.00; Friday some may be
open until 21.00 and some not open at all Monday
morning – shorter hours on Saturdays

ART GALLERIES/MUSEUMS
Usually closed Mondays and open 9.00-16.00

PUBLIC HOLIDAYS
Jan 1, Easter weekend, May 1, Ascension, Whit
Monday, Aug 15, Nov 1, Nov 11, Nov 15, Dec 25/
26

CONTACT IN THE UK
Belgian National Tourist Office, Premier House, 2
Gayton Rd, Harrow HA1 2XV tel 081 861 3300

CONTACT ABROAD
British Council, Britannia House, 30 rue Joseph II,
1040 Brussels tel 2193600
Ministry of the Interior and for the Modernisation of
Public Services and National Scientific and Cultural
Institutions, 94 rue Royale, 1000 Brussels
tel 2108411
Chamber of Commerce:
Chamber of Commerce Bruxelles, 500 ave Louise,
1050 Brussels tel 6485002; also in all major towns
Embassy/Consulate:
British Embassy, Britannia House, 28 rue Joseph II,
Brussels 1040 tel 2179000. Consulates in Antwerp,
Liege
Artists Associations:
VPK, Vlaanderenstraat 3, 2000 Brussels
Syndicat Cheretiers des Communication et de la
Culture (inc. cultural workers) 26 ave d'Auderghem,
1040 Brussels tel 2387211
Centrum voor Artistieke Confrontatie, Hoogpoort 50,
9000 Gent tel 91330324
Copyright/moral rights:
DACS initially tel 071 247 1650. In Belgium SABAM
75-77 rue d'Arlon, 1040 Brussels tel 2302660

Goele De Bruyn

How do I make a living? I often wonder about this question myself. While I was studying at the Antwerp Academy, I had several jobs. That situation has not changed much. I do some teaching, part-time, an evening course for older amateurs, and at weekends I teach children. I also manage to sell some paintings at fairly good prices. Teaching opportunities for artists are limited, like everywhere. Or maybe there are too many applicants. Most of them try harder than I do and devote most of their time to it. Many art students simply don't want to do anything else. You can teach drawing on secondary school level or in an evening academy, like I do. Evening academies are flourishing and expanding. Antwerp has at least ten of them, where people of all ages mostly come to learn drawing, painting, sculpture, printmaking or photography.

I had seven years of art education. First, I went to the Royal Academy of Fine Art of Antwerp to study in the painting department. The Antwerp Academy has a reputation for being rather old-fashioned. Other academies in Belgium like the Royal Academy of Ghent or the St Luke Institute in Brussels are more tuned into contemporary art. The training I got was very formal and technical (drawing the nude twice a week for four years, painting still lifes, and so on). The meaning or function of art was not much discussed, except in the theoretical courses, but there was no link at all between theory and practice. I did not mind because I always liked drawing. It was very quiet and even relaxing, you were just supposed to concentrate on your task, finish it and start it over again. I understood this objective and academic kind of training is becoming very rare in Europe and at times I even felt somewhat ridiculous. Maybe what got me through was I developed an individual approach. After finishing my studies, I was selected by a jury for the National Higher Institute, a kind of post-graduate study in an individual studio at the Royal Academy, which lasts for three years. There I had ample opportunity to work freely.

I am painting almost daily in my own studio. I already had this studio during my stay at the Higher Institute, because I wanted to continue working during weekends and other times when the academy was closed. It is a large one and the rent is only 3000BEF or about £50 a month, which is really cheap, even for Antwerp (rents have gone up recently, and fast). There is no heating and very little accommodation, but it is a very good place to work and I can manage easily. As long as I can keep this studio, no problem will arise.

My art is not mainstream in a Belgian context, but this doesn't mean much. Contemporary art in Belgium is influenced a great deal by the work of Magritte and Marcel Broodthaers. I like these artists very much and I like their 'offspring' too (painters like Narcisse Tordoir, Wim

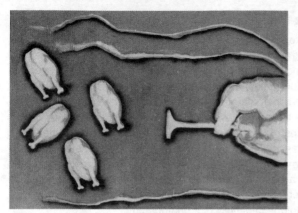

Untitled, Goele De Bruyn, **1991.**
205x150cm.

Delvoye and Walter Swennen, sculptors like Patrick Van Caeckenbergh, and others). They are witty and inventive. Nevertheless, I feel to have more affinity with painters like Milan Kunc, Peter Angermann and Jan Knap of the Düsseldorf *Gruppe Normal*. Also, I admire contemp-orary Russian painters like Komar and Melamid or Bulatov. I paint images which are very clear and open, without bothering too much about meaning. I don't feel I need a theory or an intellectual back-up.

Belgium is certainly not the best country for an artist to live in, although things have changed for the better, in recent years. The government is spending very little and sponsoring remains limited. Museums and cultural centres are very poor. They cannot even afford to buy one expensive artwork a year. So, a young artist in Belgium is not relying on the government much. On the other hand, private collectors often spend a lot, but not necessarily on Belgian art. In some other countries, they seem mostly interested in the art of their own people. Especially in France. Frence artists' go on thinking that Paris is the centre of the universe. For an artist, working in a small country means being international. This could even be an advantage in the long run.

Over the last years, I have had several exhibitions. One was in an Antwerp Cultural Centre, another in the Antwerp gallery *Parbleu,* and yet another in Prague, together with young artists from England and Germany. I don't think I will have many difficulties in finding other opportunities, as long as I can go on being productive and keeping a level of quality in accordance with my own values. But exhibiting in itself does not mean so much. Wherever you go, the public will always remain limited. The point is to find a gallery which takes a real interest in your work and is willing to defend it for some time, even if sales are not excellent. People often say money is corrupting art everywhere, because the financial possibilities are too exciting. But in my view, all art is somehow sincere, whatever its financial success. Nobody can fool the public for a long time. Anyhow, I go on thinking some people will appreciate my paintings, although I have little explanation to offer.

Belinda Swingler

When we first heard about the arts in Belgium, it was through some friends who were already teaching over there. We decided one holiday about twelve years ago to visit them and their English-speaking school.

Several years later, two jobs were advertised at this school, in the posts both my husband and I were qualified to teach. With such a coincidence, fate was with us and a month later we started the big move from England.

Help with settling in came from our employers, the school. We found a very useful magazine, in English, ideal for newcomers, called *Living in Belgium and Luxembourg*. A similar new magazine has been published *The Newcomer* but it is not as detailed as the former magazine.

Between us we had smatterings of French and German, useful in the right places. German is the third official language here. As we live in the province of Brabant, we have heard some unusual stories. One friend used his best school French, to find himself ignored. He was annoyed, he cursed aloud in English and, surprisingly, got a reply in very good English from the Belgian, they were in a Flemish/Vlaams area. This type of English reaction is not recommended as it does not improve the United Kingdom's international relations.

An unforeseen cost we had not budgeted for was the two months' rent, required as a guarantee. This is held in a blocked bank account which can only be released by the landlord. Additionally one month's rent is paid in advance. These rental contracts are normally for three, six, or nine years.

Our small apartment had a shared attic, a wonderful summer studio but uninsulated and freezing in winter. Then I worked in our living room, on small coloured porcelain pieces. I was teaching full-time, so my own work progressed slowly.

After several years in Belgium, we had to make some big decisions. We liked the country, we wanted our own house with studio space. Not being temporary residents we were paying over half our earnings in tax. Also our rent was 'lost money' and we could deduct part of the mortgage interest from our tax bills.

In an auction, my husband was lucky and we bought our present home, which was without many facilities. It took us all our spare time over two years to convert half the house into a home. The studio area in the barn would be delayed until we had enough capital.

As we live in a Vlaams-speaking commune, I am referring to their organisations. The Francophone system may in some matters be similar but in no way do these systems mirror each other.

Belgium

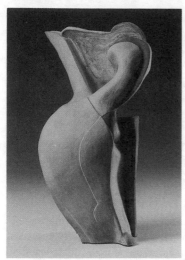

Coalite Boom. Belinda Swingler.
Stoneware clay with coloured oxides.
Photo: Charles Swingler.

Living in Belgium and Luxembourg, Insight Publications SA, 35, Av. des Erables, 1640 Brussels tel 3582340

The Newcomer, Ackroyd Publications SA, Avenue Molière 329, 1060 Brussels tel 3439909

Ministerie van de Vlaamse Gemeenschap (Ministry for the Flemish Community, services in Plastic/ Design Arts and Museums), Dienst Beeldende Kunst en Musea, Koloiënstraat 29 - 31, 1000 Brussels

Vlaams Instituut voor het Zelfstandig

Professional artists can be trained in two ways, academies or universities. They can now obtain funding and advice from two different parts of the government: the Department of Welfare and Arts Administration, and the Department of Economic Affairs.

The former department is older and plans to deal mainly with the image (visual) arts, but it still supplies grants, prizes, etc for the plastic arts. The latter department supports the technical arts, design, and plastic arts which have recently been amalgamated under the *Vlaams Instituut voor het Zelfstandig Ondernmen*, (VIZO).

Young people who have finished their education for one or more years can attain help from VIZO. It's main aims are to help with technical information and problems and also with the theory of economic practice, so enabling them to make a living from their creations. VIZO is a healthy sign of change, in aesthetic and creative training.

The trained British artists around Brussels are mainly the wives of businessmen, some join the local commune's part-time courses. However, in Belgium many of them have found problems in finding a market for their work, since the general public do not respond in the same way to the creative crafts as they do in the Netherlands or Germany. Few Belgian artists can live solely from their own artistic creations, most have a second job. Recently, an English craftsman tried to set up his business here, but he too discovered a bland market and the paperwork was too time-consuming, so he left.

Belgium utilises numerous magazines from its neighbours. At present there are only a few fine arts magazines published here, eg *Artfactum* (Artifacts), a bimonthly, *De Witte Raaf* (The White Raven), a quarterly. Antwerp's Cultural Centre probably holds the most comprehensive list of magazines and with an appointment you can browse through them before you purchase any.

Ceramic materials are readily available, but most are imported from the Netherlands, UK, and Germany. A few natural sources of earthenware clay occur in Belgium. Now I am teaching part-time, I am exploring the qualities of these different clays in my own work. There are three different categories in my work: architectural relief panels, thrown, and sculptural. A couple of the latter pieces have parallels with the Belgian ceramicists' exploratory techniques. My present temporary studio is cramped, so I am working on some small, abstract, sculptural

Ondernmen (Flemish Institute foor Advice on Self-Employment), (VIZO), ORION, Bischoffsheimlaan 23 - 25, 1000 Brussels

Culturee Centrum Berchem (Antwerp's Cultural Centre), Driekoningstraat 126, 2600 Antwerp tel 2395908

commissions. I am interested in developing the theme of conservation in my sculptures. Apparently I'm still capable of a 'very English style'!

At the end of this year, hopefully the barn conversion will be completed. I will then be able to progress with a commissioned relief panel and continue running adult classes in ceramics again, as I enjoyed them greatly in the past.

Bulgaria

LANGUAGE
Official: Bulgarian (written in Cryllic alphabet but use of Latin alphabet increasing)
Others spoken: number of minority languages including Turkish and Macedonian
English spoken: in main cities and tourist centres.

CURRENCY
Official: 100 stotinki (stotinka) = 1 lev
Others used: Dollars and other hard currency
Convertible or not: yes
Travellers cheques/Eurocheques/credit cards: larger stores in tourist centres, use is increasing but still not widely accepted.

DOCUMENTS YOU NEED
For information on visa, work and residence permits contact: Consular Division, Bulgarian Embassy, 186-188, Queen's Gate, London SW7 5HL tel 071 584 9400

BULGARIAN DTI DESK
OT 3/5d Room 316 tel 071 215 5673/4735

BANKS
Open Monday to Friday 8.00-12.00 and 13.00-17.00 (New monetary, credit and banking systems part of current changes)

POST OFFICES
Open Monday to Saturday 8.30-17.00

BUSINESS HOURS
Sofia 9.00-19.00 elsewhere 8.00-13.00 & 16.00-19.00

ART GALLERIES/MUSEUMS
Usually closed Monday or Tuesday – open 10.00-18.30

PUBLIC HOLIDAYS
Jan 1, Mar 3, Easter Monday, May 1, May 24, Sep 9, Dec 25

CONTACT IN THE UK
British Bulgarian Friendship Society, Finsbury Library, 245 St. John's St, London EC1V 4NB.
Bulgarian National Tourist Office, 18 Princess Street, London W1R 7RE tel 071 499 6988

CONTACT ABROAD
British Council, 7 Todor Strashimirov, 1504 Sofia tel 463346
Minster of Culture, Council of Ministers, Blvd. Dendukov 1, Sofia tel 8691
Ministry of Education, Blvd. A. Stamboliiski 18, 1000 Sofia tel 8481
Chamber of Commerce:
Blvd. A. Stamboliiski 11a, 1000 Sofia tel 872631
Embassy/Consulate:
British Embassy, Boulevard Marshal Tolbukhin 65-67, Sofia tel 885361/2
Artists Association:
Union of Bulgarian Artists, c/o Union of Workers in Cultural Institutions, Zhadanov St. 7, Sofia
Copyright/moral rights:
No Bulgarian organisation noted, try Design & Artists Copyright Society (DACS), St. Mary's Clergy House, 2 Whitechurch Lane, London E1 7QR tel 071 247 1650

Nedko Solakov

I am living and working as a free artist in Sofia. Before 1986 I lived in my native town of Gabrovo (by the way this is Christo's birthplace as well).

My studio in Sofia is too small, but it could be worse of course. I like to work there, to make my objects, polyptychs, books. This is my sacred space. In the days of the total crisis in my country, my studio is the only place where I could say 'I am here and three metres around me I have my own aura'. Poetic, don't you think?

Now I am here, in the studio, and I am trying to find the answer to the question why a foreign artist, or people connected with art, would want to visit my country? Difficult question. Bulgaria is in Europe, but very often people from the West don't know where exactly it is situated in Arabia, around Turkey or Albania?

So, I would simply say to you 'Come here, visit Bulgaria!'

First of all, you have to see the main historic and cultural sites. The Crypt in the Alexander Nevsky Cathedral with an excellent collection of icons; the National Historic Museum (both in Sofia); the monasteries in Rila, Bachkovo, Arbanassi, Rojen, Trojan; the old towns of Plovdiv, Turnovo, Koprivstiza, Melnik, Bojenzi, and learn a lot more about Bulgarian art and Bulgaria's people. Unfortunately it is not so easy to travel around Bulgaria, but it can be romantic in many ways.

If you want to work here as an artist, you could do that as well. You can rent a studio, it shouldn't be too expensive – for you, not Bulgarian artists! But there are still problems with artists' materials. I recommend you bring with you everything you need. There are two or three shops here where you could find Bulgarian-made artists' materials and maybe one offering brand name materials such as Rembrandt, Rowney, Pelican, etc. The addresses I could give are not reliable because everything is changing fast in Bulgaria. It is easier to ask somebody once you get here. The people are very friendly – right now they are a little bit nervous, but you will be more than welcome everywhere you go.

Maybe I am lucky, but until this moment my family and I have lived only from the sales of my works. Not the objects and polyptychs though. I used to sell pictures and drawings from my first period, which was more acceptable for the audience. Now the situation is more unfavourable. The state, the main buyer in the totalitarian past, has no money for art anymore. There are rich people (growing in numbers day after day), but their tastes, like with most of the rich people in the world, are – well, you know what they are! So now I try to sell my works mainly abroad. Most of the artists here have to work as teachers or do commercial work to survive, or they prefer to emigrate to Canada, the USA, Australia, etc.

Bulgaria

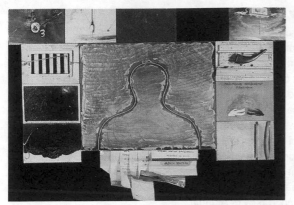

News, Nedko Solakov, 1988, polyptych in 12 parts, acrylic, oil, graphite, iron, bronze on canvas & wood, 130 x 193 x 7cm

Many artists who have stayed in Bulgaria try to unite in various groups and set up co-operative galleries in order to manage their work in the best possible way. I am a member of one of the most popular, the City Group. It consists of five artists and one art critic. Two years ago we established the City Gallery wanting to promote our projects and be more indepen-dent. I think we could survive this way.

There are some art galleries in Sofia, Varna, Plovdiv but they have no personal image as yet. The art market is still in a process of consolidation and there are no real dealers and agents either. In a way this is better for the artist since they can bypass the agent and dealer institutions and go directly to the customer, meeting them usually in the studio. But, as you know, this is not normal for the well-working art market, which I certainly prefer. You could offer your work in some of the galleries in Bulgaria, but the prices are comparatively low.

There are a lot of young artists here who are very fond of alternative forms of art production. They do installations, conceptual works, actions, performances, etc. Unfortunately, there are no foundations willing to sponsor these kinds of projects with the exception of the Open Society Fund (The Soros Foundation). The state institutions still care only about the traditional forms, which (I don't mean to ignore them) are of course more acceptable and saleable in the private art gallery scene anyway. I hope this attitude will change.

It is good to know about the groups: Art in Action, Kukuvden, Performance, RUB, DEN, Group for Objective Philosophy, the City Group – all of them focus their activities on the field of innovative art forms (sometimes innovative only for Bulgaria).

Lastly I want to say something about the system of art education in Bulgaria. There is the Academy of Fine Arts in Sofia, established at the end of the last century. There is also the Higher Institute for Art Teachers in Veliko Turnovo. Both offer very traditional education. It is still impossible for students to work in the fields of performance, video art, any type of installations, etc. Most young artists would like to make such things. The New Bulgarian Free University, which just opened in Sofia, is planning to offer more diverse possibilities for developed art education in the future.

And of course most of the young artists in my country are very eager to meet artists from abroad. I suppose such contacts will be interesting for you too. I will repeat: 'Come to Bulgaria!' and if you are already here, enjoy your stay!

Jane Ostler

In August 1990 I was the guest of Mincho Panayotov, a 45-year-old Bulgarian artist living in Plovdiv, Bulgaria's second city. He survived and supported his family in relative comfort by giving private lessons and selling paintings and etchings to foreign businessmen and local trade union clubs. Never having undertaken official art like murals and portrait he pleases himself and struck me as an uninhibited figure whose telephone never stops ringing. His work is expressive, romantic and abstract but Mincho still has to popularise it by adding stylised female forms and embracing lovers to ensure that it sells. He has built his own house on the proceeds of one very popular edition of etchings, but it took over seven years owing to the shortage of cement.

Mincho has transformed the ground floor of his studio into a gallery to show his own and friends' work. There is a growing number of galleries run by private companies and individuals. The people I met, art students, policemen, chemists, consuls, radio journalists, all viewed art as a profound pleasure and one luxury they could spend their money on.

At the Akraboff Building Firm's new art gallery I saw documentation of the exhibition 'Sign and Symbol' by a young artists group called Edge. The work attempted to debunk the common symbols of socialism which are fast becoming redundant in contemporary Bulgaria.

Punk by Kolin Karamtilov and Dimitar Mitovsky, was three variations on a head and shoulder theme, each about seven feet tall. One wore the Statue of Liberty's crown, another had hammers projecting from its wooden planks, the third bristled with sickles and basket weaving. I interpreted it as a symbolic presentation of the capitalist liberty, socialist labour, and anarchy all contained within the cultural context of Bulgaria's despoiled agricultural heritage.

At the exhibition opening there was a performance, something new and rare in Bulgaria. The artists were dressed like Pioneers, the children's communist organisation, and there was a big cake in the form of a five pointed star. An eye witness felt it was a dissection of Bulgaria's former society. *The Stomach of a Man Forced to Become a Communist* was full of undigested red stars – sharp and ugly.

Analgesic for a secular cathedral, Jane Ostler.

Other evidence of insipient rebellion was on the street: the daubing of the word 'murderer' under a statue of Lenin, two tent cities protesting against gypsies, a man on hunger strike until the Bulgarian monarchy is reinstated.

The future of a non-state subsidised arts community means support by private purchases, commissions and teaching if young artists are not to turn to creating a sub-culture of political comment. One portrait sculptor I visited relied on the support of his girlfriend. He was considered to have been very successful in the past, with many public commissions, but was now struggling in a climate of economic uncertainty.

In the studio I set up my table against one wall. My usual habits had to be modified. I was not able to stick paper to the wall or work directly against it because repainting was not as lightly undertaken as in the West due to lack of whitewash. Instead I attached large sheets of paper to three drawing boards and leaned them against the wall on a table. I made one painting and two etchings.

In and around Plovdiv there is much to see – Thracian and Roman ruins, Greek Orthodox churches, Turkish mosques and merchant's houses, National Revival buildings (a mix of Tudor, Viennese, Portmerion and Hitchcock Gothic), huge modern housing estates, libraries, post offices, and administrative centres built under Soviet Socialist guidance. The Alexander Nevsky Memorial Church in Sofia boasts some of the world's best icons.

The trouble is transport. Since Bulgaria buys all petrol from the Commonwealth of Independent States with hard currency, it is pretty scarce. My host queued one whole morning to fill up his car when we went to Bachkovo Monastery.

Mincho came on an exchange visit to London. Preferring to soak up as much visual art as possible as opposed to working in my studio, he spent his days in the Tate, the National Gallery, the Saatchi Collection and the Whitechapel. The Red Square Gallery was interested in his work and bought a painting on the strength of a slide reproduction.

For two weeks in Bulgaria I was paid the equivalent of one-and-a-half month's salary for an artist like Mincho – 500 levs (£38 @ 8 levs per £1). Mincho was paid two weeks pay for an artist like me in London – £300, more than he makes in six months in Bulgaria.

In September 1991 the work of nine British artists went over, accompanied by James Rosenthal, Matthew Carey and myself, for a joint exhibition at the Artists' Union Gallery in Plovdiv. Funded by the British Council, the Bulgarian Artists' Union and the Cultural Office of Plovdiv, we travelled by Austrian Airlines, taking the work in our luggage, via Vienna to Sofia, being met by a transit van from the airport and taken by coach back to the airport when we left. Our work returned later care of the Philippopolis Chamber Ensemble.

Staying in the magnificent Artists' Union building, a restored merchants' house in the old town, we spent a week of ceaseless activity, hanging the show and launching it to the TV and radio, plus holding a discussion for art students. Evenings were generally spent eating, drinking and talking in broken French and English. We discovered a subterranean disco, and a new Military Air Museum.

If you are visiting Bulgaria, there are a number of points to remember. Misunderstandings arise without an interpreter on hand. Some Bulgarians do speak very good English but can not always be located because of their work commitments, so if necessary, employ a professional. Organising the show from London I had the assistance of two professional interpreters now living here. Their generosity knows no bounds, so be careful! They will not accept you paying for anything with money. Gifts of tools, books, etchings and your own work are really appreciated.

When entering the country you are given a registration card which must be stamped upon arrival at your destination and stamped again on departure. Loss or failure to present this on leaving Bulgaria will result in a heavy fine of around £200.

It is illegal to take Levs (Bulgarian currency) out of Bulgaria. Unless you have a guest invitation you will have to change about £20 into Levs every day of your visit. The exchange rate is always changing, so ring the Embassy before you go. There is not a lot to buy in the shops, so buying art is the best use of your money.

The Artists' Union will consider inviting British artists to stay for several weeks in the summer rent free in exchange for one work of art made while staying there.

Commonwealth of Independent States

This section is subject to alteration, it was researched during January 1992 and was correct at that time. Soviet Embassies have become Embassies of the Russian Republic. A number of agencies formerly giving information on the entire Soviet Union often had no real contacts except in Russia itself. Each Republic has its own Parliament, Ministry of Culture, etc, and a number of the Republics, such as Ukraine, are developing their own national agencies, favouring their own language over Russian as their first language. Many organisations such as the Artists Union should still be a good starting point for information, but in general the region is in a state of flux and good research is vital before making any visit. For up to date information call the Foreign Office Eastern Europe Enquiry Desk tel 071 436 0676, Baltics Enquiry Desk tel 071 270 2423, or the Foreign Office Travel Desk tel 071 270 4179

LANGUAGE
Official: 112 recognized languages and five alphabets – Russian is the mother tongue of around 50% population
Others spoken: Wide range of languages spoken by various ethnic groups as well as border influences
English spoken: mainly in the centres

CURRENCY
Official: 100 kopeks = 1 rubl (ruble or rouble) – but the republics are developing their own currencies
Others used: dollars – almost any hard currency can get you what you want
Convertible or not: almost anyone will change money for you

Travellers cheques/Eurocheques/credit cards: limited use, mainly tourist centres but increasing

DOCUMENTS YOU NEED
For information on visa, work permit, residence permit contact: The Soviet Embassy is now the Embassy of the Russian Republic 18 Kensington Palace Gardens, London W8 4QJ tel 071 229 6412/3628 and is still the first point of contact for all other Republics and visa information or contact Intourist (see below).

You must be able to prove possession or purchase in home country of items carried in and out of the country, and there are tight regulations regarding movement of all works of art, check before travelling.

BALTIC STATES
Latvian Legation, 72 Queensbrough Terrace, London W2 tel 071 727 1698 fax 071 229 9514
Lithuanian Information Office, 2 Ladbroke Gardens, London W11 2PT tel 071 792 8450 fax 071 221 6164
Estonian Bureau, Estonia House, 18 Chepstow Villas, London W11 2PB tel 071 229 6700 fax 071 792 0218

CIS DTI DESK
OT 3/5c Room 321 tel 071 215 5265/4257

BANKS
Open Monday to Saturday 9.00-13.00

POST OFFICES
Open 8.00-20.00, otherwise 24 hours

BUSINESS HOURS
10.00-20.00 – queuing and low stocks tend to be reasons behind even longer hours than this

ART GALLERIES/MUSEUMS
Closed Mondays 10.00-20.00, with shorter hours on Saturday

PUBLIC HOLIDAYS
At the time of research many public holidays were being changed and each Republic was developing its own calendar of holidays.

CONTACT IN THE UK
Intourist, Meridian Gate, Marsh Wall, London E14 9FG tel 071 538 5902/8600
Soviet/British Chamber of Commerce, 60a Pembroke Road, London W8 tel 071 602 7692

CONTACT ABROAD
British Council, Ulyanovskaya Ulitsa, Dom 1 (VGBIL), Moscow 109189 tel 3373500
Ministry of Culture, ul. Arbat 35, Moscow tel 2410709
Chamber of Commerce:
ul. Ilyinka 6, 103684 Moscow tel 9234323

Embassy/Consulate:
British Embassy, Naberezhnaya Morisa Toreza 14, Moscow 109072 tel 2334507. Consulates: check whether the UK has developed any diplomatic links with the Republics.
Artists Associations:
Artists Union, Gogolevsky bul. 10, 121019 Moscow tel 2904110
Artists Union, ul. Gerzena 38, St. Petersburg
Artists Union, ul. Gorjkowo 46b, Moscow
Federation of Cultural Workers Unions, Zemlyanoy val. 64, 109004 Moscow tel 9273389 fax 2270943
Copyright/moral rights:
DACS initially tel 071 247 1650. In Russia VAAP, 103780 Moscow, k. 104 B Bronnaia 6a, CIS

Anastasia Ivanovna
Frolova

An artist wishing to travel through what used to be called the Soviet Union, and previous to that the Russian Empire, would do well to visit the 'cradle of Russia' – Ukraine (not *the* Ukraine, a somewhat derogatory term used by the Czars).

The capital, Kiev, was once the centre of the Kievian-Rus State, and, next to Constantinopol, the most important cultural/political city in Eastern Europe. In 988 AD Prince Vladimir had the whole city baptised in the waters of the Dnieper, and thus Russia embraced the Orthodox Church, and with it the whole tradition of Byzantine art.

It is almost a purely academic point to say 'Ukrainian art' as opposed to 'Russian art', old Russian/Ukrainian masters lived within and shared the same culture and more recently during the 'socialist realism' period the trend was toward a foistered homogeny. Though it is said Ukrainian artists tend to be more soulful, perhaps due to the nature and climate of the mother country. Russia's most popular contemporary painter, Sergey Chepik, was born in Ukraine and studied in Kiev then later Leningrad, as many other well-known artists before him, indeed Repin was Ukrainian and the writers Gogol and Dostoyevsky had 'Borderland' blood.

Our country is rich in history, culture and traditions. The travelling artist will find much to inspire them. Kiev is a tree-lined boulevard city situated on the banks of the third longest river in Europe. The Dnieper winds and bends down to Odessa on the Black Sea, which has a Mediterranean feel, and is a busy international seaport. There are mountainous regions, rich landscapes and ancient architecture.

In Kiev everything in the capital is within easy reach by a network of trams, buses and metro-trains, at a flat rate fare and served at steady regular intervals. Many of the metro stations are lavishly decorated with mosaics, sculptures (mostly of communist figures!) and paintings.

During spring and autumn the Arts Festival of Kiev takes place, (end of May and end of September), a central site for this is Andrevsky Spusk, a cobbled inclining street in the 'old' Kiev district. The playwright Bulgakov once lived here and at the top of the hill stands the beautiful church of St Andrew, built by Bartolomeo Bastrelli who designed much of St Petersburg. Today many exhibition rooms and art salons are to be found in this area (beware the tourist trap prices).

Much of historic Kiev was destroyed by the Nazi army during the Great Patriotic War (as WW2 is known to Soviets), and before then by the Mongol-Tartar invasion and occupation (1243-4) which lost Kiev its place as capital and led to the division of Russia/Ukraine. Here is where there began to appear a distinction in icon painting, which is clearly visible by the 18th century, where also strong influences had arrived from Europe.

Politics and economics, reforms and changes will surely effect the way art is created and promoted. So, what is the 'state of the arts' in our newly independent state?

Since Gorbachev, many forms of art have appeared that were previously 'forbidden' in the old USSR, though created 'underground'. Exhibitions of these works now take place, and also more recent 'agitation' art. It is possible to hire gallery space for shows (commercially run). This is usually done by art collectives. There are many small art salons where an artist can take their works, and if accepted they will be displayed and a commission taken when sold. These are some of the means by which 'unofficial' artists make a living. Something should be said about the way art had been produced in this country for the last generation or so to give the reader some idea of its psychology and perhaps an indication of the future; with the current upheavals facing us, young creative forces are looking for a soul and expression for the times in which we live.

The Soviet model of the Union of Artists of the USSR was created in 1936, its task was to protect and promote the social and economic rights of all professional painters, sculptors, graphic artists and art experts/critics. Inside this organisation is the Art Fund of the USSR which was created to solve any economic problems facing an artist. The structure of the Union divides into republic, district and city organisations. The right to open a district group is given to artists who live and work in an area and total not less than 15 persons. The Union is headed by a council and a chairperson, who is elected. An artist could become a member if they exhibited at Republican or All-Union level more than four times and attracted the attention of other artists and critics. Then they would be asked to present two characteristic works from such an exhibition where they live, a vote is taken at a plenum and this way members are created. An artist is able to show works progressively through district, republic and then all-union levels. The Artist Union has annual exhibitions for the Ministry of Culture, where works are bought for display in public institutions and the like. This is, or has been at least, the way in which the 'official' art process worked.

The foreign artist wishing to work, exhibit or sell within Ukraine would be advised to contact the Union of Artists. Though the sale of works could be problematic, non-commercial exhibition or exchange trade should be successful. The Union of Artists of Ukraine has departments in all big cities of the country (Kiev, Odessa, Zaporozhye, Kharkov, etc) with 2000 participant members. We wish you every

Meridian East
John Davis, 100 Thornhill Point, Moulins Road, London E9 7EW tel 081 985 0844. Artist organised exchange programme, art tours (includes St Petersburg, Moscow, Siberia), visas, flights, accommodation (hotels and artists' family homes)

success in your art endeavours, and would gladly welcome you to our country.

Julia Rowlands

My private visa application took seven months to be processed. However with the introduction of a new procedure in June 1991, it is said to be quicker. Financed by the Prince's Trust, 'go and see' grant award, all my costs were covered. The basic flight cost me £250, from APEX, and accommodation plus food and living costs for one month can cost as little as £250. I later found a cheaper flight, with a stop over in Paris for £150 (also APEX). On the visa application the space provided for stating where you wish to travel was only enough for one city, however once you are there, travelling with your Russian friends to parts unstated on your form is fine.

The most invaluable source of information before I left was a painter, Annabel Keatley, who had both painted and exhibited in Moscow. The next best resource for me were accidental meetings with people who had a variety of contacts in Russia.

The Society for Cultural Relations in the Soviet Union (SCRS), with a membership fee of £5 and based in Brixton, was useful for cultural events in London and visa procedures, far preferable to the Soviet Consulate and the Soviet Embassy, who on more than one occasion put the phone down on me.

Another society I used for general information was the Great Britain and the Union of Soviet Socialist Republics Association, membership £8. They have a good library, list social events, lectures, slide shows (aimed at people with no prior knowledge of Russia) and they hold some current magazines and newspapers. Occasionally their noticeboard has specialised adverts, for example offering personalised guided tours to a part of Russia of your choice, this particular one read 'please bring a flask and blanket'.

Manchester is twinned with St Petersburg. The arts department of Manchester County Council have news on contemporary exhibitions and they also have some funding available for this.

I was not able to find any other source for information before I left, apart from outdated but accurate listings of state owned artists' organisations and galleries, (from the SCRS). Soviet news agencies based in this country were and are short of resources.

I first met my Russian friend when he was living in the back of a studio/gallery, where I exhibited. Apart from a basic desire to fathom out

My Mother, Julia Rowlands, **oil on canvas, 3'x3'.**

one another, our conversation was based on the exciting opportunities we had to offer, and the necessity for arranging immediate plans.

I am a painter, my subjects are portraits depicting daily events in my life, through which I am able to see the slow change in subtleties of mood and emotion. The results are a source of comfort and understanding, much like a religion for me. My objectives in Russia were to cut out a personal view from that, which is for Westerners still an unestablished identity of the people and art.

Art education is very formal in Russia; students all reach a very high standard of traditional visual arts practice; which includes restoration and craft techniques, of which I saw examples in the art college decor itself, in silver, wood, and all traditional and local materials. Graduates (if they can afford it) are supported by their family when they leave, art holds a high spiritual value there. They produce work in studio's or in their communal home.

My friend's studio was in a block of flats, which was a housing association owned by the state, which introduced artists to encourage art in the area. A notice had been constructed by the artists to the front entrance of the flats which read 'The Ark'. Materials hold the same status as food, shared or exchanged in this case, within the cooperative. For example, artists hoard materials and may have twenty 2" paintbrushes, or thirty tubes of cobalt blue. There are art shops and we saw markets or street sellers with materials as well, but take some with you, for a present for your friends or for exchanging.

At the time I travelled to Moscow everything could be bought in three different currencies; they are pounds sterling, US dollars or the rouble. Although this is illegal it has been common practice for years, but you will have to declare how much you have spent when you leave. Goods in and out of Russia such as oils or pastels are legal.

Artists' motivations are comfortingly similar to artists anywhere. One artist living in the cooperative, Macka, had exhibited in Paris, Moscow and is soon to exhibit in Hamburg. She said of her work 'I like

Commonwealth of Independent States

Society for Cultural Relations in the Soviet Union
320 Brixton Road,
London SW9
071 274 2282

Great Britain and The Union of Soviet Socialist Republics Association
14 Grosvenor Place,
London SW1X 7HW
071 235 2116

Department of Inner City Relations
Isaakievkaia Ploshad,
St Petersburg 190107
Contact Merganka
Greniyco, head of
department

to think it documents my life and friends; a sort of diary'. She added 'priests wear very tall hats here, it is said to symbolise their contact with the spiritual world; therefore I paint all my figures with the tops of their heads protruding outside of the picture'. Her enthusiasm gave me confidence to build up a picture of the real issues they confront. Their support for free speech was echoed in the amount of styles on show within the cooperative of over 500 artists. The styles ranged from traditional visual art to live performance art, held in the courtyard entrance, once a month to an audience of friends and anyone else interested. All galleries in Russia, one per region, are state owned and managed, although I heard talk of new cooperatively managed galleries being set up.

As in England, to exhibit you choose a gallery suited to your style. Approaching them as a Westerner, you will certainly stand out, so be prepared for higher prices (the same can be said for anywhere you go in Russia). A gift is often acceptable payment for the hire fee, for instance Annabel Keatley gave three paintings. Many artists make a gift of their paintings to museums which is a way to get themselves shown. Publicity will be arranged by the state managed galleries, and critics will be invited but it is unlikely they will buy. The market at the moment therefore is mostly foreigners. However native artists market their work in other more lucrative countries.

My biggest mistake was not to learn a substantial amount of the language to give myself more independence. The friends I made in Russia are the most compassionate people I have ever met, but my heavy reliance on translation left me feeling excluded during evening meetings with artists.

Visitors will in no way be let down by any grand expectations they may have of Russia. I feel fortunate in evolving universal links with the country outside of its economic state. The growing artists' cooperatives, are the future of culture in Russia.

One result of this trip will be an exhibition with the cooperative art group TOR in London.

Czecho-Slovakia

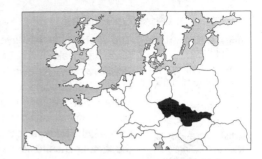

LANGUAGE
Official: Czech and Slovak
Others spoken: German, Russian was widely taught until 1989
English spoken: Rare outside Prague, Bratislava and other cities, but increasing

CURRENCY
Official: 100 heller = 1 crown (koruna)
Others used: US Dollar/Deutsch Mark
Convertible or not: yes
Travellers cheques/Eurochcques/credit cards: use growing but less likely outside main centres

DOCUMENTS YOU NEED
For information on visa, residence and work permits: Czech and Slovak Federal Republic Embassy, 25 Kensington Palace Gardens, London W8 4QY tel 071 727 9431

CZECHO-SLOVAK DTI DESK
OT 3/5b Room 335 tel 071 215 5152/5267

POST OFFICES
Monday to Friday 7.00/8.00-17.00/18.00

BUSINESS HOURS
Monday to Friday 9.00-17.00/18.00, Thursday late night, Saturday morning, some lunch-time closing

ART GALLERIES/MUSEUMS
Usually open circa 9.00-16.00, closed Monday Summer and weekend Winter

PUBLIC HOLIDAYS
Jan 1, May-day, May 9, Easter Monday, Jul 5, Oct 28, Dec 24-26 (alterations currently in progress)

CONTACT ABROAD
British Council, Cultural Attache, GB Embassy, Jungmannova 30, 11000 Prague 1 tel 224501/50

Ministry of Culture Czecho-Slovak Federal Republic, Valdstejnská 10, Prague tel 539331
Ministry of Culture Slovak Government, Suvorovova 12, 800 00 Bratislava tel 54781, fax 54140
Chamber of Commerce:
Ceskoslovenska obchodni a prumyslova komora, Argentinska 38, 170 05 Prague 7 tel 8724111
Embassy/Consulate:
British Embassy, Thunovaska 14, Prague 11800 tel 533340/70
Artists Associations:
Konfederace Umeni a Kultury (Confederation of Arts and Culture) Senovazne nam. 23, 112 82 Prague tel 21142519
Zvazslovenskych vytvarnych umelior, Partizanska 21, 81351 Bratislava
Czecho-Slovak Committee of Unions of Creative Artists, Gottwaldovo nabrezi 250, 110 00 Prague 1 tel 292441
Svazceskych vytvarnych umelu, Gottwaldovo nabrezi 250, 110 00 Prague 1 tel 232006/230001)
Sculptors Symposium Association, Revolucni nam 160, 50811 Horice v Podkvkonosi
Copyright/moral rights:
No Czecho-Slovak organisation noted, try Design & Artists Copyright Society, (DACS) St.Mary's Clergy House, 2 Whitechurch Lane, London E1 7QR tel 071 247 1650

Tomás Ruller

Office of the President
tel 3111707
National Gallery.
Hradcanské nám. 15,
Prague 02
tel x 535246
**UVU Union of Fine
Artists**, Seceretariate,
tel 292442. Foreign
Department tel 292215
**CFVU Czech Fund of
Fine Arts**, V Jirchárich
14, Prague tel 268926.
Studios for rent
tel 206393
**AVU Academy of Fine
Arts**, U akademie 4,
Prague tel 373641
**UMPRUM College of
Industrial Arts**, Nám,
Jana Palacha 80,
Prague tel 2319512
**EKK European Culture
Club**, Pálfyho palác,
Prague
**PKC Prague Cultural
Centre**,
Stroupeznického 1,
Prague
**OOA 'Protective
Authors'
Organisation**, Na
prikope 7, Prague tel
224179
**EKN C-S Committee
of European Cultural
Endowment**,
Safárikovo nám 6,
Bratislava tel 490988

The problem of the 'hyphen' is hanging over the Czecho-Slovak (Czechoslovak) federation. The Slovak Republic, represented by Bratislava with its own Ministry of Culture, Academy of Fine Arts, National Gallery and so on lives by an independent nationally-oriented culture with a problem of a strong Hungarian minority. The province of Moravia, has a traditionally special position in Czech culture. The main centre is the trade-fair city of Brno. Its artistic life is concentrated around the famous theatre scene and so inter-disciplinary activities find their home there. Music is an authentic blend of earthy underground, melancholy folklore of vintners, and cheerful contemporary-classic. Besides the school of architecture with an excellent functionalist tradition and exhibitions, an effort to establish a new college of fine arts is arising. The spiritual centres of Moravia are the town of Olomouc, where the cultural life is concentrated around the university, and popular folklore areas. The atmosphere there is marked by regionalism; on the other hand, it is not so subsidiary to trendy waves and is not corrupted the way Prague is.

The previous concentration of power and capital is still surviving. It results in a disproportion similar to the situation in London or Paris; progress towards the German pluralistic model has not been successful so far. More than half of all artists live and work in Prague. More and better opportunities are outweighed by hard competition and intrigues of special-interest groups.

The key problem of the National Gallery is introducing a modern collection which has not had a permanent exhibition due to ideological ideas for decades. Now, right before completion of reconstruction of the historical building, it seems so it will have to be given up due to economic pressures. Valdstejn riding hall, one of the most representative exhibition rooms right in the area of the Ministry of Culture, will be closed for at least one year without necessary repairs being made. Even the Ministry does not have sufficient finances. Neither frequent personnel changes in this institution nor severe changes of the structure solve the essential problem: the holes in legislation. They are supposed to be healed in 1993 at the earliest. Until then, there will not be any law about endowments (for the time being they are established under the statute of business companies or civic associations), nor a tax law which would stimulate sponsorship by a tax system. Almost all state grants, however, have been cancelled without compromise. This has resulted in seeking recovery by selling abroad (but far below the real price). Consequently it fosters a black market of artistic objects and antiques, laundering dirty money and other schemes of surviving old mafias.

8.8.88, Tomás Ruller, performance approximately 2hours long, Opatov Housing Estate, Prague. *Photo: Hana Hamplová.* 'Instead of a banned exhibition, I invited the participants for a walk in the neighbourhood. It changed into a sort of **Stations of the Cross**'.

The Czech Fund of Fine Arts is formed by artists' extra contributions of their own work. It divides the proceeds between associations and even, upon request, of individuals. Most of these associations joined together to form the Union. It has its offices in the building of Mánes which is a natural centre of fine arts not only for Prague. It is there where you can obtain information about symposiums, studios to rent, possibilities of exhibitions, etc. Reciprocity is very much in demand.

The universities generally have good reputations. After the revolution, they were staffed with new professors and gradually they are implementing fundamental reforms. Study programmes vary from the classical approach to the most modern experiments, depending on the personality of the professor and school leadership. The students gained unprecedented authority so they co-determine the course of all things, sometimes possibly too much. They have full creative freedom and exhibit and sell freely. Censorship does not exist. Both regular studies, conditioned first by talent examination and knowledge of Czech, and short study periods are open for foreign students. Besides direct contact, students can use exchanges based upon international cultural agreements through ministries or reciprocities between schools, as the Tempus Project, for example. Insurance and contingent sponsors have to be arranged at home. As far as health insurance is concerned, Czecho-Slovakia is a member of GHMSI, which means visitors are covered for health care, and has a pact with the UK preventing double taxation. Specialised legal consultations, protection of author's rights etc, are granted by OOA (Protective Authors Organisation). People interested in teaching find jobs primarily as teachers of foreign languages.

As for flats, foreign demand has driven the prices up, often to West European standard. New owners of buildings are closing studios to get higher rates per square metre. They are changing them into offices and retail spaces, preferably for Western companies. But the doors are open everywhere for those who can benefit from the advantageous rate and pay in hard currency.

Galleries are left to their own resources as well, so covering the costs connected with exhibitions and catalogues has to be done by the artists themselves. It is possible to make a living out of art but the artist's role in society is a matter of taste.

Social relations are complicated, the atmosphere tense but there is hope for finding a way out is not missing and a lot of fresh creative energy is rising from optimism. Everything is in such motion that the situation is not easy to survey. A foreigner can hardly get around without a well informed local expert in the situation. Even though frankness and cordiality generally predominate, personal recommendations help very much. To ring somebody and arrange a visit to a studio is very common. So the most important question remaining is 'how to meet the right people'.

I wish you good luck in 'the art of meeting'. (For the journey I recommend reading 'The Trial' by Franz Kafka, 'Svejk' by Jaroslav Hasek, and philosophic essays by Václav Havel – within the combination of these three one can look for the Czech soul).

Mark Pinder

I visited Czecho-Slovakia during May and June 1991 with £300, a plane ticket from the Princes' Trust 'Go and See' grant scheme, and £200 from a couple of British magazines on the understanding I shot some general material on economic and environmental issues for their picture libraries.

Finding accommodation in Prague can be quite a problem according to the guide books. Aware of this, and not being in the right frame of mind or body after the journey for running round a city I didn't yet know, I made my way straight to the accommodation office at the main train station, Havlani Nadrazi. This provided a room in a hostel, extremely basic, not too secure, but cheap, very central and it allowed me to dump most of my belongings, look around Prague and possibly find somewhere better. Finding alternative accommodation was not too difficult, private accommodation bureaux exist and enterprising Czechs seeing people coming from them would approach and offer alternative accommodation (often far cheaper than the bureaux).

It's a sad fact no city ever lives up totally to the tourist brochures and Prague is no exception. It is a very vital city with lots going on and a great cultural life which I would recommend to anyone, but crime has rocketed since the revolution, a situation exacerbated by the prison amnesties, which whilst releasing many who should never have been imprisoned, also released many other more anti-social elements too. I had one or two potentially unpleasant moments with people insisting I change money on the black market – specifically them – as well as a couple of punk-ettes in Wenceslas Square who just demanded money pure and simple!

Residential property is at a premium in Prague. Even before the revolution, flats and houses were in very short supply, housing mobility being essentially non-existent. Now the introduction of free market forces has released comparatively large amounts of property, as state assets are sold and some property reverts back to previous owners.

The price of better flats has rocketed as landlords see they can charge maybe 35 times what a Czech could pay by renting to foreign visitors, corporations and government agencies. This makes the supply of good flats to the travelling artist relatively abundant but only if the money is available. Paying $600 a month for a good flat in Prague would only be viable if you had a good income from sales of work abroad, but if you are deriving your income solely from working in Czecho-Slovakia, these prices are obviously prohibitive (I met a trainee doctor in her final year of work study whose salary was about $80 a month). Cheaper flats can be found but don't expect to find too many bargains.

Ironically, there are quite a lot of empty and decaying properties which are too decrepit, uneconomic or cash starved for habitation which could, and do, make perfectly serviceable studio spaces at quite decent rents. Contact with other artists should help here.

If photographic materials is any indicator, then Eastern European art materials are quite plentiful and extremely cheap by our standards. The quality is not up to standards and consistency in the UK, but with a little experimentation and understanding, perfectly respectable results can be achieved. Not necessarily inferior, just different.

Some Kodak, Fuji, Ilford and Agfa products could be found in Prague for slightly less than would be paid in the UK, but this was still maybe five or six times the price of an Eastern European product and whilst affordable to the relatively affluent traveller, these prices are prohibitive to the average Czech. Outside major centres such as Prague

Halo Czech Wedding. **Cheb, Czeckoslovakia.** Mark Pinder/Metaphor. or Bratislava, the availability of Western materials cannot be guaranteed. If you are planning a first trip to Czechoslovakia and the kind of work you produce relies upon specific media take any materials you think may be required just in case a serviceable alternative cannot be found.

Initially, I spent three days in Prague, then headed out to the provinces. I attended a one-week photographic workshop organised by Gallery 4 in Cheb, a town in Western Czecho-Slovakia near the border with Germany.

The provinces proved far more interesting than Prague. The week in Cheb was spent photographing a state farm in the process of privatisation. After Cheb, I headed towards the brown coal, (lignite), mining areas around Most, which proved a real eye-opener as to the scale of the environmental problems Czecho-Slovakia and Eastern Europe face. After Most and Chomutev came the Skoda car factory in Mlada Boleslav, then back to Prague for a week photographing the police and eating and drinking a lot in the company of other photographers and film makers.

I found the best currency exchange deals from the state bureau de change agencies, the agency at the airport offering a particularly good deal. I chose not to change money on the black market for a variety of reasons, one being the potential risks but more importantly, it would be blatant hypocrisy on the one hand to applaud the collapse of communism and the introduction of democracy, whilst on the other de-stabilise further an already weak economy with illegal currency transactions.

Getting around is quite easy due to the fairly comprehensive (and comparatively cheap) public transport system. In a lot of cases, it is quicker to take the bus rather than the train which can take a painfully long time.

The most obvious ways of getting to, and from, Czecho-Slovakia are air and rail. Both British Airways and the Czech airline CSA run one flight a day each from London Heathrow to Prague from around £206 to £250 return, but don't expect to find any cheap deals and book early as demand is heavy. British Rail International can arrange departures from London Victoria via Paris, taking around 29 hours. This is not necessarily much cheaper than flying, although special fares apply to those under 26 and Czecho-Slovakia can be reached by Inter-railers. Some tour operators run coach services to Czecho-Slovakia. For these I'd suggest checking out the small ads in the back of the quality press.

I spent a total of three and a half weeks in Czecho-Slovakia, by the end I was only just beginning to find my feet. I did not achieve half of what I set out to, but I gained a good understanding of how things work for the subsequent trips I am undoubtedly going to make.

On the whole, I found the Czech people to be extremely obliging and helpful (even the government departments and company reps I dealt with). I whole-heartedly recommend Czecho-Slovakia as a possible destination for the travelling artist, although, if you are like me (and have the funds), I would recommend going first only really to look and draw your own conclusions before making a return visit to get down to some serious work.

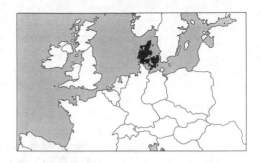

Denmark

Member of the Council of Europe and the EC

LANGUAGE
Official: Danish
Others spoken: other Scandinavian languages and German/Dutch sometimes understood
English spoken: extensively, especially cities, larger towns and young people in general

CURRENCY
Official: 100 ore = 1kr krone (kroner)
Convertible or not: yes
Travellers cheques/Eurocheques/credit cards: can be used widely

DOCUMENTS YOU NEED
For information contact: Royal Danish Embassy, 55 Sloane Street, London SW1X 9SR tel 071 235 1255

DANISH DTI DESK
OT 3/3c Room 377 tel 071 215 5341/4397/5140

BANKS
Open Monday-Friday 9.30-16.30; Thursday until 18.30

POST OFFICES
Open Monday-Friday 9.00-18.00; Saturday 9.00-13.00 (shorter hours outside main centres)

BUSINESS HOURS
Monday-Thursday 9.00-17.00; Friday 9.00-19.00/20.00; Saturday 9.00-13.00/14.00

ART GALLERIES/MUSEUMS
Often closed on Mondays, check with Danish Tourist Bureau

PUBLIC HOLIDAYS
Jan 1, Easter weekend, General Prayer Day, Ascension Day, Jun 5, Whit Monday, Dec 25-26

CONTACT IN THE UK
Danish Tourist Board, Sceptre House, 169-173 Regent St, London W1R 8PY tel 071 734 2637/8

CONTACT ABROAD
British Council, Montergade 1, 1116 Copenhagen K tel 33112044
Ministry for Cultural Affairs, Nybrogade 2, 1203 Copenhagen K tel 33923370
Chamber of Commerce:
Borsen, 1217 Copenhagen K tel 33912323
Embassy/Consulate:
British Embassy, Kastelsvej 36/40, 2100 Copenhagen O tel 31264600. Consulates in Aabenraa, Aalborg, Aarhus, Esbjerg, Odense, Frederica, Torshavn (Faroes), Rønne (Bornholm)
Artists Association:
Billedkunstnernes Forbund BKF (The Association of Pictorial Artists), Bremerholm 28, DK-1069 Copenhagen K tel 33128170
Håndværksradet (Federation of Crafts), Amaliegade 15, 1256 Copenhagen K tel 33932000
Danske Kunsthåndværkeres Landssammenslutning DKL (Danish Arts and Crafts Association), Linnesgade 20, 1361 Copenhagen K tel 33152940
Copyright/moral rights:
DACS initially tel 071 247 1650. In Denmark Copydan – Billedkunst, Ryesgade 53b, DK-1200 Copenhagen O tel 393511

Ulla Enevoldsen

Kunsthåndværkerskolen i Kolding (Kolding School for Crafts), Agtrupvej 51, DK-6000 Kolding tel 75520799

Danmarks Designskole (Design School of Denmark), Linnègade 2, DK-1361 Copenhagen K

tel 33132258

Det Jyske Kunstakademi (The Arts Academy of Judland), Mejlgade 32, DK-8000 Århus C

tel 86136919

Det Fynske Kunstakademi (The Arts Academy of Fuenen), Brandts Passage 43, DK-5000 Odense C

tel 66111288

Akademiet for de Skiønne Kunster (The Fine Arts Academy), Kgs. Nytorv 1, DK-1050 Copenhagen K tel 33126860

Grafisk Skole (Graphic School), Sct. Annagade 30-32, DK-8000 Århus C

tel 86191880

Århus Kunstakademi (Århus Arts Academy), Vestergade 29, DK-8000 Århus C tel 86138144

I do pictures and sculptures in handmade paper. It has spontaneous appeal to me, because you form the material right from the ground and are able to shape it exactly the way you want. I start out with an idea which develops through experimenting with the material.

I was trained as a textile designer at *Kunsthåndværkerskolen i Kolding* (one of the two crafts and design schools in Denmark) from 1982-86. I specialised in unique weavings and handmade paper.

From 1986-89 I shared a studio space with another textile artist. We worked at many different projects trying to find a niche for our work. I produced belts, stationery, lampshades and sold them at markets, through shops, etc. I have almost completely given up this activity because the economic gain is low compared with the effort. I've done publicity design work, interior design and decoration and given courses in papermaking. Besides this I've participated in a number of exhibitions.

In 1989-90 I went for a study tour to Mexico and Canada and spent almost a year abroad. The trip was partly financed by grants. In Canada where I stayed nine months I worked at a paper-mill, specialised in handmade paper, doing art work of my own. It was quite an experience to be on another continent, encountering the north American life-style and young Canadian artists. This year I went to Spain to be the co-leader of a World Crafts Council textile workshop with participants from all over Europe.

The incomes from the above mentioned activities have only been able to support me for periods of time. I have sold some of my art work. The buyers have been private companies, an American art dealer and the Danish Art Foundation. The rest of the time I have received unemployment insurance. The level of social security is very high in Denmark. Many artists benefit from this, so it works as an indirect subsidy for some parts of visual and performing arts. It looks as if the government will change its unemployment policy though, in the near future, because of the increasing unemployment.

There are a number of private and public funds which support cultural activities. They are being flooded with applications and are difficult to obtain. You must have a good project, be able to show results of your work and be good at writing applications.

Right now I have my studio in my house for economic reasons. Studios in the cities are hard to find at affordable prices.

I have participated in a number of exhibitions of various importance. One kind is at private companies, which are fairly easy to get. A good idea is to make a contract in advance that guarantees a minimum sale. Galleries are harder to get in touch with here, like

Wings, Ulla Enevoldsen, **1986, maquette, 50x100cm.**

Danske Billedkunstnenes Forbund DBF (The Association of Danish Pictorial Artists), Nørregade 67, DK-5000 Odense C tel 66179758

Kunstnernes Hus (The Artists' House), Hjortensgade 23, DK-8000 Århus C tel 86202086

anywhere. During my stay in Montreal I walked into one of the best galleries in town and got an exhibition on the spot. I believe being a foreign artist makes you more interesting. The story didn't have a happy ending though, the gallery owner went bankrupt and died a few months later. The third kind are the annual juried exhibitions, of which there are four important ones. It gives a good deal of prestige having participated in a number of these exhibitions and makes it easier to obtain grants, exhibitions, etc.

Paper art is relatively new media in this country. It was introduced here some ten years ago by artists who had been acquainted with it abroad. Today it is more widely known as an artistic media through courses at the art and design schools, but there are still few who work as professionals or semi-professionals and most of us know each other.

Right now we are planning an exhibition in Italy with the participation of Italian paper artists. Being a member of International Association of Hand Paper Makers and Paper Artists (IAPMA) you have access to information of what is going on in paper art worldwide and a very useful list of members.

Statens Værksteder for Kunst og Håndværk (The National Workshops for Arts and Crafts), Strandgade 27 B, DK-1401 Copenhagen K tel 32960510

International Association of Hand Paper Makers and Paper Artists IAPMA, treasurer: Eva Andresen, Molt 28, 6369 BJ Simpelveld

Dansk Kunsthåndværk (Danish Crafts), Herredsvej 7, DK-8581 Nimtofte tel 86398464

Kunstavisen (The Art Magazine), Greve Strandvej 31, DK-2670 Greve tel 426011

There are two kinds of formal training in crafts or fine arts. The arts academies and the crafts and design schools. Formal education is tuition free. You receive a study subsidy, which covers some of your living expenses, the rest you must supply yourself through working or a bank loan. At the present you have the right to receive unemployment insurance immediately after having finished a formal education, if you're member of a union. I know most about the crafts and design schools having been a student there myself. There are five different departments where you can specialise in textiles, ceramics, graphic design, clothes designing or furniture. The duration is now five years. I and my colleagues were trained to become designers in the textile industry or independent craftspeople. The jobs are few, the competition strong and many shift to other occupations after a while.

Doing fine arts like I mainly do now with a training in design has its advantages and disadvantages. You have a wide knowledge of materials, techniques and composition. It requires an effort to get beyond these considerations at times.

Lots of private schools offer art training at various levels. Many fine artists have received their training at these places. Some of the best known are *Grafisk Scole* (Graphic School), *Århus Kunstakademi* (Arts Academy of Århus). You have to pay for these courses yourself, but you are usually allowed to receive unemployment insurance or welfare while studying. Already having received a formal education, it is limited how much you can benefit from these courses apart from being introduced to new techniques.

The growing interest in creative activities means relatively good possibilities for getting part-time teaching jobs to supplement your income. The pay is decent, but the work is usually unstable.

In the town where I live (Århus, the next biggest city in Denmark with 500,000 inhabitants) we have a relatively new institution called *Kunstnernes Hus* (Artists' House). It is run with support from the town hall. It has exhibition facilities and its employees and the board try to promote art from the region through different activities. The board is formed by representatives from three different arts and crafts associations: *Danske Kunsthåndværkeres Landssammenslutning* (The Association of Danish Craftspeople), *Billedkunstnernes Forbund* (The Association of Pictorial Artists), and *Danske Billedkunstneres Forbund* (The Association of Danish Pictorial Artists). In order to become part of the house you have to be a member of one of these. Each member's work is registered with slides and on computer files. The goal is to work as an art agency taking in commissions from private people, companies and

Mark Stevens, **ceramics**

public institutions. My wish is it could be expanded with workshops for craftspeople and artists to work on special projects.

In Copenhagen they have such workshops, namely *Statens Værksteder for Kunst og Håndværk* (the National Workshops for Arts and Crafts). Artists and craftspeople can apply to use these facilities for periods of time.

Mark Stevens

Not feeling any special ties to the UK, and having travelled widely, I had no hesitations about moving to Denmark with my family in 1973. As my wife is Danish she solved many of the initial problems of settling in. At that time it was difficult for non-Danish citizens to buy property. There were also fairly strict controls on staying in Denmark for more than a certain period of time. This meant regular visits to the police, until the formalities of getting EEC status were completed. I understand that this is easier now.

The other initial problem was of course the language. Danish is not used much outside Denmark, though once mastered, you can then understand some Norwegian and Swedish. The initial period here was not so difficult as many Danes speak good English, but once a group of them get together the conversation soon reverts to Danish and, unless you have some understanding of the language, you feel pretty left out. The only way out of this problem is to learn the lingo. Fortunately, there are many good courses for beginners in most big towns. During the winter months, the days being short, there is ample opportunity for joining evening classes. In the summer months there are often short courses arranged by the Peoples University, *Folkeuniversitetet*.

Prices for materials are much the same as in the rest of Europe, marginally higher, due to the 25% VAT. There is no VAT on artworks, but there is VAT on craft items. Recently though, there has been some relaxation on the VAT on craft items, especially one-off pieces, but it is still a bit of a jungle finding your way around. This may change once financial controls are harmonised in the EC. Income tax is the other burden that everyone here has to bear. The starting rate, after various allowances, is 52%! So the tax rate plus the VAT is often enough to put many people off settling here. The UK is even regarded by the wealthy as a tax haven!

Tax and customs authorities generally seem to have little or no understanding of the plight of artists and craftworkers. In a recent controversial case, a bailiff was allowed to remove paintings from an exhibition in progress, and in the ensuing court case, this appalling action was upheld.

Once I had settled in and acclimatised (it can get as cold as minus 20 in the winter) I soon found like-minded colleagues who could give me advice on setting up and getting materials. Young artists and craftworkers often start out in jointly-owned studios, and exhibit together. The group mentality is something very Danish.

There are at least forty officially acknowledged groups, showing their work in joint exhibitions, normally on an annual basis. Some of the more established groups have someone employed to organise exhibitions, take care of publishing catalogues, and generally looking after the interests of the individual members of the group. This kind of activity can be seen in the craft field as well. There is a crafts organisation, called *Danske Kunsthåndværkeres Landssammenslutning (DKL)*. Visual artists have similar organisations such as *Billed Kunstnernes Forbund (BKF)*.

In Århus, the second largest town of Denmark and situated on the east coast of Jutland, there is an Artists' House, *Kunstnernes Hus*. This has a secretariat and information office, as well as two exhibition areas. This town is well endowed with many small galleries. Looking at the lengthy lists of exhibitions printed each week in the daily newspapers, you get an idea of the level of activity up and down the country.

Many institutions and large companies have an art club, which arranges temporary exhibitions of paintings, graphics, sculpture and crafts for their members. Usually this is on a sale or return basis.

Many of the numerous museums play an active role in promoting the visual arts. This level of activity is not just limited to the larger towns but is found the length and breadth of the country. Both state and county are active in purchasing art works for public collections.

Strangely, art has a low priority in education, and children have few opportunities for organised art teaching. Yet there is an enormous interest shown by the adult population, which can be seen from the number of evening classes that are run by various organisations.

I teach part-time at an art school in Århus, the Århus Kunst Akademi, and nearly all our evening classes fill up each term, and we have waiting lists for those wishing to take part in the day-time courses. There are three art schools with official status, one in Copenhagen, one in Odense on the island of Funen, and one in Århus. Besides these there are three design schools, one in Copenhagen, one in Kolding, and one in Herning in the west of Jutland. Industrial design can also be studied at the schools of architecture, in either Copenhagen or Århus. The students studying in all these institutions are eligible for state grants.

Those studying elsewhere must finance their studies themselves. For example, at our school the students pay for organised teaching for two days a week, and have the use of studio space the rest of the time. At the state schools, the students get an average of one day's teaching a week. At the school in Kolding the students receive four days teaching a week. It is apparent then, that teaching methods and practices vary from one school to another.

Opportunities for teaching in the main art schools are not very good. But it is not so difficult to get into part-time teaching. It is now possible to teach at evening class level without any formal teaching qualifications. This being due to a recent relaxation of the laws governing part-time education.

After having lived here for so long, I have had plenty of time to evaluate the effects Danish culture has had on my work. It is hard to give precise examples, but I notice the differences when I return to the UK. Learning about Danish history and culture, has given me a new vantage point from which to view my own background.

Through visits to museums I have learnt of the diversity of the Danish heritage, from way back to the time of nomadic peoples from around the times of the last ice age, through the Viking period, and up until the present day.

Literature on Danish arts and crafts is almost exclusively printed in Danish. Exhibition catalogues are sometimes printed in two languages, either Danish/English or Danish/German. The monthly arts magazine *North*, is one of the few journals in two languages. For those who master the language, there is a monthly paper on the arts, *Kunst Avisen (Arts Paper)*. For the crafts there is a quarterly journal called *Dansk Kunsthåndvœrk (Danish Crafts)*. Several museums have publications relating directly to the arts.

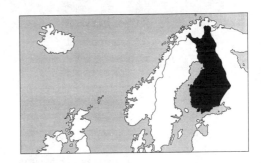

Finland

Member of the Council of Europe

LANGUAGE
Official: Finnish
Others spoken: Finno-Ugarian (Hungarian), Lapp, Swedish
English spoken: mainly in centres, but usually the first second language

CURRENCY
Official: 100 penni (pennia) = 1 markka (markkaa)(Finnmark)
Convertible or not: yes

DOCUMENTS YOU NEED
For information on visa, work permit and residence permit, etc contact: The Embassy of Finland, 32 Grosvenor Gardens, London SW1 tel 071 235 9531

FINNISH DTI DESK
OT 3/3c Room 377 tel 071 215 4783/5134

BANKS
Open Monday to Friday 9.00-16.00

POST OFFICES
Open Monday to Friday 9.00-17.00

BUSINESS HOURS
Open Monday to Friday 9.00-17.00 & Saturday morning

ART GALLERIES/MUSEUMS
Varies, some close Monday and Tuesday and many have seasonal timetables

PUBLIC HOLIDAYS
Jan 1, Jan 6, Easter weekend, May 1, Ascension Day, Whitsun, Jun 24, All Saints, Dec 6, Dec 25/26

CONTACT IN THE UK
Finnish Institute, 35 Eagle Street, London WC1R 4AJ tel 071 404 3309.
Finnish Tourist Board, Queener House, 66-68 Haymarket, London SW1Y 4RF tel 071 839 4048

CONTACT ABROAD
British Council, Erottanjankatu 7B, 00130 Helsinki tel 640505
Ministry of Culture and Education, Meritullinkatu 10, PL293, 00171 Helsinki tel 134171
Embassy/Consulate:
British Embassy, Uudenmaankatu 16/20, 00120 Helsink1, tel 647922. Consulates in Kotka, Kuopio, Oulu/Uleaborg, Pori/Bjornborg, Tampere/Tammersfors, Turko/Aho, Vaasa
Artists Association:
Artists of Finland, Ainonkatu 3, 00100 Helsinki tel 495062
Copyright/moral rights:
DACS initially tel 071 247 1650. In Finland Kuvasto, Lapinlahdenkatu 19, 00180 Helsinki

Aino Favén

little red boat	*pieni punainen vene*
tossing in the wind	*keikkuu tuulessa*
voices of work	*työn ääniä*
flashlight	*taskulamppu*
in the darkness	*pimeydessä*
sun set	*aurinko laski*
behind the island	*saaren taakse*

I am a textile artist from Finland – in English I would call myself a fibre artist but in Finland this term is not generally known. My artistic field is quite wide. I use basketry techniques for sculptures and reliefs of willow and combine it with other materials. I also paint and print textiles for works of art or clothing and interior decorating purposes, and make modern jewellery.

I used to earn my living by designing textiles for the industry but nowadays there is not much textile industry left in Finland so I do more teaching. I don't have a teacher's education but like many other artists I teach at a workers academy or other schools and courses.

My home is in Helsinki which is not a metropolis but it is the capital of Finland. My small apartment is in the centre of the town in a typical apartment building, but my studio is in a very charming place. It is on the island of Harakka (in English 'Magpie'). I walk 20 minutes or ride a bicycle to the sea shore and row in a little red boat about 100m to the island. The building is big, old and a little ghostly. It was originally the chemical laboratories of the army but since 1988 it has belonged to the city of Helsinki, which rents it to artists. There are textile artists, designers, ceramic artists, goldsmiths, paper and fashion artists, painters and so on – 22 people work in the building. The rent is moderate – usually the rents of studios are fairly high in Helsinki. We enjoy the sea and nature but the problem is occasionally the transportation from the mainland. There is a regular boat line only in summer time. Many of us row our own little boats, but during two or three months of mid-winter it is difficult or impossible because of the ice or storms. The sea freezes almost every winter but the ice is not often strong enough for walking.

I share my 40 square-metre room in Harakka with another textile artist. The room is lit by three windows and it is 3.5m high. I am quite happy with the situation because we both also teach elsewhere and don't need the studio space every day. I think it is also very important to have contacts with other artists who work there. My studio is not typical at all. Before I got the space I had a room in a cellar of an apartment building. There are lots of artists who are working in small and primitive conditions without daylight. There are a couple of artists' organisations

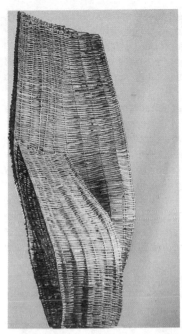

El Sol, Aino Favén**, 1991, detail, dyed willow**

which own some *ateljéappartments* which have been designed for artists as studio and living accommodation. Their rents are cheap but they are available only for a very small number of artists. It is not possible for a textile artist to get one because we belong to a separate organisation which doesn't own studios.

The materials I use are not expensive and are not difficult to buy. In contrast traditional painter's materials are expensive – all colours are imported. The standard of living is high and so are all the prices. There are a lot of artists who don't even get a minimum salary. Often the artist pays more money for the materials than she/he earns by selling art.

By international comparison the Finnish scholarship system is relatively good but only a very small proportion of artists can get scholarships. There are private grants and grants awarded by the state either for a specific project or year grants – for one, three, five or fifteen years. There are not enough scholarships available and they are related too strictly according to the field and education. For example, textile art is related to the industrial arts even though it is often closer to free visual arts.

It is very important for an artist to take part in exhibitions and organise them. I have shown my works in many design and textile art exhibitions and arranged some private exhibitions. The range of art galleries is wide. Some are very highly respected but it is also very difficult to get an exhibition. There are also a lot of other traditional or alternative galleries which may have different criteria when choosing artists. Many towns have a gallery of their own which is cheap or free of charge. Usually exhibiting is expensive. The gallery rent for three weeks is 5000-15000 Finnish marks (£800-2400) and sometimes it does not even include invitation cards or posters, etc. The commission can be 20-50% of the sale. There are still some galleries where you pay only the commission and no rental. There is no guarantee you will sell anything. People who invest in art usually follow the 'art guru's' and critic's advice or they buy old and traditional art. Textile art is not an investment. Buyers are usually private individuals who simply like the work, or companies and institutes which want to decorate their office premises or public spaces. I am interested in art in public spaces and I would like to co-operate with an architect during the design phase of a building.

Finland at the moment does not have any specific trend in art. Art is international and there are representatives of all styles and trends. My work is concerned with contemporary textile and fibre art and jewellery, not traditional Finnish textile techniques. In general fibre art is very new in Finland and it is difficult to find a proper definition for it. Art which is made with new techniques or does not have any tradition may get publicity and exhibiting possibilities but it is much more difficult to find financiers and buyers.

In Finland there are many art schools of different levels but only one academy of visual arts and one university of industrial arts which give university level education. There are lots of young people who study first in art colleges, or arts and crafts schools, and then want to get further art education. So there are a lot of applicants for those two university level schools. There are more people having an artist's education than there are work situations for artists. That is why most have to do some other work to earn their living. In most cases it is teaching art at evening schools, on courses or at children's art schools. Not everybody wants to be a teacher; it often takes up a lot of time but it is better paid than many other occasional jobs.

In Finland there are many different artists' organisations and associations. Almost all traditional fields of art have their own organisation. Nowadays this is not so good because many artists are not so strictly bound to one particular field of art. A couple of years ago a group of artists who didn't want to belong to any strictly limited organisation founded their own organisation *Muu* (Other) which arranges exhibitions and lectures, performances, video art, installations, etc.

I am myself a member of an organisation called TEXO which is a union of textile artists. Within TEXO I deal mostly with other textile artists and take part in textile exhibitions. Still I think there could be much more co-operation with other groups and associations.

Philip Dean

In comparison with most other European countries very few foreigners find their way to Finland. Tucked away in the north-eastern corner of Europe between Sweden and Russia, the country is probably better known through its sporting activities than anything else. The population of Finland is a mere five million in a land equal in size to Great Britain. But Finland is not only a land of fearless ski-jumpers and heavy-footed rally drivers as we might be led to believe. This young country has a rich cultural heritage and, despite the sparseness of pop-ulation, activity in all the arts takes place at both national and international levels.

There are many reasons for the relative lack of foreigners working here. Leaving geo-graphic and atmospheric consider-ations

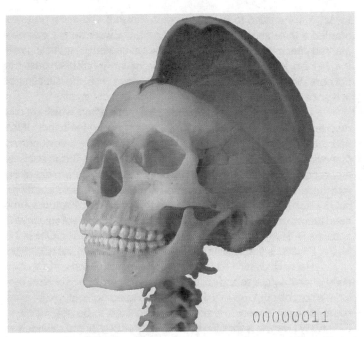

00000011

Philip Dean. **This work in progress is made using digital techniques, that is without film, darkroom etc.**

aside, Finland is an expensive country. Food is around 50-100% more expensive than in the UK and alcohol even more. Add to this the strict immigration laws, and you may understand why you know so little about Finland. But on the positive side the general standard of living is high, the social services are usually excellent, housing is warm and well built, and public transport services are well run.

I arrived in Finland nearly ten years ago as a scholarship student. Having graduated from the London College of Printing a year earlier with a BA in photography, I was glad to escape the gloom of Mrs Thatcher's Britain. My departure was a mixture of luck and opportunism and I have never really regretted packing my bags (even though I am writing this at a time when a very Thatcher-like recession is taking hold of Finland). Armed with my scholarship and its accompanying student accommodation, I was freed of the initial immigration procedures which usually await anybody intending to stay here for over three months. I spent ten months as an additional student in the department of Photographic Art at the University of Industrial Arts, Helsinki (UIAH).

I never returned to live in England. Getting married was the only way to stay here with my partner without a work permit. Obtaining a work permit was a classic 'Catch-22' affair. You could not work without a work permit but you were not allowed to apply for one from within Finland. Work had to be sought either from abroad (fat chance!) or by visiting possible employers whilst 'visiting'. I'm not sure whether this ridiculous system is still in existence but in our case it involved returning to England to make the application. My application for a freelance work permit, did not meet with approval (even though being married to a Finnish citizen

I was legally entitled to live and work in Finland) and although I was granted a three months' residence permit, the work permit was only granted after my wife Tarja spent 30 minutes heatedly negotiating with the Finnish authorities on the phone from the Finnish embassy in London. The system seemed unable to cope with the situation of freelance employment – surely the situation of most artists.

I was soon to learn the handling of these affairs which we had received was par for the course. Immigration was in the hands of the police and all foreigners were considered undesirable unless proved otherwise. Luckily things are beginning to change and British subjects are, according to studies made here, the 'most welcome' arrivals along with those from the USA. I soon started to pick up work, here and there, but my lack of cash and facilities made things difficult. Photographers need a studio and a darkroom sometimes, as well as camera equipment, and I made a few good friends who let me use their facilities. One of the joys of Finland is the smallness of everything, including social circles.

Helsinki, doesn't have the sort of rentable spaces artists often need when they are setting out on their careers. In London or New York there's no problem to rent a fully-equipped photographic studio for a few hours, or even a week. Here you are expected to be self-sufficient. Eventually I went to work full-time for the advertising photographer who let me use his studio. I worked there for over two years and produced my first solo show. Looking back now it was not very good. Unsure of myself I made too many compromises to what I imagined were Finnish expectations; my own vision began to be veiled in a strange mixture of commercial dynamism (a result of the work in the advertising studio) and an allegiance to the almost utopian view of the Finnish scene (an influence from my Finnish teachers who couldn't accept the use of a flash-gun or my experiments with the 'disrespectful' topographical landscape). Some welcome personal advice from a worthy critic led me to ignore my Finnish mentors and get on with developing my ideas.

Having regained my self-confidence my work picked up and I was even offered some teaching back in UIAH. Later we spent a year living in the country, about 80 miles west of Helsinki, and I decided to learn Finnish properly in order to communicate with my neighbours. This was critical as it has allowed me to take control of my own business and relieved my wife from the chore of translation. During this year in the country I also spent considerable time just wandering around the forests and marshes getting to know the 'real' Finland, picking berries and mushrooms and taking a few photos – very Finnish behaviour.

Returning to Helsinki four years ago I started to get more teaching and, being over 30 years old and so exempt from national service, decided to apply for Finnish citizenship. This was comparatively

FINLAND – A Guide for Foreigners by the Finnish Ministry of Labour. Published by VAPK-Publishing, 1991, ISBN 951-37-0705-9. This book should help people through the rigours of immigration, obtaining a tax book, work permit, etc.

Taide (Art) magazine covers contemporary visual art and contains some gallery information tel Helsinki 694 9517)

Valokuva-lehti, leading Finnish photography magazine tel Helsinki 663433, fax Helsinki 662422

easy as I hadn't been in trouble, had enough work and knew the language. Being a 'Finn' has allowed me to apply for some grants, which are not available for residents. Nationality is often a prerequisite to gaining financial support in Finland, unlike the UK where permanent residence will usually suffice.

Today, nearly ten years from my arrival I feel strangely indoctrinated into the Finnish way of life. I earn most of my living from teaching and in recent years I've been an editor with the leading Finnish photographic magazine, *Valokuva-lehti*. I take less photographs, produce on average about one exhibition a year and recently started postgraduate studies which deal with the integration of digital technology into photographic practice. More time is spent looking at this computer monitor than wandering the forests, which is a sad thing.

The Finnish State Scholarships for graduates are well worth investigating if you have a BA (or equivalent) and would like to study in Finland. In such a small country art colleges are few and far between but the standard of education is high. The main institutions are the Finnish Art Academy for fine art, the Sibelius Academy for music and the University of Industrial Arts for visual communications, Industrial design, art education and crafts. The Finnish embassy in London can give more details of the programme.

Although there is no problem for foreign teachers to teach in English, foreign students really need to know Finnish if they want to take part in the theoretical courses. This language bares no resemblance to other Western European language to learn it you must be seriously determined. For the casual visitor there is no language problem as English is understood and spoken by a large percentage of the population.

Finland is a land of summer festivals, ranging from folk dancing to international opera. Many foreign artists are invited to participate in these events, to exhibit, perform, lecture or to run workshops etc. These festivals are well subsidised by the state or the local community. Foreign guests are usually well established artists, although some more adventurous curators have sometimes invited relatively young artists to exhibit. If you are interested to show your work here it is well worth bombarding the galleries with examples and press cuttings. If you are lucky enough to get a show (and it's well received) this can often lead on to other commissions or possible teaching.

The Finnish press generally gives good coverage to the arts but information regarding galleries, festivals and events may not be so easy to find from outside Finland. The various artists' unions could probably give the most reliable information regarding galleries and curators.

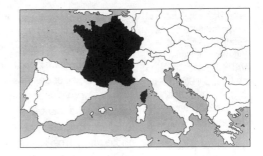

France

Member of the Council of Europe and the EC

LANGUAGE
Official: French
Others spoken: Breton, Basque, regional dialects
English spoken: more likely in towns and cities, attempts at French often appreciated

CURRENCY
Official: 100 centimes = 1 French Franc
Convertible or not: yes
Travellers cheques/Eurocheques/credit cards: not as extensive as you might expect, but certainly in centres

DOCUMENTS YOU NEED
For information contact: French Consulate General tel 071 581 5292. Visa section, 6A Cromwell Road,London SW1 2JN tel 071 823 9555

FRENCH DTI DESK
OT 3/3b Room 350 tel 071 215 4761/4762/5451/5197

BANKS
Open Monday to Saturday 9.00-12.00 to 14/16.00; Closed either Monday or Saturday

POST OFFICES
Open Monday to Friday 8.00-12.00 to 14.30/19.00 & Saturday morning

BUSINESS HOURS
8.00-12.00 and 14.00/18.00; closed Sunday or Monday

ART GALLERIES/MUSEUMS
Seasonal opening, closing days usually Monday or Tuesday

PUBLIC HOLIDAYS
Jan 1, Easter weekend, Ascension, Pentecost, May 1, May 8, Jul 14, Aug 15, Nov 1, Dec 25

CONTACT IN THE UK
French Institute, Queensberry Place, London SW7 tel 071 589 6211
French Government Tourist Office, 178 Piccadilly, London W1V 0AL tel 071 499 6911

CONTACT ABROAD
British Council, 9/11 rue de Constantine, 75007 Paris tel 49557300/45559595
Ministry of Culture, Communications and Major Works, 3 rue de Valois, 75042, Paris Cedex 01 tel 40158000
Chambers of Commerce:
All towns have one and everyone in business is a member, the agency advising small businesses is: Institut de Development Industrial (IDI), 4 rue Ancelle, 92521 Neuilly-sur-Seine, France
Embassy/Consulate:
British Embassy, 35 rue de Faubourg St. Honore, 75383 Paris, Cedex 08 tel 42669142
Artists Association:
Maison des Artistes, 9 & 11 rue Berryer, 75008 Paris
Copyright/moral rights: DACS initially tel 071 377 1650. In France ADAGP, 11 rue Berryer, 75008 Paris tel 43590979 and SPADEM 15 rue St. Nicholas, 75012 Paris tel 43425858/12 Rue Henner, 75009 Paris tel 48744039

Evelyne Iehle

Centre National des Arts Plastiques (National Centre for the Plastic Arts), 27 Avenue de l'Opéra, Paris 1 tel 42615616. (Information on awards, studios, etc)

ONI: Office National d'Immigration (Department of Immigration) PO Box 3316 Paris Cédex 16 tel 47550161

Minitel: Similar to the television information service 'Oracle' in the UK but much more advanced and comprehensive. 3616 code SICI will give you information on contacts (eg DRACS, FRACS, artists associations, gallery listings, ctc)

MAPRA (Rhône Alps Artists Association), 24, rue Ernest Rognon, Lyon 69007 tel78726580

If the decentralisation of culture realised in France in the eighties is still at work in the provinces, its effects are ambiguous. The *Direction Regionale des Affaires Culturelles* (DRAC) and the *Fond Regional d'Art Contemporain* (FRAC) organisations, established in the different regions so as to give them a real presence, with nominated posts and official offices, do not always have direct contact with regional creativity. Both organisations are often inaccessible to local artists. This has made it very unwelcome to be classified as a local artist in France. It is a defamatory label which indicates marginalisation without much hope of ever getting anywhere. Curiously, artists who live in the Ile de France region are not local artists, but Parisians!

This geographical division has brought with it an inevitable need for movement, and so it is an incessant struggle to obtain a beginnings of recognition from Paris enabling one to put on an exhibition in one's area of origin.

It is probable that a foreigner, with his or her aura of exoticism, will have less difficulties in exhibiting. They will undertake more easily the necessary visits to different institutions which will eventually give access to the several official exhibition venues active in each region.

Indeed, if the outlying regions have deliberately started to put on parades of avant garde art with elaborate displays subsidised by the government, the private galleries interested in developing present day art, seem to be relatively restrained. We could say that two levels exist, each impermeable to the other. One consists of recognition by the official galleries, and the other tends to a very traditional view of art geared towards selling.

The size of Paris and Its surroundings has permitted artistic pursuits to diversify, due to the great number of private galleries. It is still not easy to carve one's way. Friendly relations with a gallery will be rarely followed up with early possibilities of exhibition. There are many Parisian artists on their lists and the local artist suffers the handicap of working far away. Given the difficulty a curator finds in visiting a studio in the vicinity, it is a lot to ask him or her to travel to the other side of France.

Driven by necessity, the artist must aim to show work in Parisian circles. The Grand Palais, home of the FIAC and the Decouverte (fairs reserved for the use of galleries only) is also a place where exhibitions are held all year round. This venue, more or less covered by professionals, offers fruitful contacts. Other exhibition centres which should not be ignored in the outlying suburbs of Paris are Montrouge, Novembre in Vitry for painters, and Bagneux, a new centre which is making an increasing impression thanks to the talent of its administrators.

Giratoire (Monumental), Evelegne Iehle**, 1987 marble and metal.**

In several districts in Paris, the artists themselves organise associations. The Bastille district has studios and workshops open for one week during the FIAC, which increases contact with the public. These associations are not closed circles, and are interested in meeting with other European creators.

There is an interesting coming and going of alternative non-state structures. We are witnessing today an increasing desire for transversality and lateral extension which indicates a change to recognition by climbing up the ladder. To enter these fluctuating groups, it is necessary to have many friends on whom you can count to help you make sufficient new contacts. The most difficult thing is to ensure you are not forgotten.

Parisians have more possibilities for showing their work and finding the necessary materials, but have more problems with respect to space. Several artists share workshops which may be small, some have no studio. On this point we are luckier in the provinces, but it may be difficult to find a studio in a large town, and above all expensive.

The question of cost of a studio brings us to the necessary consideration of financial resources. Very few French artists earn enough to live on as a result of their creative work. Necessity obliges most of us to maintain another job alongside. Most teaching posts in the colleges of fine art are held by recognised artists who benefit in this manner from a form of state support through their salary. One can look for work in private schools, *Maisons des Jeunes,* institutions for disabled people (art therapy is a growing area) or classes for adults.

The sphere of public art may provide openings for sculptors interested in realising monuments. Several municipalities are asking themselves what heritage they will leave from the twentieth century, and it is possible there will be new opportunities in the years to come. One feels all too well a revival of interest from local public bodies. However, the aim of the municipalities in the bigger cities is to give themselves a prestigious cultural image, necessary for their identification in the race for European metropolitan status. And the state, with its *Contrat Culturel des Villes,* (cultural contract for towns) risks distancing this opening by offering it only to recognised artists. It is also true to say that at a regional level, a real need is felt by local officials for an artist's advice. The greatest difficulty is to obtain the necessary information to pose one's candidature for public works. That requires frequent provision of one's complete portfolio.

A review as short as this one does not allow for an exhaustive analysis of what happens in each province. I would only say that the region where I live, Rhône Alpes, shows a huge respect contemporary art, and is very receptive to international exchange.

Worrying that I may have painted a rather gloomy picture, I would like to add that in France it is easier to be a painter than a sculptor, preferable to be under forty, and that being female is still a problem. The true ideal is to be a very young avant-garde male artist!

Delphine Barraclough

I am a photographer engaged in community-based projects. In spring 1991 I spent a month with various Vietnamese communities in Paris to complete a photographic study funded by the Prince's Trust and the Richard Mills Fellowship.

I had gone to Paris because of the nature of a previous project. In 1990 I completed a photo-essay on the Vietnamese community in south-east London. I aimed to study different aspects of the Vietnamese communities in France and discover how they compared or contrasted with those in England. The photographs, I hoped, would form a bridge between people separated by political and economic changes in Vietnam. Eventually, the project became a more wide-ranging study of the lives of refugees in their new environment.

Running up to my departure, I was supplied with a list of names and telephone numbers by a Vietnamese community leader in London. I made initial contact by telephone while in London; I wanted everything set up so I could simply get on with the work when I got out there. I arranged to stay with a friend in Paris, and took out insurance through my bank; this was inexpensive and quickly arranged. Though this was the first time I had worked in Paris as an artist, I spent a year there as a

Nguyen Ngoc Dat, a political refugee, Southwark, London.
Delphine Barraclough

student in 1981, so I was familiar with the city and had friends there. My French was rusty so I brushed up on my vocabulary with language tapes from the local library.

I bought all my film in London as I can get a discount. I got a range of black-and-white and colour film to cover most situations. I didn't plan to do any processing or printing in Paris so didn't worry about other photographic material. My overheads were to be minimal: the accommodation was free and I had no need of studio space as I photographed people where they lived, worked or socialised. Paris is a special place in the world of photography, it has a long tradition of photography with a social conscience. It is also a good centre for photographic shops and laboratories: everything which can be bought in London can be bought in Paris.

Once there I devoted my time to taking photographs and fulfilling the proposal I had submitted to the Prince's Trust. I did not have to earn a wage since the Prince's Trust grant covered all my expenses as well as giving me spending money; I did not have enough time to carry out freelance photographic work. When I applied for the grant I outlined the details and aims of the work I proposed to do. This gave me a good structure to work from but also allowed for unexpected things to occur which then could be incorporated into the work. I had also submitted a detailed budget. I found this invaluable as I was financially prepared for all situations. Living there can be very expensive and having a budget to follow helped me to be economical and was one less worry. I have friends in Paris from whom I got information such as the price of a monthly metro ticket, the amount of money needed for food, laundry, etc. The public transport system is cheaper and more efficient than London.

Because Paris is now so easy to get to, there is no end to sources of information, from travel books to special features in listings magazines and newspapers.

The London contacts I had supplied me with names and addresses of nationalist Vietnamese in Paris who are active politically and culturally. Through people I met once out in Paris I was taken to cultural houses run by the Vietnamese consulate. The initial contacts I made from London gave access to a wide network of people which was invaluable considering the limited amount of time I had.

The initial period of thawing the ice with the Vietnamese I found to be as important as the time spent taking the photographs. Because of the political divisions there was a level of suspicion and caution exhibited towards strangers. I had also to arrive at a point where my subjects would relax and interact with me as the photographer and with the camera, as well as with each other. The recurrent problem was the lack of light in many of the places I photographed; I didn't want to use a flash since this would have intruded on the situation I was observing and photographing.

Setting up meetings could take days; the time flew by, though there were days when I was waiting to hear from someone or waiting to get in touch with another. I met a great number of people, a few who didn't want to be photographed and many who were friendly and keen to help.

I hadn't anticipated any contact with other artists in Paris but as it was I did meet a photographer interested in my work and we had discussions which will hopefully lead to us working together. I'm keen to develop my own network of artists across Europe and, through this, exchanges of ideas and opinions will occur. Speaking to photographers, I found similarities in ways of thinking and working.

Although there is a strong tradition of the French government being more sympathetic to the arts than the British, I get the impression artists still have to conform to orthodox ways of thinking and working if they wish to succeed. More money is available in France for the arts and media but to gain money the artist has to be part of the current political and social thinking. I do think it is no better or worse in Britain except there is actually less money than in France.

On my return to the UK I had a small exhibition at the Vietnamese community centre in south-east London. Exhibitions are a good way of allowing a lot of people to see my work. However they are not a way of making money: the outlay is high and my work, not being 'arty', has no market. Magazines are a better market in which to earn money from my photo-essay. Through the Prince's Trust I have been approached by other photographers and artists as well as arts administrators, who wish to learn about the project in Paris with a view to working with me in similar areas.

Germany

Member of the Council of Europe and the EC. Due to the political, social, cultural and economic upheaval of re-unification, life in Germany will continue to change and develop for a long time, this information was correct at time of research.

LANGUAGE
Official: German
Others spoken: Border influence such as French
English spoken: extensively

CURRENCY
Official: 100 pfennigs = 1 Deutsche Mark
Convertible or not: yes
Travellers cheques/Eurocheques/credit cards: more acceptable in western Germany, Berlin & larger cities in the eastern Germany; use growing – not as extensive as expected

DOCUMENTS YOU NEED
For information contact: German Embassy, 23 Belgave Square, London SW1X 9PZ tel 071 235 5033

GERMAN DTI DESK
OT 3/3a Room 361 tel 071 215 5245/4656/4796/ 4285

BANKS
Open Monday to Friday 8.30-13.00 to 14.30-16.00; open lunchtime in some main centres

POST OFFICES
Open Monday to Saturday 8.00-18.00

BUSINESS HOURS
Opening hours for shops are strictly governed by law, this is more established in western Germany and includes late opening on Thursday and early closing on Saturday

ART GALLERIES/MUSEUMS
Closed Mondays, often more out of season and in eastern Germany

PUBLIC HOLIDAYS
Jan 1, Easter weekend, May 1, Ascension, Whit Monday, Oct 3, third Wednesday in November, Nov 25/26, Dec 25/26 plus further regional and religious days

CONTACT IN THE UK
Goethe Institute, 50 Princes Gate, London SW7 2PG tel 071 581 3344.

German National Tourist Office, Nightingale House, 65 Curzon Street, London W1Y 7PE tel 071 495 3990

CONTACT ABROAD
British Council, Hahnenstrasse 6, 5000 Cologne 1 tel 206440
Embassy/Consulate:
British Embassy, Freidrich Ebert Allee 77, 5300 Bonn 1 tel 234061. Consulates in Berlin, Bremen, Düsseldorf, Frankfurt-am-Main, Freiburg, Hanover, Hamburg, Kiel, Munich, Nuremburg, Stuttgart
Artists Association:
Berufsverband der bildenden Künstler (BBK), Poppelsdorferalle 43, 5300 Bonn 1
Copyright/moral rights:
DACS initially tel 071 247 1650. In Germany Bild-Kunst, Poppelsdorferalle 43, 5300 Bonn 1 tel 219566

Claus Bach

I belong to those artists who can claim to be presently in the jungle of confusion over German unity, in the struggle between the artists of West and East Germany. Up till now I have not had to suffer any existential exodus, as so many others have done. It may be that this is linked to my occasional tendency to change course completely: in 1976 voluntarily dropping out of a course in building materials, after that working as a book printer and training to be a professional photographer, and since then self education. In the early eighties, collaboration with a literary figure from East Berlin and his companion, turning from the artistic photograph to the photo-text collage. Group and individual exhibitions, always outside the official art industry of the German Democratic Republic (GDR), in cafés, cinemas, church halls and for the most part short-lived private galleries of the Prenzlauerberg in East Berlin; collaboration on and publication of underground art booklets in Berlin and Weimar. For some years work with predominantly conceptual and directed photography.

Despite being accepted into the then Union of Fine Artists of the GDR I constantly had to look after my own existence. It was hard then and is likely to remain so, despite some successes. After a large personal exhibition in the private gallery *Eigen+Art* in Leipzig my works are now published, bought, are to be found in collections and now even occasionally get into a bigger exhibition on tour throughout the USA. However I still do not have my own studio. With the present blatantly high rent prices of the new East/West property owners, I am not likely to find one in the near future. Naturally my art does not bring in enough to live on. I finance over half through commissions, including the cost of living. But that is of course a compromise most artists everywhere have to live with. I have been able to cope with this situation up to now by means of disciplined work.

An author from East Berlin recently said to me on the telephone, 'East Germany's past has just begun'. By that he meant the entanglement of many former East German citizens in the service of the State Security. Even in the small town of Weimar, as everywhere else, I experience the contemptible transition to the general daily routine: from the ideological dogma of East German socialism to that of the new market economy, an implacable age-old capitalism is the result. The automatism of self-manipulation occasions the most jarring and comical stylistic howlers. The 'new German' is created at the push of a button. Despite the rapid spiritual metamorphosis of many, their past will catch up with them, or so I believe – ever naïve. Old and new power structures have long

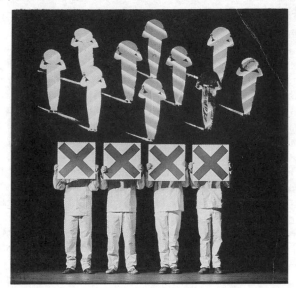

Claus Bach, *Kopfkörper.*

combined on an economic and political level. A wretched state of affairs at whose mercy we all are.

In Weimar, all contradictions and aggressions come together in the most confined space, which is normal in East German cities. Raging unemployment, xenophobia, increasing social contrasts and Neo-Nazism make life more dangerous. On the other hand, the fact Weimar still counts as provincial in the development of contemporary fine arts seems rather harmless; the influence of the dominatingly conservative bourgeois and bureaucrat mentality, which had already driven out the world-famous Bauhaus in the twenties, can still be felt in the town today – despite the enormous social changes. We are constantly confronted with the past of the Nazi concentration camp, and later Soviet prison camp, at Buchenwald, about whose existence the people of Weimar wanted to know nothing at all.

But new impulses – like the springing up of alternative private galleries, above all the 'ACC' (Autonomous Culture Centre) and the gallery *am Markt* – allow us to hope. It is mainly unknown young artists from inside and outside Germany who exhibit and who are encouraged. Even though the standard is not always outstanding, they bring a breath of fresh air into the otherwise musty museum-like tradition-entrenched swamp of the town. A vital young scene is evolving, which provides for contradiction and long overdue activity.

Like most East German artists I too stand in the field of conflict which resembles a test of tensile strength. At present, the self-dynamics of this development leave little room for reflection. Possibilities and spaces which have recently become available can often, for purely economic reasons, not be exploited at present. For most artists working on projects, such as former underground (samizdat) art booklets, time is running out, few editions remain in existence. There is a constant struggle with new legalisation and bureaucracy. But we are coming to terms with the new system, the new era.

I still remember well the words of a friend who possessed a Western visa in GDR times: 'The West is nothing more than a perfumed East'. Only now is the contradictory nature of this sentence obvious. Therein lies the old clear politico-ideologically fixed picture of the enemy. Many artists who have been inspired only by this picture, feel they have been stripped of their identity, and lapse into lethargy or flee into nostalgic reflection, as if the world had consisted solely of the GDR – a dangerous path completely clouding reality, which is becoming more and more Kafkaesque. It is better to have honest and ruthless dealings with one's own past, in order to progress. That helps us to recognise and label the apparently invisible new power structures. To want to reduce them to a single clique is a dangerous error. The realm of human behaviour is too contradictory, feelings influence those in power more than we realise.

There has never been a true East German art, we know that today. And many former state artists are following again the renewed path of conforming to the new values system of the free art market, as they did in the old days. The most abstruse changes in artistic style spring up almost overnight, at best interesting for a simple minded public. By international standards, East German artists can now claim that their work truly exudes a convincingly original power. Individuals too sometimes achieve immediate success on the appropriate Western art markets. For me a demystification of such 'Western art' took place in 1991. I saw a great deal of half-heartedly cultivated deco kitsch, few controversial or even provocative works. The art market is stagnating. The economic uncertainty is a backdrop to the more hesitant approach of many buyers and collectors in the West (forgive the restriction).

Two years have already passed since the fall of the Berlin Wall, now we East Germans also live in the world of hedonism. And most recently, since the disintegration of the Soviet Union, the world is coming apart at the apparently stable political seams; it seems to be standing on its head. Gloomy pictures of the future can again be painted, fabricated, directed. It is a long time since such an absurdly grotesque and above all dangerous situation existed. It is left to us artists regardless of our geographical situation, to make this clearer through our dreams. And may it only be for a few hope-giving, but perhaps deciding moments.

Melanie Clifford

This morning Berlin is shrill, concentrated, opaque, messy. On the front walls of the apartment buildings in Prenzlauerberg, where I am living, there are coloured, painted portions of what were inside walls but the

Melanie Clifford, **Berlin, June 1991. Installation: high-tensile, mild steel, human hair, sellotape, agar jelly, white chalk, pink and orange east wallpaper, yellow east curtain rail, tin crocodile clip curtain hangers, skylight window, suspension of dust, 4mm silver wire.**

balconies which contained them have fallen off, turning bared insides out.

Berlin's transitoriness makes it uncomfortable to work here if comfort means settling in a rented studio and getting on with it. More than just being able to improvise and move quickly, you have to have a need to do these things.

Anyway there are very few rentable studio spaces left. Until recently in the West there were many group and single studios in *Fabriketagen* (factory floors) of disused small industrial buildings, especially in the districts of Kreuzberg and Wedding. With the rush of 'big money' to Berlin as the newly reinstated German capital city, these places are just now being bought up for redevelopment or the rents raised by 200-300%, so walls are layered with posters for *sterbendes Atelier* (dying studio) exhibitions. The established studios which still exist are usually very expensive or small, dark and half full of something else.

Artists' unions are demanding money and space to be set aside within the redevelopment programmes for subsidised, or any, studio spaces. The department for cultural affairs of the Berlin Senate says it doesn't have the money from central government to compete with the big business being attracted to the city by the moving here of central government. It is hoped funding for the arts generally will be significantly increased, but expected that most of the money will go to arts institutions with obvious prestige value: big theatres, opera, substantially stocked national museums and galleries in both parts of the city. The popular fear is that from the distant stand-point of monetary concern the intricate, mobile, diverse mess of independent art work throughout the city will not only be undervalued (what's new?), but badly trampled upon.

I can't stand this pessimism. At the time of writing there are still many buildings, of all kinds, empty in the east part of Berlin and a lot of stubbornly, passionately produced work.

Using these buildings entirely legally (the rights to ownership of many are still unclear) can involve unfathomable depths of murky bureaucracy, made easier if you can work together with artists from the

Künstlerhaus Bethanien, (Bethanien Arts Centre) Mariannenplatz 2, 1000 Berlin 36. Senate-funded international arts centre with workshop facilities and studios for invited artists, average stay six to twelve months. Deadline for applications: October 1. Write for details.

Senatsverwaltung für Kulturelle Angelegenheiten, (Senate department for cultural affairs), Tauenzienstrasse 9 (Europa Center), 1000 Berlin 30

Deutscher Akademischer Austauschdienst DAAD (German Academic Exchange Service). Stienplatz 2, 1000 Berlin 12. Professional artists now by invitation only, but at the time of writing still apply to study here through the DAAD.

East. Learn some German before you come here or take cheap courses at one of the district *Volkshochschulen* (adult education schools), enrol beginning of January and July.

Independent galleries, café galleries and studio-workshop-galleries appear, disappear, reappear rapidly and are concentrated in the districts of Prenzlauerberg and Mitte in the East, and to a lessening extent, in Kreuzberg in the West. While the formal structures of previously state-controlled visual art activity in the East part of the city have been dismantled, the East is not a cultural wasteland waiting to be reclaimed. That the East has been assimilated by the West, and Easterners are as thoroughly overjoyed by the prospect of this as the Western mass-media has seemed to want us to believe, is an assumption of banal arrogance. There is now, and perhaps only for a short time, a space in the East for innovative art work outside there being any long-established structure for it: neither its production nor exhibition.

I have been making installation work in empty, condemned or otherwise unused peripheral and public spaces. I've encountered less of a need for people to see a gleaming white wall behind art before they will approach and involve themselves with it as something which is in some way meaningful within its immediate, as opposed to a traditional gallery, context.

The traditional public art of 'socialist' sculpture and murals is now juxtaposed by the spilling out of work by what were 'underground' artists, and there is a strong, if under financed, movement against billboard advertising becoming the sole communicative voice in public spaces.

Alongside the many, generally international, groups of visual artists, performers, film and video makers working and exhibiting through the gaps in Berlin's reconstruction, there is in each district of the city an official *Kunst* or *Kulturamt* (art cultural office) which organises and co-ordinates mostly grant-aided work locally. For example in Kreuzberg, which has a large Turkish population, much of this *dezentrale Kulturarbeit* (decentralised cultural work) focuses on cultural issues involving that community.

Artists of any nationality can apply to the Berlin Senate for funding for specific projects, particularly those which are publicly or community based, provided they have been legally resident here for more than just a few months or are working with an artist who has.

However you value gleaming white walls, there is a large and wide range of small galleries, cinemas and performance spaces, with varying emphasis on selling and getting work shown. Addresses and what they are showing are to be found in the two fortnightly listings magazines *Zitty* and *Tip* and on the fast-changing skins of posters which smother the walls along street and U-bahn station buildings.

Greece

Member of the Council of Europe and the EC

LANGUAGE
Official: Greek
Others spoken: German often understood
English spoken: widely, especially in cities and tourist areas

CURRENCY
Official: drachma
Convertible or not: yes
Travellers cheques/Eurocheques/credit cards: widely used due to tourism, less likely in rural areas

DOCUMENTS YOU NEED
For information contact: Embassy of Greece, 1a Holland Park, London W11 3TP tel 071 727 8040

GREEK DTI DESK
OT 3/3b Room 362 tel 071 215 5103/4776

BANKS
Open Monday-Thursday 8.00-14.00 Friday 8.00-13.30, extra hours in cities and tourist areas

POST OFFICES
Open Monday-Friday 7.30-14.00, extra hours in cities and tourist areas

BUSINESS HOURS
Opening hours for shops vary, especially between Summer and Winter – concentrate on getting things done in the mornings

ART GALLERIES/MUSEUMS
Opening hours vary, with ad hoc and sudden closing – mornings more consistent

PUBLIC HOLIDAYS
Jan 1, Jan 6, Mar 25, first Monday of Lent, Easter weekend (Orthodox calendar), May 1, Aug 15, Oct 28, and much of Christmas period; there are many other festivals/holidays

CONTACT IN THE UK
National Tourist Organisation of Greece, 4 Conduit Street, London W1R 0DJ tel 071 734 5997

CONTACT ABROAD
British Council, Plateia Philikis, Etairias 17, Kolonaki Square, PO Box 3488, Athens 102 10 tel 3633211
Ministry of Culture, Odos Aristidou 14, 101-86 Athens tel 3243015
Chamber of Commerce:
Odos Akademias 7, Athens 106 71 tel 3604815
Embassy/Consulate:
British Embassy, 1 Ploutarchou Street, Athens 106 75 tel 7236211. Other consulates in Corfu, Crete, Patras, Rhodes, Salonika, Samos, Syros, Volos.
Artists Associations:
The Chamber of Artists (EETE), Nikis 11, Athens 100 86
Greek Confederation of Labour (GSEE), Odos Patission 69, Athens tel 8834611
Copyright/moral rights: No Greek organisation noted, try Design & Artists Copyright Society (DACS), St. Mary's Clergy House, 2 Whitechurch Lane, London E1 7QR tel 071 247 1650

Ana Mathiou

Most artists, in Greek *kallitechnes* (from *kalos: good* and *techni: art*), both Greek and foreign, live and work in the busy capital city of Athens. Although living in Athens may be tiring and less pleasant than in many other cities and towns, it offers better opportunities for work. Undoubtedly, it is the cultural centre of Greece.

An increasing artistic effort has been developed within the last years in Thessaloniki, the second big city in Greece. In smaller towns, some disparate exhibitions and art events are organised mainly by municipal or private initiatives. These are often related to the traditional crafts or the promotion of local artists.

During the hot season (June to September), art people follow the touristic wave to the islands and resorts. Fine art and craft exhibitions often accompany the numerous musical or theatrical festivals. Young painters, sculptors, craftspeople move and work within an amateur tourist clientele. Some of them earn a living doing portraits outside the old town of Rhodes, or selling handmade jewellery in Paros.

Most Greek artists usually work within their flats or houses by converting a spacious room, garage or basement to a studio. Artists who can afford to pay for an individual studio are rare. In fact, there are no group studios, like old warehouses, to share in Athens.

Because of the increasing demand on rented accommodation over the last few years, it is getting harder and harder to find any spaces available in Athens. Prices vary from area to area, but remain generally cheaper compared to other European capitals.

Finding studio space is easier for painters, sculptors and craftspeople who create small artworks by using machinery operating with the standard home electric power. Artists who work with high electric power machinery face more problems, as they need to present to the Ministry of Industry a work permit and a tax declaration in order to obtain industrial electric power.

Greek weather enables artists to work outdoors, in verandas and gardens; a whole generation of Greek painters lived some decades ago in the small washing rooms on top of buildings using the roof as a studio.

A large variety of painting materials can easily be found in art and hobby shops in the centre of Athens. Materials are mainly imported from other European countries and the States and so are quite expensive.

Multi-media materials and machinery for three-dimensional constructions are quite rare and sometimes not available. Craftspeople are usually obliged to order and import their own equipment from abroad, which can take a long time and cost a lot.

Money Box, Ana Mathiou, 1988.
**From a series of wood 'Icons'
Enamelled glass, collage,
wooden frame box, inside light.
29.5x23.5x5cm.**

Since there are no large art and craft stores in Athens, materials often have to be purchased from different small shops spread all around the city. Sometimes it can be quite hard to locate them, as there are no specialised guides.

The principal body of Greek art education is the School of Fine Art in Athens and Thessaloniki. The number of students is limited, the entrance is competitive and studies last five years. The School teaches only painting and sculpture and the educational system is quite conservative and traditional. There are also some private schools, offering drawing and design courses. Various craft organisations offer seminars and short courses.

Since it is unlikely for a young artist to obtain a teaching position in the School of Fine Art, teaching opportunities are limited either to the high school where a graduate diploma is required, or to private institutions.

Most grants offered by private organisations and the European Community (EC), intend to help young people study abroad.

The Chamber of Culture and the Ministry of Civilization are the only organisations providing information and advice. Councils of most European countries are located in Athens where foreign artists can get help and information. They often organise exhibitions for artists from their countries. There are no art agencies, so artists have to contact individual galleries directly themselves.

Art magazines are few and their editorial material is limited to lists of and comments on current exhibitions taking place in Athens and other cities or towns.

Painting is represented in all its forms, but the actual mainstream with the most commercial success is neo-realism, Greek traditional and modern subjects. The most popular sculpture techniques are stone and wood carving. Most craftspeople occupy themselves with traditional pottery, metal work, embroidery, weaving and jewellery. Modern crafts also exist although they do not sell quite as well. Gold and silver work, especially jewellery are considered to be the most successful.

Artists, like myself, who do not belong to the mainstream, either because they follow different expression tendencies such as abstract painting or installations, or because they use different materials such as glass, can also be part of artistic life. This is because fashion and tendencies in Greece change more often and easily than in other European countries.

Most galleries are in the centre of Athens and belong in two categories: those which show works by well-known artists and others who promote young ones. Galleries either require a rent or more often various commission percentages. Exhibiting is competitive both for solo or group shows. Sometimes artists are invited to exhibit their work in banks or hotel halls. It is very common to visit an artist in his or her own studio.

Only very rarely can an artist earn a living from artistic work. Artists often own shops selling their own work as well as decorative objects and picture frames. Those who are trained in the Byzantine technique of icon painting, earn adequate income. Recently, many fine artists have started working in advertising which often leads them to a successful career. It is remarkable that a Greek painter who reached great commercial success recently, became famous by designing a political poster.

Tacita Dean

Thanks to Sara Wilks for assistance in writing this.

During the second year of my degree course at Falmouth School of Art and Design, we were encouraged to exchange with a student from another art school. I arranged to exchange with a student from the Supreme School of Fine Arts in Athens (ASKT) for six weeks in Spring 1987. This was my first experience of the visual arts in Greece, and it later informed my decision to spend a further year in Athens.

In March 1988 I applied through the British Council's booklet on scholarships abroad to the Embassy of Greece in London to spend some time in Greece affiliated to ASKT. Since my exchange in the previous year, my work had both mythological as well as contemporary references to Greece and I very much wanted to further my experience there. I was offered a four month scholarship and left in October the same year.

Under the terms of the scholarship, I received 40,000 drachmas a month (about £160) to cover living expenses, was able to attend comprehensive Greek language classes, receive free medical attention, and a further 10,000 drachmas to travel within Greece. I was also given a pass by the Ministry of Culture to have free entrance into all museums, galleries and historical sites. The money was given through a government scholarship organisation called IKY, who directed me to the Aliens' Bureau where I was given a residence permit, which meant I could not do any paid work or leave Greece while in receipt of scholarship money.

Mocked by its Understatement Tacita Dean, **1988.** From 'Three New Artists' at Galerie Artio.

I had received a letter inviting me to stay at the British School in Athens which is the standard accommodation offered to all Greek Government Scholars. However I decided not to live in an English speaking environment and was able to stay in a friend's flat on Aegina, the nearest island to the port of Piraeus. From here I used to commute into the Art School in Athens once or twice a week. Later I moved to Athens but again it was through a contact I'd made before arriving in Greece.

Until recently ASKT was the only art school in Greece. Now there is also a school in Thessaloniki. ASKT in Athens is run on a studio system, with its main building situated by the Archaeological Museum on Patission Street, and further studios nearby. Each studio is run by a professor who is an established artist, and assistants (also practising artists) are invited in once or twice a week.

I was in the studio of Nikos Kessanlis who has recently become the principal professor of the whole school. His was quite a popular studio, one thought to encourage alternative working practices, but generally the teaching is very conservative. Although my scholarship was only four months long, I continued to work in the studio until May; the actual course lasts five years. Several people working with me at the studio are now beginning to show in galleries in Athens, and to get teaching within the art school system. To my knowledge, no non-Greek artists are invited to teach in the school although I do know of artists giving private lessons. The best way for a native English speaker to earn money in Greece is to teach English.

The Supreme School of Fine Arts (ASKT), Patission 42, Athens tel 3616926

Photographic Centre of Athens, Sina 52, Athens 106 72 tel 3608825

Ileane Tounda Centre, Armatalon & Klefton 48, Athens 114 71 tel 6439473

ASKT has printmaking facilities in a studio in Notara Street behind the museum. There is a sculpture studio in the main school which is situated off a corridor of marble statues. However, a sign of the modernisation of the school is the advent of sculptor George Lappas as a professor, the first artist to really show internationally (recently in 'Metropolis' in Berlin) and representing Greece in the Venice Biennale. Photographic and media facilities don't really exist within the school and I know some artists, who make photographic based work, are struggling to give it comparable status to that of painting and sculpture. Finally the school owns four other buildings in Delphi, Hydra, Mykonos and Rhodes which any student or tutor may visit.

While I was at the school, another artist in my studio arranged for me to be involved in a show of three new artists at Galerie Artio, Deinocratous Street, a small commercial gallery in Kolonaki but one which is at the centre of a lot of the changes going on in the Greek visual arts. Kolonaki is where most of the art galleries can be found as well as the main British Council building. I sold most of my work in the show and I still continue to have a relationship with the gallery.

Until recently, Greek contemporary art was considered to be provincial and imitative taking its references from other European art. During the dictatorship, artists, architects and writers left Greece to live in Paris and Rome. However, Greek work is now creating its own identity and the promoting and showing of work by new, younger artists is becoming more organised. There is a new and willing market in Athens for contemporary art and many artists sell a lot while they are still quite young. The Ileane Tounda Centre is really the first contemporary art centre and is near Exarchia; its bar is a good place to meet practising artists and critics. There is, currently, a good bi-monthly art magazine called *Arti*, written in both Greek and English, the foreign language that tends to be the most widely spoken.

Studio space is quite easy to find as there is still a lot of empty property in Exarchia, the area around the Polytechnic where a lot of artists live. Materials are accessible but quite expensive. There is a good art shop on Septemvriou Street off Omonoia Square and another on Zaimi Street off Exarchia Square but it is best to buy canvas from the market on Ermou Street where there is plenty of choice. Photographic materials are expensive but colour photocopying is cheaper. It is also much cheaper to print catalogues in Greece.

Hungary

LANGUAGE
Official: Hungarian (Magyar)
Others spoken: German widely understood, minority languages include Croat, Romanian, Serbian, Slovak
English spoken: Mainly Budapest, but knowledge growing

CURRENCY
Official: 100 filler = 1 forint
Others used: Dollar and other hard currency
Convertible or not: yes
Travellers cheques/Eurocheques/credit cards: more acceptable in main centres, though use is growing

DOCUMENTS YOU NEED
For information on visa, residence and work permits contact: Hungarian Consulate, 35b, Eaton Place, London SW1X 8BY tel 071 235 2664

HUNGARIAN DTI DESK
OT 3/5d Room 316 tel 071 215 5257/4735

BANKS
Open Monday to Friday circa 9.00-14.00

POST OFFICES
Open Monday to Saturday 8.00-18.00; earlier closing outside centres

BUSINESS HOURS
Monday to Saturday 10.00-18.00; late night Thursday and shorter hours Saturday

ART GALLERIES/MUSEUMS
Closed Mondays

PUBLIC HOLIDAYS
Jan 1, Jan 15, Easter Monday, May 1, Aug 20, Oct 23, Dec 25/26

CONTACT IN THE UK
Danube Travel Agency, 6 Conduit Street, London W1R 9TG tel 071 493 0263

CONTACT ABROAD
British Council, Harmincad U.6 H-1051, Budapest V tel 182888
Ministry of Culture, Szalay u. 10/14, 1055 Budapest tel 1530600
Chamber of Commerce:
POB 106, 1389 Budapest tel 1533333
Embassy/Consulate:
British Embassy, Harmincad Utca 6, 1051 Budapest V tel 182888
Artists Associations:
Federation of Hungarian Artist's and Telecommunication Workers Unions, Gorkij fasor 38, 1068 Budapest tel 1211120
Magyar kepzomuveszek Szovetsege (Art Association), Vorosmarty ter 1, 1052 Budapest V tel 129626
Kali Basin Society, 8254 Kovagoors, Pf 9 Hungary
Copyright/moral rights:
DACS initially tel 071 247 1650. In Hungary, Hung Art, Bathory utca 10, Budapest V tel 313183

Agnes Háy

'Europe's secret spiritual centre', said M.E. a friend about Budapest, and we more or less believed that.

There was an underground group which wasn't a group but it was under the ground. I became one of their audience and friends (in about 1970) because their works and ideas were exciting and inspiring to me while the official socialist culture was quite boring. And vice-versa: they liked my works while the bureaucrats of the art policies did not accept them. We resisted the 'barbarian, Asian invaders' cultural dictatorship'. Although keeping contact with the West was a crime in the 50s, later just nearly impossible, we tried to continue a Hungarian culture which used to be European. A culture which gave the world great artists like Moholy-Nagy, Bartok, Vaserelly.

We had no posters, no newspapers to advertise our performances. We simply told each other and everybody who was interested knew 'what's on'. Once I asked two or three friends to come to my house to see some new shots which I had just developed; a few hours later twenty people arrived.

There were no art form barriers: composers went to the exhibitions, filmmakers to the concerts, poets to the theatre. We were each other's audience. And, by the way, there were a great number of mathematicians in the audience as well. Everybody worked in more than one medium. It was normal that I made graphics, animated films, theatre design and even participated in concerts. Through the 70s and 80s a group of four artists moved from painting to theatre, then to music and they also made a film. We were often involved – and gained experience – in other areas by helping fellow artists. You could always find somebody to write a preface to your book, act in your film, write and play music for your performance and we got communal help from outside too. We could illegally use the equipment of the film studios, we shot on stolen film which was developed free, we edited at night in the television building. When one artist had a budget, he put something in it for others. Lacking any financial background this type of help was essential for our work.

Maybe we were the elite where anybody who wanted to join, could. But they had to give up hope of a career. Many of us were second generation artists, others came from varied backgrounds, ranging from a housekeeper's son to a son of an executed minister. There were no class barriers, formal qualifications were of no advantage. We were sort of outlaws. In cultural politics there were three categories for artists: supported, allowed and banned (in Hungarian 'the three Ts': *támogatott, türt, tiltott*). We hoped to remain in the allowed category, but they very often banned us. Certain names were enough even to ban an event.

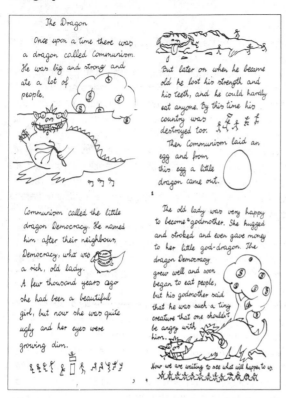

Dragon, Agnes Háy

I never understood why, and when something was dangerous for the state. I never understood why it was a scandal to perform Eric Satie's 24-hour long concert. Nor did I understand why there was a police raid at a theatre performance on an island in the Danube. We didn't speak about politics. We thought politics were a must for official 'socialist' artists and they were inferior and dirty, but at the same time we were afraid of the secret police.

Once a Jewish graphic artist drew a grotesque self-portrait and wrote many derogatory expressions against Jews, around his face. He was reprimanded by the police for anti-semitism. A few years later he went mad and burned all of his works saying that they were informers against him to the police.

In 1985, I emigrated to the UK because I felt my life was in danger in the 'communist' atmosphere. Most of my old friends either left the country, committed suicide, or went mad. In that year a film director killed himself. He was once a pioneer of experimental film, but – in my opinion – he had already given in, which had enabled him to make several large budget productions and to gain wider recognition. At the same time M.E. was dying of cancer. I believe his illness was due to never having had wider recognition, although he was a master of the underground culture. But the changes began. M.E. had his first exhibition just before he died in 1986. He was 58 years old.

The changes didn't happen from one day to the next. The Stalinist 50s socialist realist Zdanovism turned into a much more liberal system after the '56 revolution. The leaders gained power but lost their confidence. During the years they tried to find more and more liberal collaborators and dared to ban less and less things. Hungary was the 'happiest barrack in the communist camp'. Actually in the 70s – after the Czech '68 – there were no communists in the country, apart from a few old veterans. The thousands of members of the communist party were careerists.

And the changes have continued. The 'post-communist' atmosphere is more free but less warm, and money is more important than it used to be. Those *'Comrades'* who banned us changed their opinions and kept their positions. The new generation is less hungry for events and knowledge but still creative and talented.

Organising, finding contacts via the telephone is agony: it doesn't work. Sending letters is an unknown form of communication. We meet, as before, in pubs or clubs or parties or at events or just in the street. Things happen by chance – but quite well. There is a vivid cultural life with hundreds of new galleries, magazines, publishers, theatres, although the economic situation is a disaster. Several Western artists choose to participate and even live in this less 'developed' world. The Hungarian artists also participate in Western culture.

The 'old' avant-garde group is now widely recognised, publicised, exhibited, awarded. Emigrants are coming back and taking part in the artistic life. In 1988 I received the prize for the Best Hungarian Experimental Animated Film. In 'my time' the experimental category wasn't even acknowledged. In 1991 I gave lectures at the Academy where I had no chance to study. We are sort of a legend: some dead, some alive – some say it feels like being dead. I have become proud of knowing people whom I was just happy to know before.

In Budapest, in the King's Palace there is a permanent modern art exhibition. A small collection of the Western classics from the Ludwig Museum (Kolone) is shown alongside a similar Hungarian collection. The Hungarian artists are the same people I knew, and I always thought they were as good as the Western artists. But when I saw the exhibition I was shocked because the Hungarian artists were as good as the Western ones. I had to confront my feeling of inferiority – even after living for six years in London – I couldn't really believe that we are equal. It's a shame. But I don't think that I am the only person with this feeling.

Colin Foster

As in all walks of life this is a time of change. The move from a centralised communist government to a free-market capitalist economy is affecting art as it is everything else. The machinery of art management is being re-examined and may well be slowly dismantled. The information I can give here may not be valid for very long and so I concentrate on a general over-view.

Fuji Window, Colin Foster, 1989, **andersite.**
Creative Park Gallery, Fujimi Kogen

The communist regime had a long-standing centralised planning policy for the arts. The state accepted art as an important part of life and tried to provide a means of living for its artists. Art was refreshingly important on both an official and the ordinary people level. How long this will remain so is anybody's guess. The official structures established to support the arts are, sadly, inappropriate to a capitalist economy.

My own involvement with Hungary began in 1983, when on a short visit I was impressed by the enormous amount of public sculpture of all kinds. Application to the British Council in 1984 led to my paying an official visit, under the excellent exchange programme between the two countries. In 1985 I received an invitation to work at the Villány International Sculpture Park. During this visit I was invited to run the park and have been here ever since, although my official involvement with Villány ended in 1988.

The symposia which take place are one way in which the communist regime chose to support the arts. Originally they were a kind of alternative to the official Leninist art and they certainly played a considerable role in supporting such non-official art. It was the art produced by these artists which was increasingly shown in the West, although the full commercial exploitation of this art was never realised – and this was certainly not due to the quality of the work, much of which could hold its own in the Western market. These symposia soon became international forums where Hungarian artists can meet and work alongside contemporaries from other countries. They are very supportive in that workspace, tools, materials, accommodation, food and a little pocket money are provided free in exchange for the donation of one or more works produced. Conceivably one could live by moving from one symposium to another throughout the year.

The government also supported artists by extensive commissioning of work, but these opportunities are now diminishing, just as secure central funding for the symposia is under threat. The Government Art Board *(Lektoratus)* acts as a buffer between commissioned artists and the commissioner and has the added role of distributing planning permission. It advises with costings, schedules, etc, draws up contracts and determines fees to the artist. (These usually compare favourably to fees in England and, as they fix a plus payment for the artistic merit of the completed work in addition to the labour costs, the artist should not end up out of pocket). Having given the plus side, the minus is all public works go through this agency and despite changing panels it has total power in determining what kind of art is commissioned. This means the quality depends not only on the artist, but on the attitude of a handful of people. Such a body is perhaps better equipped to enforce a central policy or style than it is to make imaginative leaps essential to a liberalised open policy.

Exhibition opportunities abound in Hungary. There are many unjuried exhibitions where membership of one of the official bodies assures entry, (more of these later), and as every village, town and city has at least one arts centre, the possibilities abound. Arts centres usually pay transport, personal travel, hotels and a small sum to exhibiting artists, but with very limited selling possibilities such exhibitions are increasingly snubbed. The whole question of uncurated exhibitions is under evaluation, with many artists finding them increasingly irrelevant.

Sales are difficult. There is virtually no private market in Hungary, excluding tourists, and although there is a new class of fabulously rich emerging they are not the sort who necessarily want to buy art. Investment buying does not exist. Sales are usually to Hungarian museums or foreign collectors. Private galleries are springing up fast, but their marketing strategies are weak and dealer contracts do not exist. The government also has a chain of art shops which sell everything from leather to painting, furniture to sculpture and more like a London decor shop than a gallery.

Another government bureau takes work of Hungarian artists abroad for representative museum shows and to commercial galleries and art fairs, but again there is simply lack of experience in marketing in the way considered normal in the West. For foreign artists it is difficult to relate to this bureau, as with many official bodies, which tend to be patriotic. (Unlike British art institutions, support tends to depend on birthright rather than residency, although this is generally an unwritten law).

One advantage of the symposia, mentioned earlier, is that they do tend to have fairly good tools and materials. Private access to these is more difficult, particularly for sculptors like me working in stone. Things are improving but imported tools carry a heavy duty and are usually two or three times as expensive. I buy my tools in England, Germany and Japan and there is no duty under a certain ceiling (sadly duty-free import of tools for artists has now been abolished). Similarly on each trip abroad I come back loaded with acid-free hand-made drawing paper. I have recently heard of a private company making hand-made paper but have not had a chance to try it.

Art education here is basically the Renaissance model of master and apprentice students. This means the work of most students ends up looking like teacher's. There is only one academy of fine arts and one for applied arts, so competition is fierce. Art-orientated high schools exist, as do teacher training art departments. Some are almost like surrogate art schools and many artists originate from them. In recognition of this the school in Pécs is now starting a postgraduate fine art course in competition with the Academy in Budapest.

Dissemination of information and news of opportunities is negligible. Membership of the Hungarian Arts Fund, a body which confers professional status on artists, gives a twice-yearly publication, plus invitations to submit to certain exhibitions. Membership of the Association of Hungarian Fine and Applied Artists gives more information about commissions, etc. They did begin to produce a newsletter for members only – and it may have been my argument with the director that this newsletter should be available to all which led to her rejecting my application for membership. My application was accepted by the jury but rejected by her on the grounds of my not being Hungarian. This perhaps exemplifies the problem in the art beaurocracy. The old communist ways of thinking are no longer appropriate but in many cases the same people, with the same tired attitudes are still in place. There is a great need for an *Artists Newsletter* type publication here.

I have tried to briefly outline some aspects of art life in Hungary. As everywhere it is a mixture of good and bad. For a foreign artist it is almost impossible to make a living here, only to live and make art. Like a good many Hungarian artists I am reliant on earning money abroad, but would add, strange as it may seem, that the chance for making international contacts are very good here. With diminishing money to go round even the Hungarian stars are finding it difficult. I am sure that we will see a rapid development of the private gallery system along Western lines and an increasing commitment to the exporting of Hungarian art.

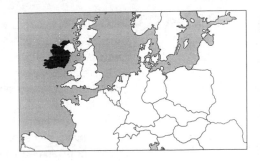

Ireland

Member of the Council of Europe and the EC

LANGUAGE
Official: Irish is the official language mainly used in the North West

Others spoken: English most widely spread and the first language for many

English spoken: Although Irish is the official language, English is in general the everyday language

CURRENCY
Official: 100 pence = 1 Punt (IR£)

Others used: Dollars and Sterling often accepted especially in large hotels

Convertible or not: yes

Travellers cheques/Eurocheques/credit cards: widely usable, less so in rural areas

DOCUMENTS YOU NEED
For information contact: Irish Embassy, 17 Grosvenor Place, London SW1X 7HR tel 071 235 2171

IRISH DTI DESK
OT 3/3c Room 377 tel 071 215 4783/4782/4786

BANKS
Open Monday to Friday 10.00-12.30 to 13.00/ 15.00 (late opening Thursday)

POST OFFICES
Open Monday to Friday 9.00-17.30 & Saturday morning

BUSINESS HOURS
Monday to Saturday 9.00-17.30 with variations

ART GALLERIES/MUSEUMS
Closed Monday – irregular hours in general

PUBLIC HOLIDAYS
Jan 1, Mar 17, Easter weekend, Jun and Oct Bank Holidays, first Monday in Aug, Dec 25/26

CONTACT IN THE UK
Irish Tourist Board, Ireland House, 150 New Bond Street, London W1 tel 071 629 7292

CONTACT ABROAD
British Council, Newmount House, 22/24 Lower Mount Street, Dublin 2 tel 764088

Arts Council of Eire (An Chomhairle Ealaion), 70 Merrion Square, Dublin 2 tel 611840

Embassy/Consulate:
British Embassy, 31-34 Merrion Road, Dublin 4 tel 695211

Chamber of Commerce of Ireland:
7 Clare Street, Dublin 2 tel 612888

Artists Associations:
Association of Artists in Ireland, Room 803, Liberty Hall, Dublin 1 tel 740529

Sculptors Society of Ireland (SSI), The City Centre, 23-28 Moss Street, Dublin 2 tel 718746

Copyright/moral rights:
No Irish organisation noted, try Design & Artists Copyright Society (DACS), St. Mary's Clergy House, 2 Whitechurch Lane, London E1 7QR tel 071 247 1650

Helen O'Donoghue

From 1975-79, I studied at the National College of Art (NCAD) and Design in Dublin. After a one year foundation course, I selected fine art for a three year diploma. I found myself in the painting area more by accident than by choice and grew dissatisfied by the possibilities offered to me. At that period NCAD had few options and fine art graduates were being funnelled into the gallery system.

During my second last year, in collaboration with a fellow student, Dervil Jordan, I decided to initiate work outside college in a local primary school. This was before there was an artists-in-schools programme in Ireland. There was a lot of opposition initially from college authorities as they complained they could not assess work produced by a partnership. Eventually after long arduous discussions and finally due to the insight of our faculty head and external assessor, we qualified with honours!

The experiences I had working in that primary school opened up new opportunities to me and formed the foundation of what I am deeply committed to as an artist – uncovering the experiences children can have through creative activity. I am committed to lobbying for improved resources in art education, in the widest sense, for all those who desire the opportunity.

On leaving NCAD, my colleague and I applied to the Arts Council for grant aid to continue working in primary schools. At that time a report on arts in education, 'The Benson Report', had been published and our proposal was compatible with many of the recommendations in this.

Dervil and I, both born and raised in Dublin were 'posted' to the West of Ireland. We were to carry out an experimental pilot scheme for the Arts Council of Ireland, to explore ways of working as artists in primary schools in counties Galway and Mayo. During a period of six months we worked in a wide variety of rural and town schools throughout the two counties.

This scheme was co-funded by the Arts Council and local authorities through the regional arts office which was based in Galway. We were well paid and the project was sufficiently funded. On completion of these six months we wrote a detailed report making recommendations for future ideas.

From this project the Arts Council designed and ran a nationwide scheme 'Paint on The Wall' from 1981-85 which was a murals in schools scheme. It had a panel of 20 artists and schools could select an artist to work for two weeks with a class group on a mural. The school paid a

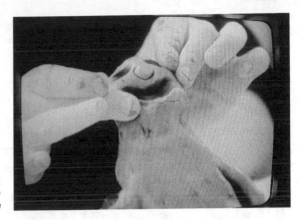

Still from *The Clay Tape* video,
Helen O'Donoghue

portion of the cost and the Arts Council the remainder. The fees and expenses equalled the average teacher's wage at the time. I worked on this for about two years intensely and it was my major income at that time.

During school holidays Dervil and I became involved in community based projects making mosaics and murals funded by local authority schemes.

In 1983 the Arts Council and the Department of Labour, (the National Employment Agency) co-funded a community art project for four months, as a pilot scheme. I was selected to run this project in counties Galway and Mayo. I worked on outdoor environmental projects and on a video drama, as I had been exploring video drama at that stage with a group of Dublin-based aspiring film makers. I was paid as a community artist for four months but, as with many such projects, the enthusiasm of the participants over-ran funding and I worked unsalaried for about six months, part-time, to complete projects.

I continued working as a part-time community artist in Dublin during 1984-85, being paid an average of IR£12.00 an hour for officially 10 hours per week but actually working 40 hours and more, I believe this to be the case of most 'arts workers' in Ireland. Most substitute a small wage with unemployment benefit.

To place ourselves in a more secure position five artists/film makers collaborated and formed a limited company called City Vision from 1984-88. This was a co-operative, non-profit making company and all grants received were reinvested into film/video productions. We rented a series of rooms in a city centre location. With this company I produced a series of programmes on child development and art. To substitute my income and to inform the content of my videos I continued part-time teaching at second and post-leaving certificate level (IR£12.35

81

Ireland

CAFE (Creative Activity For Everyone). The City Centre, 23-28 Moss Street, Dublin 2. Umbrella organisation servicing community art networking.

The Ireland Funds, Gainsboro House, 24 Suffolk Street, Dublin 2. Supports initiatives in creativity and community development.

Arts Squad, Nuala Hunt, 4 Northumberland Road, Dublin 4. A coordinating body placing artists in schools and communities.

per hour, average of 10 hours per week). Our salaries were very basic during this period, and funding came from many government agencies, and trust funds – the Department of Labour, the Arts Council, Dublin Corporation, etc. From 1986-88 I received a grant from ACE, a joint initiative of the Arts Council/Gulbenkian Foundation and the Ireland Funds.

The total project cost IR£40,500 which included fees for researcher/crew/materials, production, post-production, publication and teachers workshops in Ireland, Canada and USA. In period of '88-89 the Ireland Funds grant aided the project with IR£12,500. During this period my salary averaged IR£8,000 per annum.

I continued working freelance until 1991. I produced another video under Arts in Education productions, my own company, with a small grant – IR£6,000, from the Ireland Funds. To support my video work, I taught at vocational level, salary IR£12.35 per hour for 18 hours a week and gave teacher inservice courses for which one receives IR£50 to IR£100 per day. My videos are distributed by my own company.

From January 1991 I have been working at the Irish Museum of Modern Art here in Dublin as Curator Community/Education. It is my first time working as a full-time 'employee'. It is a wonderful opportunity as I can bring together so many of the threads of my work over the past eleven years and create opportunities through our artists' workshop programme to introduce a wide range of disciplines to a wide local community.

I have given a very broad outline of my career as it developed as I feel it necessary artists see how the content of one's work and relationship to funding agencies grows slowly from project to project. For an artist coming to Ireland for the first time or for a young artist starting out, I feel one needs to understand that while there are many structures already in place to support work I have done, it often takes time for one to find a niche and to work on a more continuous basis. If one believes passionately in one's own motivation and desires to work in a particular field I am optimistic the supports will be there. It is a long hard slog however, and young artists should not be put off by this, but should, nonetheless be aware of it.

Video production costs average at:

Equipment hire	BETA IR£350 per day
Off line edit	IR£200 per day
On line editing	IR£1,300 per day
Sound recording	IR£100 per hour
Music	IR£1,000 per production

Over the years I have built up working relationships with many technicians and companies and generally I do deals with people. I have been using my own video recording equipment, purchased in 1985 by City Vision. My videos to date have been on non-broadcast U-matic.

Anne Seagrave

By 1987 I had reached a point in my life and work where I felt as if I needed a complete change of culture and influence. I desperately wanted my work to broaden away from continually making 'shows' as I was finding this extremely artistically limiting. Keen to change these limitations, I felt I could only do this if the surroundings changed too. I'd recently met a number of very inspiring Irish artists and had performed work for the Irish Exhibition of Living Art in 1985. In England, I knew very few artists of other media apart from my own. Upon moving to Ireland all this changed.

In 1987 I attended the MA Fine Art course at the University of Ulster in Belfast. The course was led by Alastair McLennan, a prominent performance artist whose work I had long respected. The MA in Belfast is a very small course taking only ten students and was a great introduction into the local artistic community. Belfast is a small city with a big heart and an even bigger population of creative artists. I feel it important to stress I never felt any antagonism towards myself as an English person. Any long-standing grievances against 'the Brits' are aimed at the British Government and its policies. I had, though, huge misconceptions about Ireland. For example, I had been under the false impression that contraception was illegal in the Republic and that abortion was legal in the North, which was false. I felt resentful of my education which misrepresented or ignored British involvement in Ireland for hundreds of years. Having said all this, I found the move extremely inspiring.

Belfast has incredible energy, vicious humour, tension, a million conflicting opinions jostling for space in the communities. Understandably everyone living in the North is affected to different degrees by 'the troubles' and many artists deal with their experiences of and attitudes towards this through their work. I found myself creating pieces that were much less precious, less permanent than before, which seems now to reflect the uneasy stability which is always prevalent in the North.

Dublin is easy going with brilliant family-owned bars full of conversation and live music, with a very European feeling to it. A picturesque big city with a very 'local' feel about it.

Ireland

Anne Seagrave, **live peformance and tape slide, 1988**

Ireland has a very Mediterranean pace. The Celtic culture is rich with art, music, poetry, dance, storytelling, and humour with almost everyone possessing at least one of these skills.

Culture here is not separated from daily life and is certainly not linked to being able to afford it or having to be initiated into it. Ireland has high levels of unemployment and emigration and a large rural population. Many artists' works reflect these issues.

A quarter of the population of four million speak Irish and in the *Gaeltacht* regions, Irish is the first language. In the Republic, many institutions/buildings/services are referred to only in the Irish. Police are *Gardai*, the Prime Minister is the *Taioseach*. All street names in the Republic and Nationalist areas of the North are written in Irish as well as English and the news on radio and television in the Republic is broadcast in both languages. Obviously you do not need to speak Irish at all to communicate, but it is important to recognise a country's own language and understand the historical process which has replaced these languages in everyday use with English.

Originally upon moving to Belfast I was in receipt of a Department of Education and Science Bursary to study for the MA. After this, I moved to the Republic and claimed social security benefit until finding work here. As a European, you are eligible to apply for state benefits and courses in both the North and the Republic of Ireland but understandably the processes are different. Officialdom in the North of Ireland is what you would expect of British administration; longwinded and bureaucratic. Officialdom in the Republic is totally different; personal, unintimidating, minimally bureaucratic.

Through the MA in Belfast I began performing short pieces in the art college and small local galleries for free, such as the Artists Research Exchange and the Octagon Gallery, then moving on to a couple of paid

North West Artists Association, c/o Orchard Gallery, Orchard Street, Derry BT48 tel 269675

Dublin Theatre Festival, Nassau Street, Dublin 2 tel 778439

GPA Awards for Emerging Artists, GPA House, Shannon, Clare

Tyrone Guthrie Centre (Artists Retreat), Annaghmakerrig, Newbliss, Co Monaghan tel 54377

National Centre for Culture & the Arts, Declan McGonagle, Royal Hospital Kilmainham, Dublin 8 tel 718666

The Living Art Show, Mimi Behnkhe Whalley, Room 903, Liberty Hall, Dublin 1 tel 740529

Temple Bar Gallery & Studios, 4 Temple Bar, Dublin Z tel 710073

National College of Art & Design, 8 Thomas Street, Dublin 8 tel 711377

Cork College of Fashion & Design, 6 Anglesea Street, Cork. tel 966444

Limerick College of Art/Commerce & Technology, Moylish Park, Limerick tel 51344

School of Art & Design, Georges Quay, Limerick

Crawford College of Art & Design, Sharman Crawford Street, Cork

College of Marketing & Design, 40-45 Mountjoy Square, Dublin 1

School of Art & Design, Carriglea Park, Dun Laoghaire, Co Dublin

University of Ulster at Belfast, York Street, Belfast, Old Museum Building Arts Centre, 7 College Square North, Belfast, BT 1 tel 2350453

performances at Lurgan Technical college and The Old Museum Building, Belfast. Spectators here have generally seen few live art events although they are well accustomed to poetry, music, theatre etc. I performed six successful free afternoon performances at The Royal Hibernian Academy in Dublin, as part of the Sculpture Society's exhibition for the European Cultural Capital. The Sculpture Society advertised for submissions and I was awarded a bursary of £400Ir. There are quite frequently mixed exhibitions of work chosen by submission, as well as one person shows available from private and public galleries. As usual it is a case of keeping your eyes peeled for information in publications such as *Circa* magazine (an Irish bi-monthly arts review).

Dublin is not a cheap place to live, but there are excellent markets, accommodation is still half the price of a city like London and most things are within walking distance from the centre. It is possible to live very close to the heart of the city and still afford to eat (just).

Artists can work tax free in Ireland but in order to qualify you have to submit examples of your work for assessment. Not all artists are eligible. Once resident in Ireland for two years you are eligible to apply for funding from the arts councils. There are also awards for artists such as the PS 1 residency in New York and the Aer Lingus Travel Awards where any artist may apply for a free return plane ticket.

Affordable studio spaces are fiercely guarded but an alternative is to rent a cottage, miles away from anywhere, unattractive to tourists, and use one room as a studio. Cottages like this are only £20 or so a week. You can claim social security and rent allowance; you will most likely be poor and cold, but will have space and peace and quiet from which to work. The best way to go about finding a cottage is to meet artists through local studios and enquire from them.

Depending upon where you find yourself, the availability of materials and their cost will vary. The Republic is more expensive than the North of Ireland due mainly to 25 % VAT but there are artists all over who will have information as to the best places to buy materials.

There are a number of institutions offering art education in Ireland, the main ones in Belfast, Limerick, Dublin and Cork. Part-time teaching is like gold but as a visiting or foreign artist it may be possible to obtain a day's teaching in a department. I recently taught a day at NCAD, the National College of Art and Design in Dublin, in the sculpture department. The fee was £116 paid through the local authority.

Ireland is a place where its artists mix well in the local communities and are as respected as other working people for their craft. I have found it a marvellously unpretentious place that has, at its best, a quality which somehow both stimulates the imagination whilst sharpening the wits.

Italy

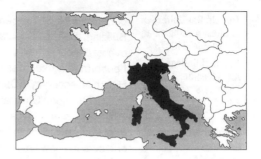

Member of the Council of Europe and the EC

LANGUAGE
Official: Italian
Others spoken: French/Spanish helpful, German & others in border areas – strong regional dialects
English spoken: not as widely as expected, but certainly in centres and amongst younger people

CURRENCY
Official: lira (lire)
Convertible or not: yes
Travellers cheques/Eurocheques/credit cards: widely in main centres, less so in rural areas and the South

DOCUMENTS YOU NEED
For information contact: Italian Embassy, 14 Three Kings Yard, Davies Street, London W1Y 2EH tel 071 629 8200

ITALIAN DTI DESK
OT 3/3B Room 362 tel 071 215 5103/4776

BANKS
Monday to Friday 8.30-13.00 and circa 15.00-16.00

POST OFFICES
Monday to Saturday 8.00-18.30; shorter hours outside main centres

BUSINESS HOURS
Closer to northern European conventions in northern Italy, otherwise circa Monday to Saturday 8.00-13.00 and 16.00-19.00/20.00

ART GALLERIES/MUSEUMS
Usually closed on Monday and shorter hours on Sunday; sporadic closing afternoons

PUBLIC HOLIDAYS
Jan 1, Jan 6, Easter weekend, Apr 25, May 1, Aug 15, All Saints, Dec 8, Dec 25/26

CONTACT IN THE UK
Accademia Italiana delle Arti e delle Arti Applicate, 24 Rutland Gate, London SW7 071 225 3474.
Italian State Tourist Office, 1 Princes Street, London W1R 8AY tel 071 408 1254

CONTACT ABROAD
British Council, Palazzo del Drago, Via Quattro Fontane 20, 00184 Rome tel 4826641/5
Ministry of Culture, Via de Collegio Romano 27, 00186 Rome tel 6723
Chamber of Commerce:
Unione Italiana delle Camere di Comercio, Industria, Artigianto e Agricoltura, Piazza Sallustio 21, 00187 Rome tel 35741
Embassy/Consulate:
British Embassy, Via XX Settembre 80A, 00187 Rome tel 4825551. Consulates in Cagliari, Florence, Genoa, Milan, Naples, Turin, Trieste, Venice
Artists Associations:
Confederazione Italiana dei Professionisti e Artisti (CIPA), Via S. Nicola da Tolentino 21, 00187 Rome tel 461849
Federazione Informazione e Spettacolo (actors, artists & media workers), Via Boncampagni 19, 00187 Rome tel 4823731
Copyright/moral rights:
DACS initially tel 071 377 1650. In Italy SIAE, Via della Letteratura 30, 00100 Rome tel 5990313

Claudia Pratelli

I left high school with a commercial diploma and did not really know what I wanted to do. I joined the Drama Academy in Bologna and I stayed there for two years, then I went to Vienna to do a German course. After this period of uncertainty regarding my direction in life, I joined the Art Academy in Ravenna, Italy, where I did a two-year course on mosaics, which I found fascinating. Maybe I had found what I was looking for! After this I joined the Albe Steiner CFP professional school for mosaicists in Ravenna. The school for mosaicists is open six days a week and there are six hours of work and study per day.

I have met a lot of difficulty since I qualified, as it is not easy to find work in Italy. Up until now I have managed to find work privately, working for architects and people with large houses and villas. Obviously I don't earn enough to survive, so as I am bilingual I often work as an interpreter or translator. In summer I usually teach at an international mosaics school in Ravenna where most of the students are American or British. The work is interesting and also well paid. Many of my old students are working as mosaicists in their own countries.

When I do find work making mosaics for private clients the fee is very good, in fact it is extremely well paid. I am not sure how other artists get on financially. If artists or craftspeople have a sponsor and are introduced to the public by way of exhibitions, they have the chance to show their work and this is often the first step to success. Otherwise it is a long, difficult road and many artists, sooner or later, change their minds and look for a safe, regularly paid job, perhaps in teaching.

Sometimes it is worthwhile producing small articles in mosaic, like clocks, frames, tables or small copies of details from famous ancient mosaics. I sometimes make and sell tables and clocks to shops.

I don't have many expenses to consider because marble and stone are found easily here in Italy and I don't have to pay for them. I usually go to marble dealers who willingly give away slabs and smaller cuts. The only problem is that I have no car so I need the help of friends. When I need glass tesserae, that is smalti, I go to Venice and buy it – it is quite expensive. One may also find gold and silver tesserae here in Italy which are splendid in mosaics.

I would very much like to hold exhibitions but this would cost a great deal. Sometimes the local council organises exhibitions for young artists and craftspeople and I did once take part in an exhibition dedicated to the art of mosaic making. In this way a large number of people were able to see our work and obtain information about mosaics and the people who make them.

Scuola Del Restauro Del Mosaico (School of Mosaic Restoration), Via San Vitale N. 17 – 48100 Ravenna

Associazione Mosaicisti Di Ravenna (Ravenna Mosaicists Association), c/o Palazzo Guiccioli, Via Cavour 54 – 48100 Ravenna

Albe Steiner (C.F.P.) Via Delle Industrie N. 76 – 48100 Ravenna.

Segreteria Cisim – Comune Di Ravenna – Assessorato Pubblica Istruzione E.F.P (Ravenna Town Council – Department of Public Art), Via Corrado Ricci N. 29 – 48100 Ravenna

Accademia Di Belle Arti (Academy of Fine Art), Via Di Roma 13 – 48100 Ravenna

Copy of an ancient mosaic found in Piazza Armerina, Sicily, Claudia Pratelli**, 1992, 1 metre diameter.**
Photo: Monica Pratelli

Perhaps the biggest problem for mosaicists in Italy is finding premises where they can store marble, usually large quantities, and work without disturbing anyone. This is important as the work may be noisy. Perhaps the ideal solution would be to organise a group of crafts-people and share the working area – thus the cost of rent and rates could be divided. At present I am working in the country outside Rimini at a friend's house so I can work whenever I wish without disturbing anyone. I don't pay rent either but in a few months I shall have to look for new premises which will not be easy or economical.

There are possibilities for Italian artists to work in the Italian state schools, very often optional courses are held in the afternoons outside school hours but usually these are only available in the big cities like Rome, Florence, Milan and Ravenna.

I recently discovered *Artists Newsletter* and *Mosaic Matters* and I am very enthusiastic about the possibility of communicating with other mosaicists in Great Britain perhaps through these two papers. I think it is necessary to exchange ideas regarding methods and to pass on information about work possibilities throughout Europe.

The artist in Italy gets very little or no financial help from the government or local authorities, so very often during unemployed periods one often feels like giving it all up, but as the satisfaction in this field is great, many do not give up that easily.

There is work to be found in Italy and other countries in the restoration of ancient mosaics but I must emphasise one needs to be qualified and have a lot of experience. The restoration work carried out on ancient mosaics must be done accurately especially when removing and relaying the mosaic, if not it may be irrevocably damaged. In Italy there are too few experts in this field compared to the work which needs to be done, I would advise anyone to take this career into consideration. There is, for example, a very good restoration school in Ravenna. The course lasts three years and after this one would need to get as much experience as possible, perhaps working with restorers as assistants, before being able to tackle mosaic restoration.

Another problem is that there are several factories in Italy which produce mosaics at a low cost and they have a thriving business. Obviously craftspeople who make mosaics following the ancient procedures and cut their own tesserae from marble they choose themselves, cannot work very fast but nonetheless they do compete with the factories, as one presumes that the buyer who knows about art will always insist on quality and originality.

Said Adrus

As a practising artist the idea of working and showing my artwork away from home in Britain let alone Europe sounds exciting. I felt the need to explore and meet fellow artists and thought this experience, particularly abroad, must be a challenge and should enhance my own development. Initially, I remember feeling enthusiastic about showing my latest work to an entirely new audience on the continent.

I suppose for me, it all started with my exhibition at the Horizon Gallery in London in the summer of 1988. An Italian art critic and curator on his regular visit to the capital for exhibitions and meetings saw my work on display at the gallery near Russell Square. From this initial meeting came the actual invitation to do a short residency at a museum in north Italy. Although he seemed impressed at what he saw, and was keen for me to go to Italy and do a project, I still felt unsure and was not convinced that something definite would come of this.

A few months later I received a couple of registered letters from Italy. To be honest, I had almost forgotten I had met Mr Enzo Santese in August. He wanted to know for sure whether I was still interested in the idea of working in Italy. Also at this stage he was inviting me formally to do a residency for August/September 1989. The invitation outlined a month's residency in Claut, a small village high in the Dolomite mountains. The museum *Museo d'Arte Contemporanea della Valcellina* would pay for my materials and provide accommodation. The work I produced during my residency would be exhibited in the museum. On my part I paid for the return flight to Italy, plus personal expenses.

So that was the deal with no cash mentioned in Lire or Sterling. Do I accept or reject? If I go ahead, where the hell am I going to get the money from? And if I don't, have I missed a life time's opportunity? Endless questions prevail, and in this confusion and frustration it is easy to forget that at least you were invited for a project abroad.

Mais Noir, Said Adrus, **computer generated image.**

I contacted my regional arts board explaining the project to the visual arts officer who told me it might be difficult for them to fund such an initiative and I should seek financial assistance from the British Council, which is normally re-sponsible for exhibitions abroad. So I put an application together with slides, CV, and details of the project, including a copy of the museum's letter. Unfortunately, I did not receive any funding from the UK and was later told by the British Council that it was extremely competitive and of course there is a lack of funds generally. Who knows, perhaps my name was not familiar with the British Council or the respective visual arts committee responsible in assessing applications.

In the meantime, I wrote to the museum's Director expressing my interest in the residency. I realised I had to get some money together somehow. Over Christmas 1988 I visited my family in Switzerland and decided to spend extra money and travel to Venice with the intention of meeting the art critic. We met up in Pordenone where my Italian contact works as a lecturer in acollege of further education. The town is about a couple of hours train ride from Venice. I discussed the project further and left some information for him for publicity purposes. At this stage he was determined to show me the museum in case I had any doubts. In Claut I was able to see the set-up, the environment, the museum and its growing collection. I really liked the place.

In 1986 I showed my work at Loeb gallery in Berne, Switzerland. This experience, although it wasn't a residency as such, did help in some ways in terms of my approach to working in Claut. Between 1972 and 1976 I lived in Switzerland as a political refugee. I went to school in the German speaking part of the country where I met Turkish and Italian kids from migrant families.

The language wasn't a problem. I understand some Italian and can converse in basics regarding food and drink, or when going to buy something and some people I met spoke English. As I had intended to stay in Italy for a month there was no need for a work permit. For the immigration and customs officials, I was on holiday as a tourist, and I knew I would not be doing any paid work.

The museum in Claut provided all the materials asked for, canvas, acrylic paint, drawing paper, and some oil pastels. From England I took some materials with me like crayons, charcoal, a sketch pad and some paint brushes. I must have spent about three weeks painting and preparing the show. Looking back, I really enjoyed the experience working out my ideas and exploring issues which interest me.

The accommodation and studio space consisted of two separate rooms in the basement area of the museum where in fact the Church library was located. The space was reasonable and I often worked on the floor, spreading my canvas over newspaper and plastic sheets. This suited me fine and I liked the process of working on several paintings at the same time.

During the mid-eighties I worked on a series of mixed-media works on the theme of identity and nationality. These were mainly influenced from my personal experience of being a political refugee in Western Europe. In 1989 I tried to push this idea further on the subject of racism and examine the concept of 'Europeaness', as we were embarking on a new decade of European union. Whatever 1992 may offer in terms of opportunity, free trade and movement for people within the EEC, the central question remains, how does this affect people of non-European origin? Particularly so as we witness a growing right wing element in France, Germany and Italy. This rather disturbing situation has once again brought the issues of 'race' and 'colour' to the top of the political agenda.

These points had a strong impact on the work I was to produce during my residency in Claut. As the only Black resident (however temporarily) in that scenic village, the immediate environment of beautiful landscape did not steer me away from my aims in confronting issues of social and political significance. I say this because I was less inspired by the locality and was determined to deal with the subject, commonly associated with industrial cities of Italy and the rest of Europe where migrants have settled.

My own history has been of living in three very different countries where I was confronted by various languages, religions and cultures. This journey of migration, alongside my Indian origin, has left a strong mark in establishing an identity with diverse experience. I had the opportunity to discuss this with the Director of the museum and decided to title my exhibition 'Art Beyond Frontiers' *(Per Un Arte Oltre La Frontiera)*.

The exhibition in Claut consisted mainly of two-dimensional work with about 15 paintings of various sizes. The museum produced a small monchrome pamphlet with an introductory essay by the art critic in Italian. This was well produced with an English translation, including several illustrations and was free to the general public. The pamphlet was also used for publicity along with some reprinted posters which arrived from England. East Midlands Arts had made full colour posters of my exhibitions in England which we could also use in Italy. On the day of the private view two regional papers reported on the exhibition and residency. After its completion in Claut, the work would tour to another venue 'Juliets Room' in Trieste, in October 1989.

None of the paintings I produced during my residency in Claut were for sale – this was the policy of the museum. In fact I had to donate at least a couple of works for their collection. I asked for the remainder of my paintings to stay in Italy after their showing in Claut and Trieste. My attitude was that what I produced there could possibly be used for other exhibitions in Italy or neighbouring countries.

While in Italy I met only three artists. My contact with them was through the art critic, but was limited to visiting art studios or exhibitions. Neither a workshop or slide talk was arranged, I was informed the Museum did not have educational activity resources. This was disappointing because in a workshop situation one can be in contact with the local public. It can also be a source of income for the artist.

In recent years I have participated in several group shows abroad. A couple of these exhibitions have been in Switzerland, one in Sicily, and last year in Havana, Cuba. For these I made sure proper contracts were available with insurance plus the safety of collection and return of artworks. My attitude has changed since Claut and it is extremely important to consider these points before embarking on a project abroad. Altogether I must have spent about £300 over the four weeks, keeping in mind my limited budget and time. I also feel funding must come from official UK sources, like the RABs and the British Council. Private sponsorship also needs to be explored. Informed advice on these matters is essential, particularly when one is not working through a gallery or dealer/agent system. Of course, if one intends to sell the work, there are a lot more considerations to take into account, but I do not have this experience.

Luxembourg

Member of the Council of Europe and the EC

LANGUAGE
Official: Letzeburgisch
Others spoken: French and German
English spoken: extensively

CURRENCY
Official: 100 centimes = 1 Luxembourg Franc
Others used: Belgian Franc
Convertible or not: yes, equivalent to Belgian Franc
Travellers cheques/Eurocheques/credit cards: extensive acceptability

DOCUMENTS YOU NEED
For information contact: Embassy of Luxembourg, 27 Wilton Crescent, London 3W1X 8SD tel 071 235 6961

LUXEMBOURG DTI DESK
OT 3/3a Room 369 tel 071 215 4790/5486/4794

BANKS
Open Monday to Friday 9.00-12.00 to 14.00-16.30

POST OFFICES
Open Monday to Friday 8.00-12.00 to 13.30-17.00

BUSINESS HOURS
Weekdays (look out for Monday morning closing) 9.00-circa 18.00; some late nights and shorter hours on Saturday

ART GALLERIES/MUSEUMS
Often affected by short hours or complete closure out of season, usually closed Monday and Sunday, though Sunday opening is more likely

PUBLIC HOLIDAYS
Jan 1, Easter Monday, May 1, Ascension, Whit Monday, Jun 23, Assumption, All Saints, Nov 11, Dec 25/26

CONTACT IN THE UK
Luxembourg National Trade and Tourist Office, 36/37 Piccadilly, London W1V 9PA tel 071 434 2800

CONTACTS ABROAD
British Council, Britannia House, 30 rue Joseph II, 1040 Brussels tel 2193600

Ministry of Cultural Affairs and Scientific Research, 19-21 rue Goethe, 1637 Luxembourg tel 47181

Embassy/Consulate:
British Embassy, 14 Boulevard Roosevelt, 2450 Luxembourg City tel 29864

Chamber of Commerce:
rue Alcide de Gasperi 7, 2981 Luxembourg-Kirchberg tel 435853

Artists Associations:
Dokumentationszentrum fur die zeitgenossische Kunst, Contemporary Art Institute, 5 ave de X Septembre, 2551 Luxembourg

The Art Circle, Banque Nationale, 7 rue Plaetis, Luxembourg

The following unions may be helpful: Onofhaengege Gewerkschaftsbond-Letzeburg (Confederation of Independent Trade Unions), BP149, 4002 Esch-sur-Alzelte, Luxembourg tel 540545

Federation des Artisans du Grand-Duche de Luxembourg, rue Glesener 41, 1631 Luxembourg

Copyright/moral rights:
No Luxembourg organisation noted, try Design & Artists Copyright Society, (DACS) St. Mary's Clergy House, 2 Whitechurch Lane, London E1 7QR tel 071 247 1650

Helen Webb

Cooperations a.s.b.l.
Centre de Projets
Gruberbierg B.P. 81,
L-9501 Wiltz,
Luxembourg Nord tel
957783

In June 1990, Anneké Pettican, an environmental artist, asked me if I would be interested in being involved with a sculpture project in Luxembourg together with two English landscape architects, Jo Guatelli and John Constable.

Anneké met the co-ordinators of Cooperations a.s.b.l project during the Manchester Landscape and Sculpture Symposium in 1989. Cooperations asked her to select a group of artists and landscape architects to work on projects in the Jardin de Wiltz for a three month period. At this time, I was completing my textile degree course at Manchester Polytechnic and I felt this was an opportunity not to be missed. During my final year at college, I had been working on environmental art projects and this opportunity to work in a sculpture garden, in a foreign country, with a material I knew little about seemed ideal. With the knowledge I had about the project in Wiltz, I was sufficiently excited to say 'Yes!'.

Cooperations evolved ten years ago in 1982 from a group of artists who had been running workshops in Capellan, a rehabilitation centre for disabled people in the south of Luxembourg. After realising their success, the artists (eleven – from Austria, Germany, England and Luxembourg) started the project in Wiltz, in the north of Luxembourg.

The project was given 2.5 hectares of sloping grass land by the Wiltz council together with buildings which had previously been an old brewery. The artists lived in these run-down buildings for some time, with small groups of disabled people during the first year. The collaboration of disabled and non-disabled artists in garden projects interested me. Also, various European artists would be arriving at the centre throughout the summer to run their own workshops which seemed exciting.

Cooperations is an independent organisation and receives funding from a variety of sources – the European Community, the National Ministry of Education, *Association Européenne pour la créativité des personnes handicapées* (EUCREA), and private donations.

The town of Wiltz is situated near the Belgian border. It has 4,200 inhabitants. The area of land given to the project has become a garden for the community of Wiltz and a place where disabled and non-disabled artists can work.

The project encourages professional and social integration with people who have special needs, such as disabled people or those who have been unemployed for a long time for health or social reasons. These people are given the choice of various avenues of work, eg in the

The Wall. Helen Webb.
Jardin De Wiltz, Luxembourg

garden, café, administration, in the hope they will eventually feel able to integrate into the community socially and professionally.

Disabled and non-disabled artists are encouraged to work together on various projects such as sculpture, film, design, drawing and painting, working with people one-to-one and also as a group, building relationships and realising people's own ideas. It is intended that artists reveal their own knowledge and experiences of their disciplines and cultures into this field of education-building activities.

Cooperations has steadily grown in size and reputation. As a result of the achievements, the Wiltz council has given the project a building close to the garden. This has become *Le Centre de Projets Gruberbierg*. Workshops for adults and children will be held in this new building together with other garden events and exhibitions. The art projects are often undertaken by visiting artists from various European countries adding new approaches and cultures to the workshops.

Jardin de Wiltz, the garden project, is the largest in the centre. The development and maintenance of the garden offers numerous other possibilities for artists, unemployed and other interested people. *Kunstkooperationen* is an exchange with a disabled artist and a non-disabled artist. Projects can vary from sculpture, painting and drawing, utilizing and developing a space, cooking, taking part in films, etc. *Kannersummer* are children's workshops which take place during the summer holidays for Wiltz and surrounding areas. These involve dance, music, making costumes and stage sets, performances in the garden, using the garden as a stage.

As the project is multi-cultural, it provides an ideal opportunity to meet and work with other artists from all over Europe. Language in Luxembourg is not a problem. Most of the Luxembourgish people speak French and German and a little English. Of course, there is a Luxembourgish language but I found it easier to be understood by stringing a few French and German words together!

When we arrived, we were able to choose which project we would like to work on, I chose 'the wall'. This was initiated by Herbert Nagel, a German sociologist, writer and artist. Herbert had been working with the disabled artists from Capellan and they had planned and prepared the foundations of the area before we arrived in July. It involved building a dry stone wall, typical to those built in the north of Luxembourg. The research into design and materials was extensive, but if it was going to last more than 20 years the effort would be worth it and, of course, interesting. We made studies of the various walls in the area, making drawings and photographs.

During our 'wall search' around the countryside in the north of Luxembourg, we discovered an interesting one in a village called Bavigne. We were also fortunate to find the two men who had built it were still alive. The Toch brothers, 84 and 86 years old, were very helpful and advised us on how to build our wall in the traditional way. We had many questions which needed to be answered – drainage, materials, how to curve the wall so it would remain stable, etc.

Various people came to help us build the wall over the two month period – visiting artists, disabled artists from Capellan and other interested volunteers.

Cooperations does exhibit work by the disabled and non-disabled artists. These exhibitions are becoming more frequent as the project gains greater recognition. Other organisations are becoming more and more interested in their work and their ideas about social integration.

An exhibition in Brussels supported by EUCREA and the European Community, and representing work done with the project in Wiltz, led to a number of future exhibitions in Europe.

Because we were working on established projects, we received a weekly wage which covered living expenses. This was not so important to me. I was excited about the project as a new experience which may lead to other work possibilities in the future.

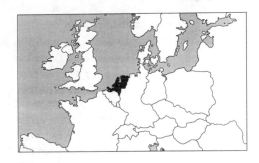

Netherlands

Member of the Council of Europe and the EC

LANGUAGE
Official: Dutch
Others spoken: wide knowledge of many European languages
English spoken: extensively

CURRENCY
Official: 100 cents = 1 guilder (fl or Dfl)
Convertible or not: yes
Travellers cheques/Eurocheques/credit cards: widely accepted

DOCUMENTS YOU NEED
Information contact: Royal Netherlands Embassy, 38 Hyde Park Gate, London SW7 5DP tel 071 584 5040

DUTCH DTI DESK
OT 3/3a Room 369 tel 071 215 4790/4794/5586

BANKS
Monday to Friday 9.00-16.00, centres late night Thursday and some Saturday morning

POST OFFICES
Monday to Friday 8.30-17.00, some Saturday morning

BUSINESS HOURS
Tuesday to Friday 9.00-circa 18.00, often a late night towards the end of the week (often closed Monday morning and early on Saturday)

ART GALLERIES/MUSEUMS
Tuesday to Saturday 10.00-17.00, Sunday afternoon (contact Tourist Board for details of cards offering discounts on entry in advance of travelling)

PUBLIC HOLIDAYS
Apr 30, May 5, Ascension, Whit Monday, Aug 15, Dec 5, Dec 25/26

CONTACT IN THE UK
Netherlands Board of Tourism, 25-28 Buckingham Gate, London SW1E 6LD tel 071 630 0451

CONTACTS ABROAD
British Council, Keizersgracht 343, 1016 EH Amsterdam tel 6223644
Ministry of Welfare, Health and Cultural Affairs: Steenvoordelaan 370, PO Box 5406, 2280 HK Rijswijk tel 3407911
Embassy/Consulate:
British Embassy, Lange Voorhout 10, 2514 ED The Hague, Netherlands tel 645000.Consulate in Konigslaan 44, 1057 AE Amsterdam tel 764343
Chamber of Commerce:
One in most towns and cities eg, Kamer van Koophandel en Fabrieken voor Amsterdam, De Ruyterkate 5, 1013 AA Amsterdam tel 5236600
Artists Association:
Beroepsverenigingen Beeldende Kunstenaars BBK (Professional Plastic Arts Association), Niewe Herengracht 29, 1011 R1 Amsterdam
Federatie van Kunstenaars Verenigingen (Federation of Artists Associations), Passeerdersgracht 321, 1016 XH Amsterdam tel 237761
Copyright/moral rights:
DACS initially tel 071 247 1650. In Netherlands Beeldrecht, Kerkstraat 310, 1017 HC Amsterdam tel 6277147

Erik Odijk

When I was asked to write about my situation as an artist in the Netherlands, I wasn't sure at all if 'the situation' for artists in my country is a good or a bad one. It can vary individually, depending on your kind of art, the effort you put into your 'career' concerning getting exhibitions and connections, the choice of galleries, spaces, is your art appealing and does it have a place in the mainstream? I for myself detest any form of commercialism practised in so-called fancy galleries and museums, where colonisation of the artist's ideas and work are a matter of fact. So I never put too much effort in showing or selling my work on a commercial basis. For me it always was more important to work and take initiative in organising artist manifestations and exchanges.

My own art has almost nothing to do with the Netherlands. I make 'neo-romantic' realistic drawings and paintings of landscapes in which I deal with disappearing nature: its beauty and cruelty, craftsmanship (I am a man) and aesthetic values. Apart from this I'm experimenting with installations, creating a context of serenity and purity for the presentation of the photos and drawings. For this I use fabric and coloured light, as well as sound and aromatic data, to express feelings of colour, temperature and atmosphere. These installations have the image of shrines, for a worshipping and careful, dignified approach. In this way I can deal with walls and two-dimensional work. So the audience can approach the work in a different way. I was inspired on my journeys through deserts and tropic regions far away from the Netherlands.

After three presentations of these installations I was finally asked to prepare an exhibition in a gallery outside the city of Nijmegen. Recognition and more shows seem to be coming slowly. Before that it was just waiting: for opportunities, for contacts to work out, for a good private studio, but I only came across rejection after rejection.

I have lived and worked in Nijmegen since 1977, including six years of study at an art-teachers school and three years at art school in Arnhem (very near Nijmegen). During these years I got involved in several artist initiatives, music and festival organisations. With colleagues, I set up two foundations which deal with art disciplines as printed matter, books, Dadaist and surrealist manifestations, experimental audio-visual arts and an artist residence. From 1983 till 1989 I worked in the initiative *KNUST*, later *Extrapool*. We operated from a squat, where we had studios, printshops and room for our manifestations. Our projects were low-budget and, concerning our printed matter, very revolutionary. The artists' books we made were a good way of showing our work to the public. A group is stronger. Getting individual exhibitions of paintings, sculpture and so on was far more difficult. Once thrown out of our squat,

Tenger Highlands (East Java), Erik Odijk, **oil on canvas.**

we legalised our initiative through political actions supported by declarations of solidarity from all kinds of artist initiatives: galleries, boards, other art groups, the music scene, and important individual artists from all over the country. Thus we obtained a new building, a storehouse, which still exists as the *Extrapool* initiative.

In 1988 we started the Elba artist-residence where we invite mostly foreign artists to realise a new work of temporary art during a residency, basically focused on disciplines such as live art, installation and multi-disciplinary experiments. The actual buildings we inherited from former initiatives and through lobbying at the city council. Elba is funded by the city council as well. WVC (the Department of Culture in our country) turned us down and criticised our entire programme as being insignificant and non-categorised.

I also helped promote the AVE festival in Arnhem from 1986 till 1988 and travelled a lot for the festival as a scout. I met a lot of artists in those years.

I think artists' initiatives, and there are quite a few in the cities, are the places where topical art and experiment are visible in the Netherlands. The initiatives are, it's in the name, run by artists who have no other goal than making art and exchanging ideas and projects with others. They strive for an independent view. The buildings they operate from are either squats or former squats now legalised, and quite beautiful in their roughness and architectural qualities, so art projects are almost always related to these spaces through various experiments. As a tradition in the Netherlands (like our many co-existing political, religious and social movements) the initiatives also have very different characters and represent different spheres of ideas. But there is exchange and solidarity, in this so called 'second art circuit'. Raising money for these initiatives is difficult. Of course we have to deal with the trend of budget-cutting by local, regional and national governments, so competition is even at hand between the initiatives themselves, but there still is money available as subsidies and it just takes a good programme and some skill to lay hands on this. Also, because the work of the initiatives is beneficial to the public interest, it is, as a tradition in this country, rewarded with public money, although it's clear the biggest budgets are for big theatre, music, monuments and other so called 'high art' structural projects. As a matter of fact, most initiatives have to depend on small subsidies from their own town, or maybe the province; government money is difficult to get, you have to face art-boards who have no feeling whatsoever for what you're actually doing and the importance of it. To be honest, what some initiatives get, is just a fee.

All the work mentioned above isn't paid, it's voluntary and idealistic. The seventy-five per cent of the time left is for my own work, which means thinking about it and actually making it. I lack the time to promote it, if I would wish to.

When you leave art school, or any school, you'll get the status, and the money of an unemployed person. The money is a minimum, enough to stay alive, pay the rent, buy some materials and have a subsidised studio. I waited a long time for a studio as there is a waiting list, but then I squatted in the space anyway because it was empty and not used for almost a year. Materials are expensive and I cannot spend a lot. So, life is hard, trying to make extra money and not losing my social security money is possible as long as you play it fair (according to my own moral standards). The occasional selling of paintings, drawings and books does not yield much profit to live off. Normally I deal with these transactions through one of the two foundations I belong to. The general rules of a foundation prescribe the members should not make profit so that earnings can only be used for investments in art supplies and studio rent, which is good, I think. I even get VAT back when I spend more on my work than it brings in. A negative point is that, officially, nothing you create belongs to you personally.

Getting individual grants is difficult in my situation. My work isn't mainstream enough, I guess, to get a grant from the so called *Fonds voor Beeldende Kunsten, fotografie en architectuur* in Amsterdam. It's due to their ignorance, I think, but also the competition is severe. The thing is to keep trying and maybe one day hit the jackpot. Every artist in Holland will confirm this. When applying, I must also deal with national standards which means with important and senseless artists in the selection boards. And then there is *Randstad* (Amsterdam, Rotterdam, Den Haag) and the sometimes embarrassing neglect of other parts of the Netherlands.

Luckily I received a project grant from the regional arts council. It's a good province I live in, they even give subsidies for having an exhibition (100 guilders for every week of the exhibition). For me there is no money left for the luxurious items of life, even though I have to face a society which is doing this day in day out, which makes me sick. Probably one day my social security councillor will put the thumbscrews on me. Because officially I'm still unemployed and have to apply for jobs, which is of course impossible, since I have no time.

Anyway, most people like to spend their 'free' time on shopping. Even those, who should be interested in what is going on in art, seem to take the easy way out. Television gets more attention than paintings, that is a fact. I know it, I live in the middle of the town in which I put so much cultural effort. Couch potatoes and shopping addicts don't contribute a lot to the development of art – do they?

My studio is a little bit outside the centre, more quiet. I ought to spend more time there and do some work.

Amanda Benson

In the summer of 1990 I spent two months in Nijmegen, Holland. I had been invited there by the artists organisation ELBA, an initiative set up by artists for artists.

The previous year I met one of the artists involved in the project. During a visit to my studio he showed me material on ELBA and other art events which took place in his town. Having seen my work first hand he felt my way of working would be sympathetic.

Prior to this I had experience of working in France and knew the stimulus of working in another country. So I decided to apply to ELBA which could provide a free studio and accommodation, but the problem was the cost of travel and of supporting myself for two months.

The year before I had been commissioned to make a sculpture for an educational programme in Notting Hill which was sponsored to some extent by the Prince's Trust. I telephoned the Trust and found they offered a 'go and see' grant, basically intended for someone to investigate what possible links could be made with a foreign organisation working in a similar sphere, but they did not see any problem if I actually did some work whilst abroad. Even if I was not accepted for ELBA I still had an invitation to go to Holland and so I applied. After an interview my proposal was accepted and I received £200 and my return air fare. Around this time I was asked by ELBA to send documentation and slides of my work and later I was sent an invitation contract. It all seemed so simple after years of complicated application procedures.

La Vache, Amanda Benson,
1990, part of a room installation

I was offered limitless use of a studio for two months, at the end have a private view and a publication paid for by them, and the help of the artists in the organisation when I needed it. Foundation ELBA is a voluntary organisation partly funded by the municipality of Nijmegen. Established in 1987, it is managed by an executive board of four artists with ten others making up the rest of the core of the group. Allocation of jobs within the groups is fluid and there are frequent meetings to discuss any relevant issues. This all seems to work well and people do get involved. I had considerable support from the other artists.

I spent my first week getting to know Nijmegen and going to Amsterdam. A Dutch friend was doing a show there in an artist-run gallery, an installation piece using oil. There was no language problem, everyone spoke English and things cost about the same as in London.

Rijksacademie Voor Beeldende Kunsten (State Academy for Fine Arts), Contact Director for Academic Affairs, Rietveld Academie, Fred Rockestraat 96, 1076 ED Amsterdam tel 799912

Contact the **Royal Netherlands Embassy Cultural Department** for information about scholarships for advanced study at universities and institutions of comparable status in the Netherlands (normally for a period of nine months September – June). Application forms available November and closing date January for courses commencing in following September.

ELBA Foundation, Artist Residence, Pijkestraat 4 Nijmegen, PO Box 488, 6500 AL Nijmegen tel 240308

Most of my time was spent collecting materials, meetings with the group, arranging shoots for the publication and scripting a video which along with the leaflet was the organisation's documentation.

It was an ambitious set of tasks – and I felt too much to do in such a space of time – the video had to be finished after I had left. I made an installation titled *La vache est un plat qui se mange froid*, using wire, milk, wax, muslin and a very large shallow steel sink. The studio was light with a high ceiling and at least twice as big as my space in London. There was a separate living area contained within the studio which meant I could work at any hour and I really enjoyed that freedom.

The town of Nijmegen on the German border is on the river Rhine surrounded by countryside and cows. Being in Holland meant it was easier to get to other countries, Cologne was quite near and a few friends I met had private views whilst I was there. I also went to Berlin which is not so near but cheap to get to.

The artists I met were in the main on state benefit. This being around £70 for a single person but with no rent paid makes it similar to here. From talking to people it seems for years it was easy to be an artist in Holland and be accepted by the state and supported, but now it is not so easy and becoming comparative to England.

As I left ELBA was in the process of obtaining another building, to be a temporary museum with an archive – again to invite artists from other countries. The idea being to show (make) installations the life of which extends only to the life of the show. ELBA was also obtaining buildings, mainly old schools, to make into cheap studio spaces for foreign artists, similar to those set up already in Berlin.

Most artists I met were working in a sculptural/installation way. Installations and video and film seemed to be very popular with festivals happening all over Holland, but many Dutch artists look to Germany for exhibiting, that is the place with a dominant market.

ELBA invites an artist in any discipline from any country and hopes 'to present all these activities within a context of the transcultural reality of art in today's society, establishing an exchange between different backgrounds and aesthetic values'.

Being large, my work is stored by one of my Dutch friends maybe to be used at a later date in their temporary museum or another European venue. I believe really one would have to stay in a country for a while to fully understand and benefit from the artistic happenings and gallery system and I do not claim to have done so. The experience has been invaluable to my own artistic development and the confidence to work somewhere else – the knowledge that I can do it. I had little contact with the official gallery system, more with artist projects which seemed very set up and established.

Norway

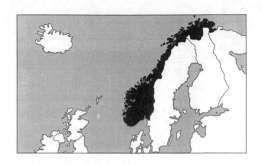

Member of the Council of Europe

LANGUAGE
Official: Norwegian (Bokmal/Nynorsk)
Others spoken: Lappish
English spoken: usually spoken and understood in centres and amongst younger people

CURRENCY
Official: 100 ore = 1 Norwegian Krone
Convertible or not: yes
Travellers cheques/Eurocheques/credit cards: more widely accepted in centres, but extensive

DOCUMENTS YOU NEED
For information on visa and residence and work permits contact: Royal Norwegian Embassy, 25 Belgrave Square, London SW1X 8QD tel 071 235 7151

NORWEGIAN DTI DESK
OT 3/3c Room 377 tel 071 215 5341/4397/5140

BANKS
Open Monday to Friday 8.00-16.00, shorter hours Summer months

POST OFFICES
Open Monday to Friday 8.00-17.00, Saturday morning

BUSINESS HOURS
Monday to Friday 9.00-17.00, longer hours Thursday, shorter Saturday

ART GALLERIES/MUSEUMS
Look out for shorter hours and even complete closing in Autumn and Winter

PUBLIC HOLIDAYS
Jan 1, Easter Weekend, May 1, May 17, Ascension Day, Whit Monday, Dec 25/26

CONTACT IN THE UK
Norwegian National Tourist Office, 5-11 Lower Regent Street, London SW1 tel 071 839 6255

CONTACT ABROAD
British Council, Fridtjof Nansens Plass 5, 0160 Oslo 1 tel 426848
Arts Council, Radhusgt. 7, Oslo 1
Ministry of Culture, Akersgt. 42, PO Box 8030 Dep, 0030 Oslo 1 tel 249090
Embassy/Consulate
British Embassy, Thomas Heftyesgate 8, 0264 Oslo 2 tel 552400. Consulates in Alesund, Bergen, Harstad, Haugesund, Kristansand, Kristansund, Stavanger, Tromso, Trondheim
Chambers of Commerce:
Bergen, Oslo and Trondheim: Oslo Handelskammer, Drammensvn 30, 0255 Oslo 2
Arts Association:
Kunsterforbundet, Kjeld Stubs gt 3, 0160 Oslo tel 414029
Kunstnernes Hus (The Artists House), Wergelandsveien 17, 0167 Oslo tel 607423
LNBK (The Association of Norwegian Visual Artists), Kongensgt. 3, N-0153 Oslo
Copyright/moral rights:
DACS initially tel 071 247 1650. In Norway NORWACO, Storgata 14, 0184 Oslo 1 tel 170117

Alf Edgar

I came into art by accident. At the time, 1977, I was doing laboratory work at the Agricultural University of Norway. I'd had one-and-a-half years of agricultural training, and was wondering if I should study on. I had been an amateur photographer for some years, and done a little press photography for local papers. In 1976 I had exhibited prints at the stock exchange hall of my home town.

At the university I soon found myself maybe too often in the darkroom at night, and too little in the digestion-lab at daytime. I did a lot of experiments on non-silver processes like gum-bicromate printing, carbro, cyanotype and others.

I started sending my prints to various exhibitions. The Association of Fine Art Photographers had been established in 1974, and the interest for artistic photography was rising in Norway. Due to this I came into it at a favourable time. Some of my first work was well received, experimental as it was.

In 1979 I received a travel scholarship from the state (travelled Eire, Great Britain and the Faroes), and in 1982 I entered the Association of Norwegian Visual Artists, which today has about 2,500 members.

The first years of my artistic career I had no studio or darkroom of my own. I worked under quite primitive conditions in attics, cellars and bathrooms, until 1982 when I luckily could join the Myren Grafikk workshop for five years. This is a collective workshop owned by the Kristiansand Town Council. It is situated in the buildings of an old farm, and graphic and textile artists, painters and other artists can work here at low cost in well-equipped studios.

Conditions like this are not to be found all over the country, but some councils are offering establishing funding, and even scholarships for up to three years. This is mainly in the western and northern part of the country.

Visual arts education is well established on all levels. Recently five regional art schools for children have been established, with the support of the central culture authorities. At the moment this is a temporary arrangement for three years, but it will probably become permanent.

Art schools on secondary level, as we find them in Stavanger and Kabelvåg, act as preparation to the art colleges and academies. Colleges for arts and crafts are found in Oslo, Bergen and Trondheim, academies for fine arts in Oslo and Bergen.

Until 1990 it was necessary to go abroad if one wanted artistic photography education. Sweden, UK and the US used to be the alternatives. However an Institute for Photography is now established at

First Projection, Alf Edgar, **1989, Gum-bicromate print, cyanotype, bee-wax and wood. In Centre for North Norwegian Artists, Svolvær.**

the Bergen College of Arts, Crafts and Design, under the leadership of professor Robert Meyer. A five-year theoretical and practical photography course is offered, five students accepted each year.

This is a modest start, and still no formalised photographic education is offered at any of the academies of fine arts. Photography though appears frequently in relation to other subjects, as at the 'intermedia' section at the Trondheim Academy of Fine Arts. This institute was founded in 1988 for film, video and computer arts.

The opportunity of teaching painting, drawing, etc, is good at all levels. Payment is fair inside the art school system, but at other schools artists' salaries are poorer than other teachers' because of their lack of academic knowledge.

There are various opportunities of exhibiting in Norway. It is said no other country has as many art galleries in proportion to the population.

Among public galleries we first find the art societies, about 200 of them all over the country. These are run by their members, and only the bigger has a permanent gallery. Their exhibitions are often found in schools, libraries or the council hall. The policy of selecting artists vary, but amateurs are usually excluded.

Second, there are the artist-owned galleries. Fifteen regional artists' centres run their galleries supported by the Cultural Ministry. The central artist associations are all situated in Oslo, and have their galleries mainly in the Kongensgate area. Exhibitors are selected by a jury once or twice a year. The artist gets exhibition remuneration.

The central national art institutions, like the National Gallery and the National Museum of Contemporary Art, are not for the majority – at least if you're not dead.

Public galleries usually take a 25-30% share of the sales. Private galleries and art dealers will take a 30-50% share depending on the location, promotion and so on. Exhibition charges are unusual in Norway.

Due to necessity most artists' income has various sources, and so has mine. To illustrate this I have made a list of my income 1991, in order of its importance to me:

• Public commissions: psychiatric clinic, Rana; and health centre, Bergen.

FFF (The Association of Norwegian Fine Art Photographers), Box 173 - Sentrum, N-0102 Oslo

KIK (Information Centre for Contemporary Arts and Crafts), Kongensgt, 3, N-0153 Oslo

KEM (artist-owned material dealer), Chr. Krohgsgt. 32 B, N-0186 Oslo

Hans Ekjord Fargehandel (Colourman), St Olavsgt. 3, N-0165 Oslo

Fellesverkstedet Myren Grafikk (Collective workshops), Myren Gård, N-4621 Kristiansand

- Art consultant on public commissions: the Norwegian Cultural Council: Harstad cultural activity house; the National Foundation for Public Commissional Arts: Longyearbyen Hospital, Spitsbergen.
- Exhibition remuneration: two solo exhibitions and one collective. This is an agreed payment for exhibitions supported by the state.
- Fundings: from artist foundation for video project to be realised in 1992. From local council for solo exhibition.
- Artwork sales: from exhibitions and studio.
- Teaching: guest teacher at art college.
- Posters and postcards.

From 1987 to '89 I received a three year scholarship from the state, but since then most of the money seems to have come from public commissions. Incomes vary a lot, and although my activities are spread over a lot of different areas, I am not able to support a family. Luckily my wife's income is twice that of mine, which makes us able to live in a small house of our own, in the countryside.

In 1987 I moved from the south coast to northern Norway, to Brønnøysund, not far from the Polar Circle (geographically Brønnøysund is exactly in the middle of the country). I do not know if it has affected my art to live far from the art metropolis, but I guess it has stimulated my interest in art and telecommunications. The effort made to create a worldwide electronic 'gallery' is exciting.

My interest in this 'virtual' reality, created with the help of computers, may have been stimulated by the nature of photography. Photography is dealing with reality in a way which differs from other arts. This made me in the first place bring the photographed objects into the exhibition room, and also do installations in nature.

Sophie Henderson

My first trip to Norway in 1983 was a whirlwind affair travelling around in a converted ambulance. I returned in 1988, on completing a fine art degree at Exeter College of Art and Design, to work on a farm in the Sognefjord, picking fruit. This was through the Atlantis 'working guest' scheme for students.

Afterwards I visited Oslo and looked round the Oslo Art Academy, *Statens kunstakademi* (SKA). I discovered there was a scholarship to study at the SKA. After working in the Sognefjord I was inspired, but I had been unable to fully visualise my ideas, as I had had neither the time nor the space.

Footprints, Sophie Henderson, 1990, 190x115cm.

On returning to Britain I applied for the Norwegian Government Scholarship, through the Royal Norwegian Embassy, in London. After a written application I was short-listed, attended an interview, with portfolio, and was accepted. It was for nine months to study at SKA, funded by the Norwegian Research Council for Science and the Humanities, *Norges allmennvitens kapelige forskningsrad* (NAVF).

I arrived in Oslo in September 1989 and applied for a resident's permit on arrival, to the main police station. This proved no problem as I was a scholarship student and being financed by NAVF. You can stay in Norway as a tourist, without requiring a visa for up to three months. For longer periods of time you need a resident's permit and to be working, studying or have sufficient funds to support yourself. It is best to find a job before you go and apply for a work permit well in advance.

The majority of Norwegians can speak fluent English, especially in the cities. There are two official languages, *Bokmal* and *Nynorsk*. The former is more Danish-based and more widely spoken, especially on television and radio. The latter is based upon 'old' pre-Danish Norwegian, made up of dialect words.

I only started learning Norwegian after being in Norway for four months. It did make a difference. People really appreciated it if you tried to speak to them in their own language, rather than taking it for granted they can speak English. It was quite entertaining at times as well. As the population is only 4.2 million, Norwegian is not very widely spoken outside the country. Through learning Norwegian I gained a better understanding of what was going on around me. I did not feel isolated or 'deaf'. I felt I was actually living in Norway rather than just being a tourist.

There are two main places for learning Norwegian: the University of Oslo (Blindern), which has entrance requirements, is more academic and you should apply in advance; and the Rosenhof School.

I received nine monthly payments of 4900 Norwegian Kroner (NK) from the NAVF. I also received an extra initial payment of 1200NK to cover the accommodation deposit costs. The NAVF provided a 1500NK travel allowance, which I used to travel to the Lofoten Islands.

As I was exhibiting work in the final year show in November, I decided it was easier to stay and work over the summer. Especially after I had survived the long winter nights. Through advertising in a farming magazine I found a job milking goats and making goat cheese. I earned 1000NK per week, including food and accommodation. The job gave me a chance to live in the mountains and experience a completely different way of life from what I had been leading in Oslo.

Since returning to the UK I have had four exhibitions of the work I made in Norway. I am approaching Norwegian companies based in Britain and continuing to exhibit my Norwegian paintings. There is also a proposal for a Norway-Cumbria link, but this is still in the pipeline.

I was provided with a studio space in the academy, in the centre of Oslo, with the freedom to work there from 8am-11pm, seven days a week. Materials such as turpentine, linseed oil and scrap paper were freely available. The academy also provided a materials allowance each semester (twice a year) of 330NK. The working atmosphere was in isolated pockets and it was difficult to see the other students' work as individual studios were frequently locked.

The students are expected to work independently, although there are set courses available, eg colour, materials. Each student has their own personal tutor for a year, who they see on a regular basis. The tutors are professional artists who teach at the academy over a four year period. I found there was a strong emphasis on the theory rather than solving practical problems. A lot of the work was abstract-based and more conceptually influenced, particularly in the sculpture department. There are three main art academies – Oslo, Bergen and Trondheim. The equivalent to a postgraduate course in Britain lasts for four years, a fifth year is available but there is usually a gap in between. Students quite frequently transfer from one academy to another during their course, and there are also quite a few students from other countries.

Atlantis (Working Guest), Rolf Hofmosgate 18 0655 Oslo 6, tel 670043

Statens kunstakademi (Oslo Art Acadamy), St Olavsgate 32, 0166 OSLO 1, tel 200150

NAVF (Norweigian Research Council for Science and the Humanities), Sandakerveien 99, 0483 Oslo 4, tel 157012

The Aliens Office, Politihuset, Gronlandsleiret 44, Oslo, tel 669050

Norway

The University of Oslo, Blindern, 0313 Oslo 3

Unge Kunstners Samfund (Young Artists Association), Radhusgate 19, 0158 Oslo 1 tel 426666

There is a strong arts policy funded by the state. Artwork and sculpture are frequently incorporated into both public and private developments. They are seen as part of a building or environment rather than in isolation.

Textiles, weaving and tapestry have a higher profile and are exhibited on the same level as painting and sculpture, but outside the main cities, art can only be seen in isolated pockets. Though on a local level the Norwegian people are still very much in touch with creating, using traditional craft skills. There is also a strong awareness of what is going on outside Norway, especially Europe.

As a landscape painter it was important for me to travel outside Oslo. With the help of the NAVF travel allowance I travelled to Svolvar, Lofoten Islands in north-west Norway. I stayed in the Artists' House, *Kunstners hus*, for a month in November, which is specially for artists to live and work in. There are living quarters on the ground floor and studio space upstairs, with panoramic views all round. It was also a good place to meet and work with other artists. I also visited the Sognefjord, Telemark, Kristiansand and the Hardanger Vidda.

I enjoyed the sheer variety and strength of the Norwegian sea and landscape. Both the subtlety and impressiveness. I found it difficult to comprehend at first, as the landscape was like a foreign language, I had to slowly build up a new vocabulary of marks and colours to make sense of the awe-inspiring scale and images for my paintings.

I found Norway unusual as a country because of the strong links which still exist between the people and the land, with many people having connections with their agricultural roots and the *hytta* tradition. This underlies the culture, customs and way of life which exists in the modern day society of Norway.

I enjoyed the time and space I had in Norway. The only stipulation was to submit a report to NAVF about my work. I returned to England more visually aware, fully inspired and wanting to practice a little English.

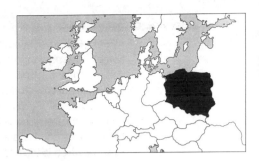

Poland

LANGUAGE
Official: Polish
Others spoken: German widespread and some French; Russian used to be taught in all schools
English spoken: use growing, though mainly in cities

CURRENCY
Official: zloty
Others used: dollar, deutsch mark
Convertible or not: yes
Travellers cheques/credit cards: only in centres, use of credit cards growing

DOCUMENTS YOU NEED
Information contact: Polish Consulate General, 19 Weymouth Street, London W1N 4EA tel 071 580 0476. Embassy of the Republic of Poland, 47 Portland Place, London W1N 3AG tel 071 580 4324

POLISH DTI DESK
OT 3/5d Room 316 tel 071 215 4734

BANKS
More usual to be open in the morning and maybe to early afternoon, later in main centres

POST OFFICES
Monday to Saturday 7.00/8.00-20.00 main branches (18.00 at latest elsewhere)

BUSINESS HOURS
10.00-18.00 Monday to Friday (often 6.00-14.00 in rural areas) and Saturday morning

ART GALLERIES/MUSEUMS
Usually closed Mondays and often closed by 15.00

PUBLIC HOLIDAYS
Jan 1, Easter Monday, May 1, May 3, Corpus Christi, Assumption, All Saints, Dec 25/26

CONTACTS IN THE UK
Polish Cultural Institute, 34 Portland Place, London W1N 4HQ tel 071 636 6032
Polorbis Travel, 82 Mortimer Street, London W1N 7DE tel 071 636 2217

CONTACTS ABROAD
British Council, Al Jerozolimskie 59, 00-697 Warsaw tel 7211981/2/3/4
Ministry of Culture, ul. Krakowskie Przedmiescie 15/17, 00 916 Warsaw tel 200231
Chamber of Commerce:
Krajowa Izba Gospodarcza, Trebacka 4, PO Box 361, 00-950 Warsaw, tel 260221
Embassy/Consulate:
British Embassy, Aleje Roz 1, 00-556 Warsaw tel 281001
Artists Association:
Zwiesek Artystow Rzezbiarzy, ul. Nowyswiet 21, 00-029 Warsaw
Zwiezek Polskich Artystow Malazy i Jrafikow, ul. Foksal 2, 00-366 Warsaw
Copyright/moral rights:
DACS initially tel 071 247 1650. In Poland ZAIKS 2 ul. Hippoteczna, 00-092 Warsaw

Jadwiga Sawicka

I live in Przemysl in southern east Poland, 13km from the Ukrainian border. Przemysl is not a small city but very quiet and without many cultural options. It was not quite a free and conscious choice that I came back here after my studies in Kraków but I have never regretted it. I found the slow pace of provincial life is my own. Out of three friends who graduated in the same year and returned to Przemysl, two want to move further in the country and live in isolation, one is going to move back to Kraków which is the nearest (240km away) big cultural centre.

I am not happy about living with my parents although the fact I don't pay rent has made my life a lot easier. There has been a shortage of flats in Poland ever since I remember. Under the communist regime an artist was lucky to get hold of a studio space 10-15 years after finishing studies, providing they put some effort into doing a lot of paper work. Now it's only a question of money. The consequences may be similar but at least the situation is clear. You need £30-60 to rent a studio, the average wage is £100, a teacher earns £50-60, unemployment benefit is £35.

I work in my room which luckily is big enough; such a situation is common among artists. Some of them have converted cellars or attics for studio space. Two of my friends, printmakers, have started building a house in the country (8km from Przemysl) in beautiful surroundings. They are not able to finish the building for financial reasons. They are looking for a person or a group of artists who could assist them in finishing the house. In return they offer the use of spacious studio with excellent light and view for many years to come. There is also etching workshop and wood in a large garden with a workshop.

For details of this building project contact Alina Czernecka, ul.Wybrzeze Focha 5, 37-700 Przemysl.

The artists' union had its glorious moment during the martial law (introduced in 1981) when it managed to organise many important exhibitions and other events independently from state supported galleries. After the definite collapse of communism (in 1989) there have been fierce and prolonged discussions concerning political attitudes in former times. It has affected artists and their union as well. It is difficult to avoid a question of the legacy of communism in Poland because it is still present in all areas of life. For 40 years society had been split up. Art had been treated as a tool in either of opposing camps. Because of this usefulness artists have had quite high social status but involvement in political issues very often resulted in artistic compromise.

There are regions where the union has recovered its proper function and tries to help its members by negotiating a reduction in studio rent with the city authorities, sponsoring events, etc. In Przemysl, together with a few smaller cities, there are about 50 artists and craftspeople but very few of them are really committed. There are not

many problems which these people could have in common. The union
meetings suffer from chronic lack of quorum.

Since Solidarity artists have taken initiative from bureaucrats. It
was a group of enthusiasts who set up international meetings of avant-
garde artists, Construction in Process in Lodz (central Poland). During
the third meeting in October 1990, 100 participants were offered halls
and gardens of the city museums as well as streets, sub-ways and
squares in Lodz. This, and the WRO-Sound Basis Visual Art Festival, a
festival of new media held annually in December in Wroclaw, are
sponsored by sources other than the Ministry of Culture from Poland and
abroad.

Residential artists' workshops had been organised before but
under close state supervision they showed rather mean results. The two
workshops in which I took part in 1990 and 1991 were organised and
co-ordinated by one of my friends, a man of vision and a very committed
artist. For three weeks a group of 15-20 people had the opportunity to
work in a huge partly derelict castle in Krasiczyn (10km from Przemysl)
and we all agreed it was an extremely stimulating and important
experience. A group of English artists who were invited to Krasiczyn
organised a similar event in England (Sutton Courtney Abbey 1991).
Together with the Krasiczyn workshop organiser and another Polish
painter I went to England and spent a month painting and meeting artists
from other countries.

In Oronsko (central Poland) international sculpture meetings are
held; artists who were invited to work there have a high opinion of it.

Centrum Rzezby Polskiej, CRP (The Centre of Polish Sculpture)
in Oronsko offers 14 sculpture and technical studios (ceramics/casting,
bronze, stonemasons, smiths and carpenters), there is also a hotel, a
sculpture gallery and a large park. CRP organises international sculpture
meetings financed by the government of Poland, and rents to artists its
studios and all social and technical equipment.

The future of these events is unclear. The law encouraging
private sponsorship has been talked about but hasn't been passed yet.
In consequence of the catastrophic state of our economy, money
provided for culture is scarce and public art commissions don't exist. In
the late 80s foreign tourists started buying Polish art which was cheap.
Due to inflation 100 dollars made a small fortune in Polish currency.
Private galleries were abundant. This artificial boom was soon over. The
galleries either closed down or became very commercial which doesn't
help much. People don't have money even for pretty landscapes and the
newly rich prefer antiques. In bigger cities like Warsaw or Poznan there
are more ambitious galleries promoting avant-garde art. They are

A nude., Jadwiga Sawicka, **1991, oil on canvas 120x110 cm.**

sponsored by the Ministry of Culture or the city council. I am not very avant-garde as far as medium is concerned (oil painting) and definitely non-commercial. I paint big figurative pictures using mainly white, grey and black colours and I know that my work may be disturbing to look at. As a result there are not many galleries suitable for me at the moment.

Artists who sell abroad are able to make their living but these are few. Mostly people make designs and advertising for developing private enterprises and shops. Such jobs are easier to get in big cities. It is not easy to get work teaching because art is a small part of the curriculum in schools. There is a shortage of English teachers so I decided to start a newly founded English Teacher's College but this is not typical. Some of my friends make jewellery or toys. Generally the standard of living has deteriorated much in recent years.

There is no problem with availability of art materials but not all of them are of satisfactory quality. Usually I do my shopping in Kraków. Supply may be erratic but the main problem is cost. A 150ml tube of oil titanium white costs £3. Stretchers and canvas size 150x150cm, £5. This is expensive and prices are rising.

The oldest and most prestigious art schools are the Academies of Fine Arts in Warsaw and Kraków. There are several other art schools which specialise, such as tapestry and cloth design in Lodz, glass making and ceramics in Wroclaw. There are entrance exams in drawing and painting and then in the history of art and foreign language.

I graduated from the Kraków Academy in 1984. I studied graphics for one year and then changed to painting. Although the graphics department has a very high reputation I found it too strict and rather frustrating. The atmosphere at the painting department was more encouraging for individual studying, though we were obliged to draw from the nude for five years and too much experimenting was frowned upon. The Academy in Warsaw has always enjoyed being more open to new trends.

We share with all other people the consequences of our ruined economy but I believe that out of the whole society artists will benefit most from freedom and the end of cultural isolation. It is an exciting time to be an artist in Poland.

Helen Ganly

For several years I had been travelling to Czechoslovakia to make contact with dissident artists and intellectuals. Through these contacts I was asked to give some slide lectures at an independent symposium in Przemysl in south east Poland, seven miles from the Russian border. It was 1988 and the communists were in power. The first lecture was a formal one, held in a church and open to the general public. The second was to a group of intellectuals and artists, Solidarity supporters, who met regularly in the attic of an old farmhouse.

I showed the work of artists in Germany and Czechoslovakia and work by painters and sculptors taking part in the ArtWeek festival in Oxford. On the strength of the slides I was asked to return with two or three others to take part in a 'plener' or workshop-symposium in September 1989, one of many held all over Poland and traditionally funded by the communist authorities for officially acknowledged artists.

When martial law was introduced in 1981, the Catholic church had provided sympathetic support for many of the artists and intellectuals. Exhibitions and meetings were often held in the spacious crypts of the churches. There had been an uneasy communication between the official Union of Artists, who in many towns ran their own government-subsidised galleries, and the independents, who showed in churches and other spaces.

Our official invitation, which exempted us from the then compulsory currency exchange, was issued by the regional head of the Artists' Union, but we ended up living and working alongside independent Polish artists in the rambling attic rooms of a presbytery. A lot of people speak some English but true discourse doesn't take place unless there are enough fluent interpreters. We had our fares paid by a trust fund and our board and lodging in Poland was free. We in our turn left money behind to help two Polish artists come to Oxford for ArtWeek 1990, although in that year the cost of a return flight from Warsaw rose from $60 (£35) to $300 (£176). A return coach ticket from either Poland or England costs about $150 (£88).

2D installation, Helen Ganly, **1990, work on show in one of the studio spaces in Krasiczyn castle**
Photo: Roger Perkins

The Polish artists both sold work in England and took home useful money. Another five of us travelled out in September 1990 to join the next plener. This time Solidarity was in power and the independent artists were able to use money from old communist funds to run a wonderful plener where the artists lived in a small hotel and were able to use a semi-derelict 16th century castle as studio space.

Materials can be a problem. I asked one artist where he had got his quantities of black paint. He looked at me with some amusement, 'I mix chimney soot with oil' he said. I had asked someone if they could buy me some clay. 'We won't be able to buy it' they said. 'We'll try and dig some up'. Oil paint is used more frequently than acrylic. It is worth trying to find out what materials are available in your area.

On our first trip, we travelled by train, carting heavy paints across to Poland, only to find that high-quality artists' oil paint was made and distributed from a small factory in the town – and by our standards, was extremely inexpensive. Supplies of artists' materials may be erratic, and it's best to take as much as you can with you, including film. Polish artists are full of enterprise and initiative, but they often have to stockpile – when and if they can. Incidentally, slide film is expensive, and not widely-used in Poland, whereas VHS videos of exhibitions are quite common.

£58 (or $100) is an average monthly wage. In Poland it will buy proportionally more, but the illogical exchange rate means English people will feel ridiculously wealthy. Because of the exchange rate, it is not financially rewarding for visitors to sell work in Poland, and it may be almost impossible for Polish buyers. Artists give and exchange work out of interest and friendship; on the other hand, we bought some beautiful etchings very cheaply from some printmaking graduates from Kraków who had a small press in their flat.

I used the time in Poland to make work which I have shown in exhibitions elsewhere. Teaching jobs are not plentiful, school jobs are poorly-paid, and academic subjects are concentrated on at the expense of the creative arts. We enjoyed doing an unpaid workshop in a primary school, but there is no tradition of artists doing residencies in the way that has developed in the United Kingdom.

The small galleries are closing down as people switch from buying prints and paintings to newly-accessible books and videos. Many artists are having to give up their studios as privatisation pushes up the rents. I met a few fortunate artists in Kraków, who had taken over unconverted lofty attics in huge old apartment blocks where they lived. Like artists everywhere, many worked in their living quarters. That can be difficult. It is very common to find hardworking professional families with several children living in two small rooms with a bathroom and kitchen.

The Poles are wonderfully kind and hospitable, proud of their language and rich cultural heritage, but space is at a premium and consumer goods (now plentiful) are very expensive. Life is difficult as the country moves painfully towards a free-market economy. Visitors should take sleeping-bags and dollars to help pay their way.

The Polish artists we worked with were mainly graduates from Kraków. The other academies are in Warsaw and Poznan. Most of the work was painterly and expressionist. Three dimensional work including soft sculptures were used in installations. Of the artists we met in the plener, the oldest (in his late fifties) was established and successful, selling work in Poland and Germany. Amongst the others, one was a technician in the sculpture department at Kraków, one did odd teaching jobs, also buying and selling artefacts and antiques, one designed labels and packaging, also selling the occasional large canvas, one had survived for some years through selling work and teaching privately in his studio, and one was basically supported by her parents. It was a very familiar scene.

During the three years I have been going to Poland, my work has been directly inspired by the experience of being there. The subject-matter has reflected my feelings and observations. I have used metaphor in my large-scale drawings, have referred to pollution and ecology in my acrylic paintings, and have conveyed a sense of a shared central European culture in my installation in the castle.

Through living and working alongside each other, sympathies and interests developed. Inspired by the Polish example, we organised the first International Artists' Plener in Oxford in 1991, inviting artists from seven different European countries with support from the Arts Council and a number of other sponsors. We had to raise the money for the fares of the artists from Czechoslovakia and Poland, but the others were expected to pay their own fares.

This September, the Poles have raised money from their regional Ministry of Culture to fund artists from England, Germany, Austria and the USSR. We will all pay our own fares. The studio space will again be the 16th century castle. Some oil paint, canvas, stretchers, and paper will be provided for the artists. The exhibitions of experimental art will again be held in the castle (to the amazement of the local community) and in the crypt of the Franciscan church in Przemysl. It is less expensive to look after visiting artists in your own homes and studios, but nothing can replace the intensity and excitement of living and working together for three weeks under the same roof.

Bringing work back can be fraught with bureaucratic problems. Transporting large quantities of work for cultural exchange exhibitions is best done through the Customs and Excise, with carnets detailing precise descriptions of works, and their weights and sizes, but as an individual artist, I have found the simplest way is to carry the work with you. I have found saying it is 'incomplete' or 'work-in-progress' or 'not valuable' is quite acceptable if one is questioned.

The sculptors documented their large-scale work and left it behind to disintegrate; the painters also left large-scale paintings behind. Retrieving my large-scale drawings by post or rail seemed impossible; the paperwork was daunting. I decided to go over and fetch them myself, taking a length of grey plastic drainpipe to pack them in. If it wasn't taller than a person or a pair of skis I argued, how could the airline object?

I will always treasure the memory of the incredulous expression on the customs officer's face at Warsaw airport as I explained first that I was carrying a drainpipe, and secondly, that it had *nothing* in it.

Portugal

Member of the Council of Europe and the EC
Many telephone numbers in Portugal are changing
In 1992

LANGUAGE
Official: Portuguese
Others spoken: French/Spanish sometimes understood in border areas
English spoken: mainly in centres and amongst younger people

CURRENCY
Official: 100 centavos = 1 Portuguese escudo (1,000 escudos = 1 conto)
Convertible or not: yes
Travellers cheques/Eurocheques/credit cards: widely accepted, especially in tourist centres and cities

DOCUMENTS YOU NEED
Information contact: Portuguese Consulate General, Silver City House, 62 Brompton Rd, London SW3 1BJ tel 071 581 8722

PORTUGUESE DTI DESK
OT 3/3b Room 362 tel 071 215 4776/5103

BANKS
Monday to Friday 8.30-11.45 and 13.00-14.45

POST OFFICES
Monday to Friday 9.00-18.00, Saturday morning in main centres

BUSINESS HOURS
Monday to Friday 9.00-12.30 and circa 14.30-circa 19.00, Saturday morning

ART GALLERIES/MUSEUMS
Closed Mondays

PUBLIC HOLIDAYS
Jan 1, Apr 25, Good Friday, May Day, Corpus Christl, Jun 10, Aug 15, Oct 5, Nov 1, Dec 1, Dec 8, Dec 25

CONTACT IN THE UK
Portugal 600, Palingswick House, 241 King Street, London W6 9LP tel 081 748 0884
Portuguese National Tourist Office, New Bond Street House, 1-5 New Bond Street, London W1Y 0NP tel 071 493 3873

CONTACT ABROAD
British Council, Rua de Sao Marcal 174, 1294 Lisbon tel 3476141
Ministry of Culture, Directorate-General for Cultural Action, Av. da Republica no 16 4, 1004 Lisbon
Embassy/Consulate:
British Embassy, Rua san Domingo a Lapa 37, 1296 Lisbon tel 3961191. Consulates in Maderia, Orporto, Ponta Delgada, Portimao
Chamber of Commerce:
Rua das Portas de Santo Antao 89, 1194 Lisbon tel 327179/3423277
Artists Association:
Sociedade Nacionale de Belas Artes (National Society of Fine Arts), Rua Barata Solgueriro 36, Lisbon tel 521046
Copyright/moral rights:
DACS initially tel 071 247 1650. In Portugal, SPA Rebello/Av Duque de Loule 31, 1098 Lisbon tel 578320

Ines Amado

I had lived in England for a number of years before returning to Portugal to work as a sculptor. Being Portuguese I did not suffer any language difficulty but it was really a new experience for me; I had become used to London, the people, the facilities, and of course, new friends and colleagues were in their majority in London.

I established my base in Lisbon, the capital city. Although not my home town I had lived and studied there previously and was fortunate enough, through my family, to have the use of an apartment in Lisbon; what I lacked was a studio. I rapidly discovered it would be very difficult to rent studio space. The old part of Lisbon has masses of workshops often part of mixed occupancy properties with offices above workshops and apartments at the higher levels. Unfortunately the rent laws then prevalent in Portugal restricted vacant properties being offered for rental. It was very frustrating given that there was a lot of vacant property available, particularly in the docks' area. This situation has now changed and some specific studio lettings are available to artists within twenty minutes drive from Lisbon.

Eventually I found an attic for rent in an old building which would provide about 350 square feet of studio space but it required fully converting being without water, electricity and windows. Working with my husband we managed to create a very good studio, even opening the attic onto an adjoining terrace giving me an open air working space with magnificent views across the river Tejo estuary to Lisbon. The one drawback was that the studio was on the fourth floor with no lift, this was not ideal for a sculptor and I was forced, for a while, to adapt my work to match the facilities available.

Establishing contact with other working artists was essential and I decided the quickest way would be through the art schools. There are two principal schools in Lisbon, the *Academia das Belas Artes* (Fine Art Academy) near the Chiado district and the ARCO School; the latter is a privately sponsored and relatively new 'alternative' established in a beautiful 17th century building in the old Alfama part of the city.

I was very fortunate to be offered more or less immediately part-time teaching at ARCO and in the following years I taught both sculpture and drawing to the new intake of students on a part-time basis. The school gave me the opportunity to meet and discuss with my contemporaries our work, 'the arts', and to assimilate rapidly into an artistic framework of which I had limited previous experience in Portugal.

ARCO is located in one of the oldest and most beautiful parts of Lisbon. The Alfama district is very hilly, criss-crossed by tramways, and topped by St George's Castle from which there are the best views across

In/between, Ines Amado, **aluminium, copper and wood, 92x62cm, 1991**

the city; the streets are narrow and shaded from the heat of the day ever opening into small squares encroached by cafés and restaurants. It provides a rich and stimulating environment for student and tutors alike!

My contact with the school opened access to galleries, art events and symposiums throughout Portugal. Particularly recommended for sculptors are the annual stone symposiums organised with the sculptor João Cutileiro that take place near Portugal's marble quarries.

There are however many differences between working in Portugal and England. It took me some time to readjust to the pace of life in Portugal. It is generally more relaxed, fluid and languid, a great deal can be achieved as long as you accept the rhythm and flow of the city and its people, and you will gain reward and enjoyment from a prolonged stay in Portugal. This is not an onerous duty, much time is spent socialising with and getting to know your new-found friends in one of the many cafés or inexpensive restaurants scattered across the city. This is not as outrageously expensive as is the case in London. Lisbon is still a very cheap city in which to live and, as always, the limited pockets of artists and students seek out those establishments which offer value for money. I had somehow forgotten this most important factor of Portuguese life, quite foolish really as I had spent so much of my own student days in and out of cafés between study. This way of daily life is so different from working in London where artists tend to enclose themselves in their studios, only emerging occasionally to attend an opening or preview and meet up with friends and acquaintances and berate the art world and how it is treating them, perhaps going on for a beer or curry afterwards.

In Portugal you must be prepared to give time to those who will willingly give time and friendship to you, people will always be 'dropping in' to inquire after you, share a coffee, invite you to lunch, the cinema or just to talk. The day stretches long in Lisbon, night life starts after 10pm; unlike England the bars don't close at a set hour, and if you want to spend the night theorising and intellectualising about art there are a thousand places open to you. Even the bars where the great Portuguese writers and artists in history congregated such as *Café Nicola* and *A Brasileira* will be happy to accommodate you for the price of a cup of coffee or beer.

There are many art galleries in Lisbon ranging, as ever, from the excellent to the poor. There is always a good cross-section of Portuguese and international work on show, many of the major international exhibitions find their way to the Gulbenkian Foundation which is the premier arts centre in Portugal. Its facilities just off Praça de Espanha are similar to the South Bank in London offering music, dance, ballet and avant-garde theatre. The permanent collection is displayed in the superb modern gallery generally accompanied by special exhibitions of Portuguese or international artists. The major touring exhibitions are generally held in the main building that is located across the beautifully landscaped sculpture park. Not to be missed is the excellent restaurant attached to the art gallery and the summer open air performances, these embrace a broad performing arts spectrum, idyllic on a balmy summer evening. Cinema is wonderfully catered for in Lisbon, international films are shown often before they are released in the UK, not just the box office success productions but also the 'fringe', so called 'art films' of worldwide directors infrequently screened in London.

Recent years have seen an expansion in the number of galleries in and around Lisbon. Exhibited work does sell, there is a healthy market at prices equivalent and quite often higher than in the UK. Collectors are in the market as in any other country, however there is a distinct element of spontaneous purchase which is generally unlike London, if they like what they see they will buy the work.

Ray Smith

I went to Portugal originally with a commission to make some practical researches into the Portuguese ceramic tile tradition. During those initial two weeks, I found myself working in tiny craft workshops, large modern factories and also in medium-size factories which did not seem to have changed much in 250 years and which turned out thousands of clay tiles each day.

**River Park Leisure Centre,
Winchester,** Ray Smith

That initial experience remains vivid, I had never been to Portugal before and I found Lisbon extra-ordinarily alive at all times of the day and night. What was it about the place? Perhaps it had something to do with a sense of scale. From the *Castello de Sao Jorge* or from the other side of the city in the *Bairro Alto*, you would overlook the whole central part of the city, from the *Avenida da Liberdade* to the *Baixa*, with every building sharp and clear in the early summer light. The buildings seemed tiny but also close-up, so there was a sense of being both present and distant. At night, looking down, there was a similar impression, with the *Rossio* railway station lit up like a stage set and with the large-scale neon signs perched like great birds on the illuminated city below. In a similar way, standing under the *Ponte 25 de Abril* suspension bridge leading from the city across the *Tagus* to *Almada*, you were conscious of a great over-arching curvilinear perspective with tiny passing lorries and cars seemingly miles above you. You were either in among the action, with the busy city pressing in on you, with its shoe-shine men, its bank clerks in suits with jumpers, its beggars, and women in heavy grey suits with wide shoulder pads and chunky gold jewellery, or you were overlooking a city which led you down to the broad river, with the massive *Lisnave* shipyard on the opposite bank and the statue of Christ in Majesty above, and the sea beyond.

Portugal

Cultura, magazine on cultural exchange with Portugal published three times a year by Portugal 600, Palingswick House, 241 King Street, London W6 9LP tel 081 748 0884

Anglo/Portugese Society, Canning House, 2 Belgrave Square, London SW1 tel 071 245 9738

Gulbenkian Foundation (UK), Gulbenkian is a Portugese organisation that is virtually an unofficial ministry of culture or arts council in Portugal, 93 Portland Place, London W1 tel 071 636 5313

The Portuguese are working fiercely to improve their position on the European economic ladder. Everywhere there is new building work. Taking the train from Lisbon out to Sintra, you see countless new blocks of flats, their floors supported by rough-hewn timbers as the concrete sets. But right next to the new flats with their new shopping centres, are the shanty towns where families who provide cheap labour, scratch a living in third world conditions. Such contrasts abound in Portugal and the Portuguese are very conscious of them. They are a proud people and their pride can take the form of a kind of defensiveness. There is a sense of conformity, of doing the right thing at the right time, of wearing the right clothes for the right occasion: perhaps there is an element of insecurity which underlies this. On the other hand, the Portuguese also have the most extraordinary capacity for tolerance, accepting people as they are.

On the first point, I found when I was working in one tile factory it was difficult for them to understand that the client who had paid a great deal of his own money for a large order for hand-made tiles, should also be the one to don overalls and paint them himself, coming into the factory early in the morning and leaving late at night just like the workers. For large-scale work at least and sometimes even for individual tiles, the tradition in Portugal is for the artist to make the design which is translated onto the tiles by the painters employed at the factory. They even go so far as to copy the artist's signature. But having accepted there was now a new convention established by this creature in a moon suit and dust mask, everyone accepted my idiosyncratic behaviour with amused tolerance. One might have foreseen at least some resentment from those who work long hours for little pay, but if there was any, I did not come across it.

One of the great things about making work in a new medium in a country other than your own, is that you tend not to be too constrained by the stylistic conventions with which it is associated. But the influences can be felt everywhere. The long and unbroken *Azulejos* tradition has left stunning examples of work in every part of Portugal. From the extraordinary sculptural plain tiles in various hues of warm and cool white in the vast kitchens with their massive rising chimneys in the Royal Palace at Sintra, to the magnificent sequence of knights on rearing horseback in the tiled arches of the gardens at the *Fronteira Palace*, there are examples wherever you look. A simple baker's shop will be entirely decorated with its own original art nouveau tile scheme. You will come across a bar such as the *Cervejaria Trinidade* in Lisbon where the simply painted rugged tile panels are striking in their power and immediacy. Or you might wander into a chapel where the whole barrel-vaulted ceiling is of painted tiles or where the seventeenth century altar facings are not made of material at all but are painted illusionistically onto ceramic tiles.

It is not therefore surprising many Portuguese tile factories and workshops seem to spend much of their time recreating designs of the past. There is an understandable national pride in cultural tradition and clearly a commercial demand to be met. But no great claims would necessarily be made for this kind of work and there is a quite separate contemporary movement which is encouraged by the exhibitions at galleries such as *Ratton* in the *Rua Academia das Ciencias* and by the commissioning of major new tile schemes from important contemporary artists for stations on the extension to the underground.

The tile museum in the cloisters of the church of *Madre de Deus* has excellent examples of *azulejos* from all periods, including a sensational sparkling panel of birds made by primary school children. There is art to be seen everywhere, from the renaissance collection in the *Museu Nacional de Arte Antiga* to contemporary work In commercial galleries like *Modulo* or *Comicos*. There is some wonderful art to be seen in the cool modern interiors of the Gulbenkian Museum where temporary exhibitions of contemporary work by artists such as Vieira da Silva or Paula Rego, are featured along with work from the permanent collection. In the modern collection, Paula Rego's 'Prole's Wall' of 1984 is an extraordinary and unique achievement from one of her most original periods of work. Among magnificent earlier works such as Van der Weyden's 'St Catharine or the Virgin' and Rubens' 'Portrait of Helena Fourment', is a small 'Portrait of a young woman' by Domenico Ghirlandaio. This one breathtaking painting is worth making a special trip to Lisbon to see.

Romania

As with other Eastern European countries, good research is important before you travel, the whole area is undergoing dramatic change, some regions more violently than others. The information below could alter at anytime, but was correct at the time of research.

LANGUAGE
Official: Romanian is a Romance language with Slavonic, Turkish, Magyar and French additions
Others spoken: German, Hungarian, Spanish, Italian – French the most widely understood
English spoken: yes – but not widely, mainly amongst younger people and in tourist areas

CURRENCY
Official: 100 bani = 1 Leu (Lei)
Others used: Hard currency such a dollars, also basic goods such as soap very helpful
Convertible or not: yes
Travellers cheques/Eurocheques/credit cards: Limited, especially check restaurants & shops

DOCUMENTS YOU NEED
For information on visa, work and residence permits contact: Romanian Consulate, 4 Palace Green, London W8 4QD tel 071 937 9666. Do this well in advance (Consulate recommends at least 7 days) of travelling and note that visas are only dealt with between 10.00 and 12.00 Monday-Friday

ROMANIAN DTI DESK
OT 3/5b Room 355 tel 071 215 5152/5267

BANKS
Open Monday to Friday 9.00-12.00 and 13.00-15.00; Saturday 9.00-12.00

POST OFFICES
Open Monday to Saturday 7.00-20.00; Sunday 7.00-12.00

BUSINESS HOURS
Monday to Saturday, early morning to circa 20.00; Sunday early morning to circa 12.00

ART GALLERIES/MUSEUMS
Closed Mondays with wide range of and sporadic opening times

PUBLIC HOLIDAYS
Jan 1/2, May 1/2, Aug 23/24

CONTACT IN THE UK
Romanian National Tourist Office, 17 Nottingham Street, London W1M 3RD tel 071 224 3692

CONTACTS ABROAD
British Council, Calea Dorobantilor 14, Bucharest tel 118444
Ministry of Culture, Piata Presi Libere 1, Sector 1, 71341 Bucharest tel 505020
Embassy/Consulate:
24 Strada Jules, Michelet, 70154 Bucharest tel 111634
Chamber of Commerce:
Bd. Nicolae Balcescu 22, 79502 Bucharest tel 154707
Artists Associations:
Uniunea Artistilor Plastici din Romania, str. Nicolae Iorga nr. 21, 7000 Bucharest tel 504920
Trade Union of Workers in Education, Science and Cultural Institutions, c/o Confereratia Nationala a Sindicatelor Libere din Romania (Unions belong to this organisation), Str.Ministerului 1-3, 70109 Oucharest tel 136579
Copyright/moral rights:
No Romanian organisation noted, try Design & Artists Copyright Society (DACS), St. Mary's Clergy House, 2 Whitechurch Lane, London E1 7QR tel 071 247 1650

Adrian Branea

After many years of difficulty in the environment of Romanian art, I think I am now a lucky man. Art and culture is one of the main ways of expression of people in our country, so there is a good know-how in this area. On the other hand Romania is a poor country but artists couldn't be touched by the deep economic recession so hard, because one can use any materials in comparison with other activities and art principally depends on human qualities. I was not able to follow a typical career after graduation because the institutions which managed artists' affairs before the events of 1989 were for a time closed to newcomers.

I started my free career after ten years of waiting. My first step in the new situation, after the changes in Eastern Europe, was to find enough time to work. This is a very difficult task because living is expensive and a full-time job provides only half of basic income. Getting work outside your speciality might seem like abandoning your art, but it is acceptable with the current problems. Selling my paintings is the best way of combining use of time with income but it is also unsafe when I'm not successful. So I have to take some other jobs, as a teacher of drawing and a photographer, which allow me to deal with lack of sales.

Maybe the story sounds like a sad one in contrast with what I said at the beginning. But that was true. There are strong feelings that art and culture can help us rise to an up-to-date standard. Our society has developed secret ways of supporting the long bad periods, and learning and culture are among them.

The first need of all in my art is to see enough in order to understand people and represent what I see. I like to play an active role, with many meetings and exchanges of opinions. My personal belief is we have to grow a Romanian style of art, instead of trying to take other experiences too directly. I'm not a traditionalist but I like to understand how ideas appear.

I can show my work in several ways. One of the most traditional is to participate at national salons, which are very large exhibitions of art at regular dates. One can see trends in our art, as a whole, and representative works of masters. The exhibitions are organised by the Ministry of Culture and are non-profitable shows. The shows specialise in painting, sculpture, graphics, decorative art and design. They last about two months in Bucharest and then they travel to other big cities. The Ministry of Culture also is the host of the international exhibitions. The smaller shows are organised by the National Organisation of Visual Arts (UAP). This organisation is quite old, has 2000 members all over the country, it also has several galleries in Bucharest and in the main cities of the country. Each member can exhibit in the place they want, but they often use local galleries. The organisation also has art shops where each artist can have works on the wall for several months. The shops also have decorative art, crafts and modern jewellery. The organisation was founded in the totalitarian times as an expression of centralisation, but luckily was always an independent organisation. Now it has to face the dilemma of remaining a big organisation or breaking into smaller units.

A new wave in exhibiting has started by private galleries, adding antiquities to contemporary art, which is a good service for clients.

Several Romanian artists show their work abroad. I know many friends who were well accepted by Western countries, this means perhaps Romanians belong to Europe, because they don't have big problems in communicating their feelings internationally. Or perhaps our new works are cheaper, about £200 for a piece, in Romanian galleries. I hope both of these are true. The Romanians who visit exhibitions are mainly our own colleagues and the informed public. This is not the same with foreign visitors who understand art better!

Artists work in their studios which are also places where they can meet those people interested in their work and personality. There are also summer camps for painting and sculpture. There are very interesting open air shows of sculpture as a result of the camps, a good school for experimental and environmental art.

The right way of using these opportunities is another difficult task. For each form of show or activity one must pass a kind of exam and, as in all countries, it's a very competitive environment. The jury is made up of artists and critics who play an important role in selecting works. But the most difficult thing for me is to make a painting able to make someone like it and this takes me hours of work daily at my studio finding out what is also good for me.

Jacqueline Norris

In response to an article in the Southern Arts Board newsletter, I visited Baia Mare in northern Romania on a cultural exchange. Curiosity was the driving force which determined our decision to go. Information on Romania was minimal and what I read implied parts of northern Romania are heavily polluted. We opted to go and see for ourselves.

I am a ceramicist, I work with intense colour and am particularly interested in religious artefacts as source material. Romania, I discovered later, holds these qualities in abundance.

My partner and I travelled together by car. Obtaining visas was no problem, a simple matter of a letter to the Embassy including dates and reasons for travel. Visas can be purchased on the Romanian border using hard currency but we were pleased not to have taken this option as we drove past all those waiting for their visa documentation. We discovered just in time that the 'green card' insurance does not include Romania and took out additional cover.

The journey took five days. We crossed into Romania without problems but had slight reservations about the long queue of cars waiting to leave the country. We assured ourselves that they were all Romanian vehicles and were told visitors are entitled to queue jump.

Romanian time is one hour ahead of Central Europe, a fact we did not know at this stage. Close to dusk, we soon discovered that traffic (mostly bicycles, horses and carts) continues after dark and with no lights! Despite the roads being of reasonable quality, this slowed us to a crawl as we kept a constant look-out for pigs and geese in our path. The final leg of our journey took far longer than anticipated with our unknowing hosts being rudely awakened in the middle of the night.

Language problems did not arise despite the fact neither of us spoke a word of Romanian on arrival. By pointing, miming and repeating a few Romanian words we managed, and our host spoke impeccable English. We occasionally found French to be a useful common language but generally relied on the patience of local people to understand our gesticulations.

My visit was short and intense with the purpose of investigating future possibilities for longer term study. My aim was to visit studios, factories and artists at work and to get a feel for the country. I did not spend enough time away to produce my own work, but was offered the opportunity to stay and work if I wished. In general, studios are enormous with artists friendly and willing to share their spaces, or even vacate them temporarily for a visitor. Most studios include a bed and simple wash/cook facilities. In general, artists' studios are housed in the older buildings of Baia Mare. With enormous windows and high ceilings, they are ideal. With most people living in uninspiring concrete blocks of flats it surprises me these old buildings are not returned to living accommodation.

Outside the large, unattractive towns lie an abundance of small villages where peasants live a simple farming life. Local women still wear colourful traditional costume as everyday dress while Sunday brings music and dancing onto the streets. Each village boasts one or more church with a towering spire constructed entirely from wood; the interior decor bearing a wealth of textiles and icons. Without a car, transport to these areas would be very difficult as public transport is minimal.

There is a large gallery space in the artist complex of Baia Mare showing paintings, ceramics and sculpture. It was suggested I could

Fishy Candle Casket No. 13,
Jacqueline Norris, **ceramic.**

exhibit here or maybe go for a larger exhibition in Bucharest. To exhibit is one thing, but to sell is another. Judging by the inexpensive prices we paid for handmade ceramics, I cannot imagine selling any work brought over from Britain at realistic prices.

The countryside around Transylvania is rich in minerals and metals which are mined extensively. For a potter, these materials, used in conjunction with the local clay would provide the means to make and glaze work. Traditional Romanian pottery remains relatively unchanged. Using red clay, thrown with amazing skill and lightness, decoration is fast and fine using coloured slips and slip trailing techniques. Clear lead glaze is common. Other ceramicists were slip casting and decorating with enamels. A close link between factory and artist allows access to materials and firing facilities otherwise unobtainable. Many potters work for local ceramic factories and in return are provided with studio space and materials on site. The factories we visited were hot, dusty and antiquated environments, although the workers maintained drive and enthusiasm.

Artists' subject matter deals generally with the changing landscape and figurative work. This reflects a country which until 1989 was dominated by Ceaucescu who gave his personal approval or disapproval to everything. With secret police everywhere it was unwise to produce work concerning political issues. After the revolution in December 1989, the country has undergone such a change that the people are still re-adjusting to their freedom.

Colour photographic film is not available in Romania and books are also in short supply. One artist showed me his copy of an English book on Raku which he had photographed page by page.

Living costs are low by European standards. Banks open for short periods only and exchange rates vary enormously. On reflection we should have taken more money in sterling or dollars, not travellers cheques. It is impossible to change these anywhere except the bank whereas dollars are readily accepted with enthusiasm. While we were visiting, petrol was in demand with queues several miles long and car owners camping overnight to fill their tanks. Owing to the kindness of our friends, we were constantly supplied with cans of fuel which relieved us the burden of queuing. We are assured this was unusual but be warned – when you go (and I hope you will) take a spare can!

Spain

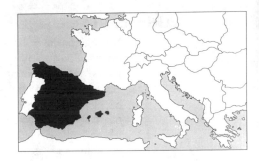

Member of the Council of Europe and the EC

LANGUAGE
Official: Castilian Spanish
Others spoken: Catalan, Basque, Galician
English spoken: mainly in centres and amongst younger people

CURRENCY
Official: 100 centimos = 1 Spanish peseta
Convertible or not: yes
Travellers cheques/Eurocheques/credit cards: widely acceptable, particularly centres

DOCUMENTS YOU NEED
Information contact: Spanish Embassy, 16th Floor, Portland House, Stag Place, London SW1E 5SE tel 071 235 5555
Consular Section, 20 Draycott Place, London SW3 tel 071 581 5921

SPANISH DTI DESK
OT 3/3b Room 356 tel 071 215 4772

BANKS
Open Monday to Friday 9.00-14.00 (longer hours in Winter)

POST OFFICES
Monday to Friday 8.00-12.00 and 16.00-19.30

BUSINESS HOURS
Monday to Saturday 9.30-13.30 and 16.30-19.30 some open all day; variations in Winter

ART GALLERIES/MUSEUMS
Closed Monday and Sunday afternoon, note substantial break circa 13.00-16.00 weekdays

PUBLIC HOLIDAYS
Jan 1, Jan 6, Easter weekend, May Day, Corpus Christl, June 24, Jul 25, Aug 15, Oct 12, Nov 1, Dec 6, Dec 8, Dec 25, plus regional holidays

CONTACT IN THE UK
Spanish Institute 102 Eaton Square, London SW1W 9AN tel 071 235 1484
Spanish National Tourist Office, 57/58 St James' Street, London SW1A 1LD tel 071 499 0901

CONTACTS ABROAD
British Council, Calle Almagro 5, Madrid 28010 tel 3373500
Ministry of Culture, Reina Sofia, Madrid 28071 tel 468 7951
Embassy/Consulate:
British Embassy, Calle de Fernando el Santo 16, Madrid 28010 tel 3190200. Consulates in Algeciras, Alicante, Barcelona, Bilbao, Ibiza, lanzarote, Las Palmas, Malaga, Menorca, Palma de Mallorca, Santa Cruz de Tenerife, Santander, Seville, Tarragona, Vigo
Artists Associations:
Asociacion de Escritores y Artistas Espanoles (Spanish Artists and Writers Association), Leganitos 10, Madrid 28013 tel 2489067
Asociacion Española de Pintores y Escultores (Spanish Sculptors and Painters Association), Infantas 30, Madrid 28004 tel 5224961
Copyright/moral rights:
DACS initially tel 071 247 1650. In Spain VISUAL, Museo Espanol de Arte Contemporaneo, c/Juan de Herrera 2, Madrid 28040 tel 5497150

Gonzalo Torne

Nobody can doubt the multiple and positive changes which have taken place in Spain over the last decade. In some aspects these have been splendid years, even if many of the shadows from the past have not disappeared; and what is worse some of our defects have evolved. Our country has grown closer to its European surroundings culturally, politically and economically, opening a great stream of relations.

In the visual arts, works produced in Spain are sent abroad, at the same time as some works which circle through international art channels are shown here in Spain. In spite of policies with a tendency towards big and forceful exhibitions with astronomical budgets, the result is only to fulfil the functions of window dressing and official propaganda. In this setting, the artist's reality is a life submerged in exhibition circles kept alive by certain social sectors and promoted by the state, with suspiciously coinciding interests between private and public sectors.

Already in the first State Congress for plastic artists held in the Reina Sofia Art Centre in Madrid 1988, they concluded to 'recommend the Cultural Ministry and other public offices not to excessively spiral the profit interests of the private middle-man'. Artists claimed the ministry acted like a promotion and marketing agency for some artists, to the detriment of others. Panoramic and collective exhibits, and promotion of Spanish art abroad is manipulated by special interest groups.

The Spanish art market is comparatively small and secretive. There is little public or private information, one may even say what dominates is 'the occult'. The market for Spanish work is concentrated in Madrid and Barcelona. Until recently, foreign artists have achieved minor volume.

Official awareness of artistic production has been extremely low. Public budgets for cultural use have been very limited, lacking adequate funds for art education. Schools are overfilled, located in old, unsuitable buildings without appropriate spaces. There is a lack of educational support programmes. Professional specialisation and economic resources for creative activities are few and far between. There are few public scholarships, although lately, some banks and large private enterprises have given out stipends.

There are no public studios to be lent or rented out to artists: neither at a state nor at a local level are workshops made available for professional artists.

Artist unions and collectives are very rare and have no strength or capacity to make their voices heard by society or by official bodies.

Desjarretes y Estructuras, Gonzalo Torne, 1990.
Mixed media on canvas.

Neither society at large nor official bodies consider artists' opinions. There is no doubt a dismal outlook for the professional visual artist.

On the other hand the two big promotional centres for art, Madrid and Barcelona, are highly populated cities with serious pollution, traffic, and noise problems where speculation has forced rental prices for studios and housing to new heights. These cities have a very high cost of living, adequate materials are hard to locate and, since they are often imported, expensive. Neither city provides proper professional centres or equipment at reasonable prices, especially for artists who work with new visual media.

My situation as an artist is exceptional and cannot be considered representative. I have one rented studio with living area in Madrid, and another in a little town 40 kilometres outside the city where I can work, hidden and shielded from the tremendous aggressiveness of this city. I have been able to make a living for many years through my professional art activities, of course, with great effort and concurrently pursuing other activities related to my work as a painter. To make this possible, it has been of great importance for me that my work has been sold abroad, in addition to the normal commercialisation through galleries and national Spanish collectors. As a matter of fact, in some years I have sold more abroad than in my own country.

In any case one should not forget that recent questionnaires confirm only about 2% of Spanish artists can live from their profession. In most cases they have to perform other forms of work. Many teach or work in advertising. Within teaching, we have state centres and municipal cultural centres in which one teaches classes or direct workshops. In the bigger cities, it is also easy to find a job in an academy or a private school. In advertising, the majority of artists work freelance from their own studio with temporary contracts for national or international agencies.

I genuinely think if one wants to work in Spain, and has a minimum financial backing, and access to sales channels for work, the best place for artistic production is in some little village in the south of my country. In the mountains of Andalucia there still exist marvellous *pueblos*, filled with light, a good climate, and a non-expensive life. These are definitely not the best locations for promoting or selling one's art, but they are marvellous places for creation. And that, in the end, is for the artist the most important thing.

Jill Randall

In May 1991, I returned to Britain, having spent three months living and working as a freelance artist in Barcelona.

My stay was financed largely by a £2000 travel award, which I won in an open competition (advertised in *Artists Newsletter*), from the McColl Arts Foundation, to enable artists to fulfil a proposed project in the country of their choice.

A combination of excitement and panic engulfed me on hearing the news; an opportunity to turn dreams into reality! I now had the money, but it was up to me to arrange all other aspects of the trip.

I had spent two weeks in Barcelona the previous summer, and was instantly struck by the city's chaotic vitality, colour, contrasts and visual richness, plus excellent bars with seafood tapas! It's an exotic and unique place, between sea and mountains, with palms and cacti sprouting on every street corner.

I was impressed with the wonderful collection of sculpture at the Fundaçio Joan Mirò, and the Gaudi and Modernist architecture which makes Barcelona streets feel like parts of one enormous sculpture.

I had found much in terms of content and imagery which reflected my own ideas and concerns, and needed new impetus and stimulation after a long and demanding period of constantly producing and exhibiting sculpture. I wanted to view my work in a broader European context, and also to try and set up an exhibition in Barcelona for the future.

Spain has tremendous variety and richness in its landscape and architecture, and a quality of wildness, which pervades the landscape history and art, and sets it apart in Europe, linking it to other continents.

My main difficulties in planning the trip were lack of information and going to Barcelona as a freelance artist, not attached to a specific body or institution. This had advantages and disadvantages. An advantage was that I gained a very broad view of the Spanish arts scene, society and culture, through the experience of having to find everything out myself, which was challenging and interesting. Disadvantages were 'getting a foot in the door' of the arts world, and the possibility of feeling like a tourist on an interminable vacation! Fortunately, I lived for the first few weeks with a sculptor, Julia Castro, who provided me with that link, enabling me to experience Spanish life from the inside.

I had two and a half months to plan the trip. I had few other commitments, allowing me time for the essential letters and phone calls,

End of the line., Jill Randall, plaster and steel, 4ftx4ftx2ft.
Photo: *David Bennett*

and most importantly, learning Spanish. Having a grasp of the language made all the difference to my stay, especially as I lived exclusively with Spanish people. I was thrown in the deep end by having to show slides and talk about my work on my first night in Spain. After that, ordering a beer in a bar was no problem!

I found Spanish people incredibly friendly, generous and hospitable, with both artists and non-artists curious and interested in my work. Galleries were well used, and seemingly accessible to a wide cross-section of the general public.

I slowly built up a network of contacts in Barcelona, by following up anything connected with the place. I knew of student exchange schemes operating there, like the one from Winchester School of Art, and they proved helpful, as did the British Council. I also wrote to the Fundaçio Joan Mirò, and academic institutions. The Spanish post is painfully slow, and phone calls are really the preferred means of communication. Do take into account the high cost of calls when budgeting, especially phone calls to your partner, if away for months, as this can add literally hundreds of pounds onto your expenses.

I decided to use my time to collect visual information to make new work on my return. There's so much to adjust to and absorb working in a different country, that it's difficult to also be very productive, ie to start making large sculptures straightaway. I found it a better use of the experience to go out every day, to look, record and respond to the place, and this took many forms; observational drawing, collages, rubbings, and a set of 20 small relief sculptures, constructed from found objects. Barcelona is incredibly rich in interesting things to pick up, and colours, surfaces and textures all seem sharper and more fascinating. It's all too easy to be overwhelmed by the profusion of art, and it's important to find a focus which can relate to your work and interests. For me, it was a luxury to rediscover drawing as an end in itself, rather than 'for sculpture', and to return many times to the same place to draw. I found new forms appearing in the sketch books, instead of the well-worn, familiar ones.

When looking for a studio in Barcelona, be patient, and be prepared to pay. Industrial space is expensive, and group studios do not appear to exist on the same basis as Britain, possibly because many artists have full-time jobs, and it's more practical to work at home.

Accommodation in Barcelona is expensive if you are used to cheaper northern prices, but not difficult to find. If you're looking for a

large, light room, which can also double as a studio, then remember –
so is everyone else! The average rent for a room in a shared flat
exclusive of bills was around £175 per month. I shared a flat with a
Spanish woman who halved my rent in return for English lessons, which
cut my costs considerably.

After accommodation, Spain is very cheap for food, drink, and
travel.

Numerous exhibition spaces exist in Barcelona. New galleries
are setting up all the time, in competition with the more established ones,
and some of the most exciting work is to be seen on the fringe, in suburbs
like Hospitalet and Poble Nou. Only a handful of galleries at present will
show foreign artists, but if you are determined, it should be possible to
show in an alternative space.

I had expected the city's visual wealth and tradition of great
twentieth-century innovative artists to be reflected both in the art
schools, and what was to be sampled in the galleries, but this was
generally not the case. The arts scene appeared to be in a state of some
confusion and regression, with 70s minimalism much in evidence,
especially in sculpture. My own work, which has more in common with
Miro than Carl André was somewhat at odds with this, though I am
hoping to exhibit my work at Galeria Vicent Bernat in 1992/93.

What I did enjoy immensely was Spain's rich tradition of mixed
media two-dimensional work, and an exhibition by Tapies, 'Extensions
de la realitiat' at the Fundaçio Mirò was definitely one of the highlights of
my time in Barcelona.

Sweden

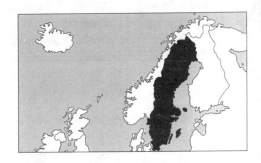

Member of the Council of Europe

LANGUAGE
Official: Swedish
Others spoken: Finnish, Lappish
English spoken: extensively

CURRENCY
Official: 100 ore = 1 Swedish Krona (Krone)
Convertible or not: yes
Travellers cheques/Eurocheques/credit cards:
widely accepted

DOCUMENTS YOU NEED
*For information on visa, residence and work
permits contact:* Swedish Embassy, 11 Montagu
Place, London W1H 2AL tel 071 724 2101

SWEDISH DTI DESK
OT 3/3c Room 377 tel 071 215 5341/4397/5140

BANKS
Monday to Friday 9.30-15.00

POST OFFICES
Monday to Friday 9.00-18.00, open Saturday
afternoon

BUSINESS HOURS
Monday to Friday 9.00-18.00 and open Saturday
afternoon, much longer hours in main centres

ART GALLERIES/MUSEUMS
Often closed Monday and short hours on Sunday;
as with other Scandinavian countries there are
often shorter hours or closures during autumn and
winter

PUBLIC HOLIDAYS
Jan 1, Jan 6, Easter weekend, May 1, Ascension,
Midsummer Day, All Saints, Dec 25/26

CONTACT IN THE UK
Swedish National Tourist Office, 5th floor, 29/31
Oxford St, London W1R 1RE tel 071 437 5876

CONTACTS ABROAD
British Council, Skarpögatan 6, S-11527 Stockholm
tel 6670140
Ministry of Culture, Jakobsgatan 26, 11152
Stockholm
Embassy/Consulate:
British Embassy, Skarpogatan 6-8, 115 27
Stockholm tel 670140. Consulates in Gavle,
Gothenberg, Malmo
Copyright/moral rights:
DACS initially tel 071 247 1650. In Sweden, BUS
Dalgaton 7, 4tr.o.g, 1123 Stockholm tel 107090
Artists Associations:
Svenska Konstnarsfordundet, Fiskhanmagatan 8,
41458, Gotenberg tel 424731
Konstnarernas Riksorganisation, Norrtullsgatan 45,
11345 Stockholm tel 349086
Konstnarhuset, Smarlandgatan 7, 111 46 Stockholm
tel 694230
Foreningen Sveriges Konsthantverkere och
Industriformivare, Wallingartan 38, 11124
Stockholm tel 213334

Leif Lindberg

In 1983 I was admitted as one of five students to *Akademin för Fotografi* (Academy of Photography) at *Konstfackskolan* (National College of Arts, Crafts and Design) in Stockholm, one of the two courses in photography at university level in Sweden. The course at the Academy of Photography is three years with the possibility of a one-year extension. The other course, at the University of Gothenburg, is also for three years. During my four years at the school (1983-87), the contents of the course changed rather dramatically, from learning different techniques and workshops in, for instance, the different disciplines of photography to longer projects with themes such as archetypes, the view on nature and man, postmodernism. This change happened, to a great extent, because of the more and more important role of photography within contemporary art in Europe and USA. The lectures at the school were altered from Swedish photographers coming and showing pictures from their own production, to theorists and critics discussing different approaches within art, but above all showing imagery from contemporary artists outside Scandinavia. The references for the pupils were broadened, from the traditional names such as August Sander, Irving Penn, Bill Brandt, to artists that do not call themselves photographers in the traditional sense, but who work with photographic techniques, such as Cindy Sherman, Richard Prince, Victor Burgin.

For me it was a freeing experience to see the works of artists with various presentations of different problems. The mass media language and the challenge to advance this approach in my own work was more attractive and motivating than to follow the inter-photographic tradition within, for instance, documentary or studio photography. Despite the fact it was in these areas that opportunity lay for support after leaving school. I think this was the general attitude amongst most of the pupils.

After a year or so of having some identification problems and after some half-hearted attempts to survive as a commercial photographer, I got a full-time job at another school, *Dramatiska Institutet* (College of Theatre, Film, Radio and Television). For three years I worked there at the course for media studies, with administrative and technical assignments and elementary teaching in still photography, slide shows and video. Alongside, I worked to a limited extent, with my own photographic projects, which in 1990 gave me a scholarship from *Sveriges Bildkonstnärsnämnd* (the Arts Grants Committee) for 45,000 Krone. In connection to this, I took some time off from *Dramatiska Institutet*, to carry out one of my projects called 'The Swedish Model'. Part of this material was a reconstruction in images of the evolution of Sweden from peasant society to industrial state. I started out from the

Leif Lindberg **from the *The Swedish Model***

photo albums and collection of negatives of my own family (my father was an amateur photographer).

When the work was coming to an end, I sent out proposals to show my exhibition to galleries and institutions that I knew show photographic work. Of these, three were interested: one newly opened private photographic gallery in Malmö, *IRVING; Fotograficentrum* (the Centre of Photography) in Stockholm, subsidised by the Swedish Board of Culture; and *Konsthallen* in Härnösand, a local government art gallery. *IRVING* had no money for either transport or trip, *Fotograficentrum* usually only pay freight one way, the same goes for *Konsthallen* in Härnösand, I paid the trip there myself (Härnösand is approx 600 kilometres from Stockholm). None of these places pay any exhibition fee. At *Fotograficentrum* I sold two smaller works for about 2000 Krone each.

When I received a positive answer from these three places, I decided to, with private means, print a smaller book/catalogue of the material. I paid about 30,000 Krone for a monochrome publication of 64 pages, in the format 23x17cm, with an edition of 1500 copies.

Owing to these three shows, I was invited to some group exhibitions outside Sweden, amongst others 'New Space of Photography' in Wroclaw, Poland in 1991. For exhibiting outside Sweden, you can relatively easily get a travelling and freight grant from *Sveriges Bildkonstnärsfond*. For the trip to Poland I received a grant for 6,000 Krone.

I think there is a great interest in Sweden, both from the audience and the media, for the type of artistic photography I represent. Unfortunately, I do not know many who can live off the fruits of their work. There are very few artists working with photographic techniques who are

Sweden

Fotograficientrum
(Photography Center),
Paulsgatan 3, PO Box
15152, S-104 65
Stockholm, Sweden
tel 6406069, fax
6419608

IRVING, Stora Nygatan
79, S-211 37 Malmö,
Sweden tel 11286

**Göteborgs Universitet
Institutionen för
fotografi** (Gothenburg
University
Photographic Institute)
Mölndalsvägen 85, S-
412 85 Göteborg
tel 631000

**Konstfackskolan
Akademin for
fotografi** (National
College of Arts, Crafts
and Design, Acadamy
of Photography), PO
Box 27116, S-102 52
Stockholm, Sweden
tel 6679550

FFF/Fotogalleriet,
Kongens gate 6, N-
0120 Oslo, Norway
tel 424924

represented in the commercial galleries. Almost nothing is bought privately when it comes to photographic art, neither in Sweden nor in Norway. There are no large collectors, the biggest buyers are institutions which have a certain responsibility to purchase the respective country's contemporary photography for their collections. In Sweden there are about five people working with photography who have life-time grants from the Swedish state. They are all between 50 and 65 years old.

I live on teaching at *Dramatiska Institutet*, where I receive 1600 Krone a day for four weeks a year, and at the Academy of Arts in Oslo, where I work about seven weeks a year, for 1,200 Krone a day. I also have some curator assignments at *Fotogalleriet* (The Photo Gallery) in Oslo and I do some freelance photography and graphic design. Apart from that, I take ordinary extra jobs. At the moment I share a studio with another photographer. It is about 45 square metres and the rent, including electricity, is 3,000 Krone per month. These days it is relatively easy to find studio localities, the rent varies between 500 Krone and 1,000 Krone per square metre per year.

When it comes to the possibilities of exhibiting, Sweden is a small country and artistic photographic work is a relatively small area. It has become more common for artists go outside the Scandinavian borders, also because of the possibility to teach, lecture and publish. During the past years, there has been quite an exchange of exhibitions between Scandinavia and the Baltic states.

For Swedish citizens and foreign citizens living in Sweden, there are scholarships granted by *Sveriges Bildkonstnärsnämnd*, that are especially intended for photographers. The scholarships are granted every year, but in principle you can only receive one every other year. The scholarships are between 25,000 Krone and 60,000 Krone. The criteria selection are based on are how active you are as an exhibitor, along with examples of your work. Every year approx 30-40 scholarships are granted. For those who would like contact with organisations in Sweden and Norway which work with photography, I recommend *Fotograficentrum* in Stockholm, which runs several galleries around the country and publishes *Bildtidningen*, a magazine for photography (mostly Scandinavian), and theory, with texts in Swedish and English. And in Norway, *Förbundet Fria Fotografer* (the Association for Independent Photographers), which run *Fotogalleriet* (the Photo Gallery) in Oslo.

Geoffrey Cooper

Sweden to many people is synonymous with pornography, high taxes and successful tennis players. Luckily this is far from the truth. A country of its size and small population means, along with the rest of northern Scandinavia, there exists a vast open landscape of virtually undisturbed natural beauty. Add to this the bizarre phenomenon of 24-hour daylight during the summer months and the north of the country offers some truly phenomenal experiences. Winter is no less spectacular with deep snow and freezing long nights. It is perhaps these dramatic environmental conditions which have resulted in the country's high rates of suicide and divorce. Its warped attitude to alcohol is however a little more difficult to explain. The overwhelming feature of Swedish society is its high level of organisation, though this does seem to make people passive.

The decision to up and move from the UK was not a difficult one to make. The opportunity arose after being together with a Swede for a number of years who was keen on returning 'home'. Four years of unemployment after art school made it seem like an exciting opportunity for a change of scenery, though the consequences of the move were not really considered.

The mechanics of moving proved to be very straightforward. A short interview at the Swedish Embassy in London, which was mostly concerned with establishing I was together with my girlfriend, resulted in a temporary work permit which lasted six months. After six months we were called for an interview in Sweden where the main emphasis was again on checking that we were actually living together. This continued for two years at the end of which I was given a permanent work permit which requires renewal every third year. The permit procedure is not always so smooth, this applies particularly if you come from a country less 'desirable' than the UK.

There is an organised system of free language education for foreigners which seems to be reasonably successful in integrating them into society. I had actually been introduced to Swedish through evening classes in London so I found picking up the language relatively easy. Having an 'adopted' Swedish family helped. Language classes were a good place for meeting other foreigners and hearing their experiences. Having English as a native language can be a real handicap as most Swedes love to speak English. It is a real confidence crusher to receive a reply in English to an enquiry in Swedish but some Swedes seem to delight in this! The only advice is not to let them grind you down!

Until recently unemployment has been virtually non-existent, in Stockholm at least. This has meant an abundance of part-time cleaning, caretaking, cashier jobs, etc requiring minimum effort whilst being

Oscar, Geoffrey Cooper,
pen & ink, 1991.
Photo: *Factory Floor*

relatively well paid. The last few months have however seen a dramatic rise in unemployment which inevitably makes finding work considerably more difficult, especially for foreigners. The high cost of living makes everything expensive, from studios to materials, but this is of course compensated by higher wages.

The Swedish model aims to give professional artists security from the 'art school cradle' to grave. The system is built up around Swedish artists having been to Swedish art school. Acceptance into the national artists organisation, *Konstnärernas Riksorganisation* (RKO) means official acceptance as a professional artist with studio queues, access to studios in Paris, members' materials shop at discount prices, free admittance to all state museums, etc.

Problems arise however when artists with foreign degrees apply for membership. The admittance procedure for these (along with non-degree Swedish artists) requires a folder of six works to be assessed by a jury along with a CV. Difficulties in assessing foreign degrees suggests assessing foreign exhibitions may be even more problematic and the success rate for foreign artists is not high. Not being a member of KRO makes convincing official institutions you are a serious artist a little more difficult. It is only recently, after several applications, that I have been accepted as a member.

KRO has its own job centre, *Konst Centrum* (KC), which I have found a more manageable organisation to deal with. The consultants I have spoken with have been encouraging (which is always something), and have answered practical questions about suitable galleries, funding, etc. They are mostly practising artists. The idea is that artists have a number of slides (20) at the KC which potential buyers/commissioners can view. The size of the slide bank no doubt makes it difficult to use. However, in autumn 1990 I successfully secured a three-month employment with the Stockholm City Council through KC as a full-time artist. I produced a number of works for which I received a fixed salary and materials cost. As these works are now hanging in public buildings I will hopefully receive 3,000 Krone (£300) a year reimbursement.

There is also an organisation for foreign artists in Sweden, *Internationella Konstnärer i Sverige* (IKIS) but small membership and lack of finances make raising the profile of foreign artists difficult.

Luckily it is possible to continue living and working as an artist outside of the official scene. For some reason there is an almost

Konst Centrum KC
(Artists Job Centre),
Kulturarbetsformed-
lingen, Hollandargatan
17, Box 3190, 103 63
Stockholm

**Konstnars Kollektiv
verkstan** (Print
Workshop),
Planiavagen 28, 131
34 Nacka

Filmverkstan (Film
Workshop),
Slupskjulsvagen 3,
111 49 Stockholm

Konst Akademien (Art
School), Fredsgatan
12, Box 16317, 103 26
Stockholm

**Intonationella
Konstnärer i Sverige
IKIS** (International
Artists in Sweden),
Immigrant Institutet,
Kvarngatan 16, 50233
Boråf

complete lack of open exhibitions, the exception being the annual spring show at *Liljevalchs*. This means if you are interested in exhibiting the alternatives are few. The major galleries seem most interested in established names or well-exhibited (in Sweden) artists. Their complete lack of interest has led me to hire gallery space and organise exhibitions myself, no small task. Though these exhibitions do not carry too much weight with the establishment they have in fact paid off financially, so far, and the group of people keen to be invited to coming exhibitions is gradually growing, amongst these art associations.

Art associations can be a major source of income. Most larger companies have a monthly lottery where employees can win an original work of art. This makes art associations regular buyers and the nature of those groups usually means they buy a varied cross-section of work.

The size of Sweden's population, with Stockholm at its head, makes for a small audience for 'alternative' areas of culture. The vast majority of cultural workers are products of the conservative painterly traditions expounded by the two art institutions in Stockhlom, *Konstfack* and *Konst Akademien*. Experimental film and video along with performance art are minority activities mostly interesting to the few who practice them; a useful film workshop however is *Filmverkstan*, where selected independent films are given financial backing and loan of equipment.

The relatively small scene in Stockholm is considerably more manageable than say London. It is easier to get things done, but the move from the UK involved a move away from the network of contacts, however limited, which existed as a result of years at art school and the exhibitions which followed. Moving to another country requires a large degree of determination to continue working. The re-establishment of contacts with artists or art groups can require years, during which time you stand virtually alone.

The recent change of government to a conservative coalition has created a new air of uncertainty within the ranks of most cultural institutions. Government subsidies are sure to be reduced or withdrawn in an effort to increase 'effectivity' and encourage private sponsorship. Sweden is also in the process of applying for membership of the European Community which, if accepted, should make it considerably easier to obtain access to the country. Hopefully this will also result in an internationalisation of a country that has been on the periphery of Europe long enough.

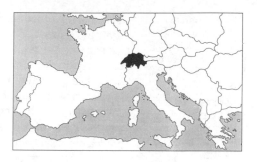

Switzerland

Member of the Council of Europe

LANGUAGE
Official: French, German, Italian, Romansch
Others spoken: Raeto-Romansch (small area in east)
English spoken: quite widely

CURRENCY
Official: 100 rappen (centimes in French area) = 1 Swiss Franc
Convertible or not: yes
Travellers cheques/Eurocheques/credit cards: widely accepted

DOCUMENTS YOU NEED
Information on visa, residence and work permits contact: Swiss Embassy, 16-18 Montagu Place, London W1H 2BQ tel 071 723 0701

SWISS DTI DESK
OT 3/3c Room 373 tel 071 215 4798/4359

BANKS
Monday to Friday 8.30-16.30/15.00

POST OFFICES
Average Monday to Friday 7.30-12.00 to 13.30-18.30, Saturday morning

BUSINESS HOURS
Monday to Friday 7.30-12.00 to 13.30-18.30, Saturday morning; some Saturdays to 16.00 or closed Monday morning

ART GALLERIES/MUSEUMS
Often closed on Monday

PUBLIC HOLIDAYS
Jan 1/2, Easter weekend, May Day, Ascension, Pentecost, Aug 1, Dec 25/26

CONTACT IN THE UK
Swiss National Tourist Office, Swiss Centre, New Coventry Street, London W1V 8EE tel 071 734 1921
British Council, Contact Europe Division (West), British Council Enquiry Point tel 071 389 4795

CONTACTS ABROAD
Ministry of Culture, Federal Department of Home Affairs, Bundeshaus Inselgasse, 303 Berne tel 619111
Embassy/Consulate:
British Embassy, Thunstrasse 50, 3000 Berne 15, Switzerland tel 445021. Consulates in Geneva, Lugano, Montreaux, Zurich
Chamber of Commerce:
Zentralscweizerische Handelskammer, Kapellplatz 2, 6002 Lucerne tel 516865
Artists Associations
Gesellschaft Schweizerischer Maler, Bildhauer und Architeken – GSMBA (Swiss Association of Painters, Sculptors and Architects, Kirchplatz 9, CH-4132 Muttenz tel 617480
Gesellschaft Schweizerischer Malerinnen, Bildhauerinnen und Kunstgewerblerinnen (Swiss Association of Painters, Sculptors and Craftspeople), St. Alban, Anlage 50, 4052 Basel tel 232882
Copyright/moral rights:
DACS initially tel 071 247 1650. In Switzerland, COSMOPRESS, 11 Chemin Falletti, 1208 Geneva tel 493233 and PROLITTERIS, Universitatstr 96, 8033 Zurich tel 3631350

Ursula Jakob

ESAU Ecole Supérieure d'Arts Visuels (National College of Art), 9 Blvd Hélvétique, CH-1205 Geneve

Ecole Cantonale des Beaux Arts (Cantonal School of Fine Art), Rue des Châteaux, CH-1950 Sion/Valals (a partly private school)

F+F Farbe und Form (Colour and Form), Zielquai 67, CH-8005 Zurich

Schule für Gestaltung (School of Applied Arts), Schänzlihalde 31, Postfach, CH-3000 Bern 25

Kunst-Bulletin (Art Bulletin – magazine), Hallwag Ag, Nordring 4, CH-3001 Bern. The following are all studio groups and workshops:

Kulturfabrik Burgdorf, (Culture Factory) Lyssachstr. 112, CH-3400 Burgdorf

Interessengemeinschaft KIFF (KIFF Collective), Postfach 3147, CH-5001 Aarau

Werkverein Bildzwang (Collective for Compulsive Image Making), Reussinsel 59, CH-6003 Luzern

Kulturwerkstatt Kaserne Basel (Basel Barracks Culture Workshops), Klybeckstr. 1b, CH-4057 Basel

When I began my professional life as an artist in Switzerland after a year of study at the Glasgow Print Studio, I felt as if I had been suddenly thrown into a void. I was completely on my own. In Glasgow, everything seemed to be immediately available: materials were provided by the print studio, I could observe and study other students' evolution, etc. It was not quite the same in Switzerland. I had already began to notice the difference between the situation in the UK and Switzerland when people would ask questions as simple as what made up the traditional Christmas meal in Switzerland. I would explain that there really wasn't any one traditional meal, since it varied in relation to which part of the country you were talking about – the French, German, Italian, or Romansh. An overall national feeling is hard to define. Switzerland is marked by cultural and political decentralisation. Our neutrality has more or less kept us out of the mainstream of European history, and has also had its effect on the arts. It has produced individualists and at its most extreme eccentrics. There is no mainstream tradition to guide you or to which you may compare yourself.

The only universally recognised art academy is in Geneva. Recently, in Bern, a fine arts section was created as part of the applied arts school. The situation is similar in Zürich and Basel. This is due to the fact we do not have a national centre like Paris or London. Nevertheless, there are many artists about, most of whom, including myself, have had a totally informal art education. After studying lithography at the applied arts school in Bern, silk-screen printing with an English friend with whom I shared a studio, and etching with an artist who gave classes in the evening to survive, I spent a year working in Glasgow.

The artistic climate in Switzerland has been the subject of much critical discussion – something that leads many artists to go abroad in order to develop their ideas. This usually helps to develop their artistic independence, something I personally appreciate.

I have already noted Switzerland does not have a large national centre. However, there are many smaller regional centres with a comparatively high cultural standard. My own town of Burgdorf (16,000 inhabitants) has five galleries, a municipal theatre, an avant-garde theatre, two cinemas, two clubs for jazz and rock music, a large hall for larger events, and the *Kulturfabrik*, where I have my studio. Bern, Lausanne, and Basel (population of between 100,000 and 140,000) have about twenty galleries each; Zürich, by far the largest city with 450,000 inhabitants, has sixty galleries. The *Kunst-Bulletin* (Art Bulletin) is a comprehensive periodical which provides news of exhibitions throughout Switzerland as well as abroad. Because of the relative prosperity of the population, exhibiting and selling one's work is not as

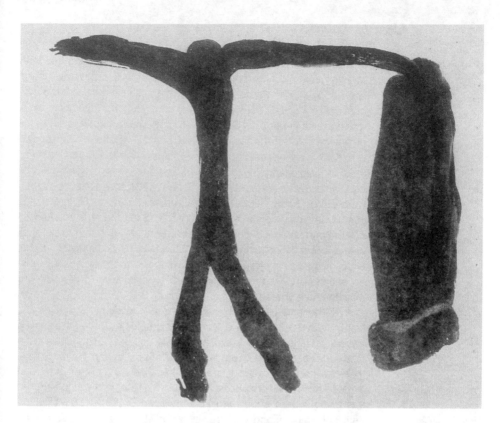

Untitled, Ursula Jakob, **aquatint, image size 24.5x31cm, 1990**

Rote Fabric (Red Factory), Seestr. 395, Postfach, 8038 Zurich CH

Eisenwerke Frauenfeld (Frauenfeld Ironworks), Industriestr. 23, 8500 Frauenfeld CH

Print Studios, Michelle + Arno Hassler, Route de Soleure 25, 2740 Moutier CH

difficult as elsewhere. It is difficult to say how much this will change once Switzerland becomes part of the EC, something that will effectively put an end to its isolation.

In any case, at the present time, public and private support for the arts is quite good. Apart from the annual national grants, each of the 26 cantons holds competitions for its resident artists. A very valuable source of information regarding public and private sponsorship for cultural activities is the *Handbuch der öffentlichen und privaten Kulturförderung* (Orell Füssli, 1991).

I should also mention the *Gesellschaft der schweizerlschen Maler, Bildhauer und Architekten* (GSMBA), the professional organisation of painters, sculptors and architects. Each canton has at least one section. It provides a variety of services, such as insurance, discounts on art materials, as well as publishing a bulletin providing information regarding exhibitions, competitions, etc.

Centre de la Gravure Contemporaine (Centre for Contemporary Gravure), Route Malagnon 17, 1208 Geneve CH

The last few years has seen the appearance of a new phenomenon both in Switzerland as well as other countries: the leasing of abandoned factories by artists as well as other culturally active groups. These premises usually provide space for studios, concerts, plays, performances, etc. For contributing to the local cultural life, they are usually subsidised by the municipality, and in a parallel fashion by the cantons in which they are located.

On my return from Glasgow in 1986, I eventually found a studio in such a place: the *Kulturfabrik* in Burgdorf. Although the name ('culture factory') does not particularly appeal to me, I like it. Currently, there are four sculptors, two painters, a printmaker (myself), a musician, and a woodworker in residence, each with an independent studio. A communal space is shared by six potters and a painter. There is also a vast hall for cultural events. Although someone has been appointed to administrate the 'factory', most of the decisions are made communally at frequent meetings. The latter usually concern financing as well as maintenance. Despite the independent nature of the work of each individual, we must function as a group in order to avoid friction, and in general this has been rewarding socially.

My own studio is large enough to accommodate five or six people. In order to finance my own work, I teach etching classes twice a week. Along with exhibitions and the occasional odd job, I manage to make ends meet. This is not very easy since the cost of living and materials here are quite high. Most of the artists I know are obliged to work on the side, and most are involved in teaching art. Although it took some time to find my way about, I find that after six years at the *Kulturfabrik* the art scene in Switzerland is generally positive.

Shaun Smyth

So you want to go to Switzerland? Starting logically where everyone does, at the frontier post (it's a very conspicuously law-conscious country), you must ask yourself whether you are going to install yourself on a semi-permanent basis and live and work in Switzerland, or are you just going to sell exquisite works to rich burghers, and then leave to live in happy luxury ever after? I 'installed', ie married a Swiss, so I really had little choice in the matter. Even so, I gained experience in the Swiss art market only by a series of trials and errors over a period of years. The present situation, which is not at all the same as in England, probably has as many pitfalls as it had a few years ago.

First, you must bear in mind that Switzerland is broken into three linguistic groups, several cantons (regions) and hundreds of communes

Lukim Pisin (Looking for birds), Shaun Smyth,
oil on aluminium50x70cm

(cities, towns and villages). All these cultural groups are proud of their individual 'flavour'.

The question is what to sell, and where to sell it? Minimalist art and clean and orderly abstracts were the rule rather than the exception. Conceptual and throw-away art are suspect, and the new figurative is to be treated with circumspection. The exceptions to every rule are concentrated in the main centres, of which Geneva, Zurich and Basel are the principals. Even in Geneva times are now hard, and although the 'grand old galleries' are still there (Krugier, Kramer, etc), most of them are looking across the Atlantic for support and profits. This is really 'la plaque tournant' of the high rise sellers of impressive impressionists, who are more interested in the millions of dollars in a patch of sunflowers than a few cents in new buds of doubtful value.

Basel and Zurich are the most affluent cities of the 'golden Triangle', but there is an artistic rivalry between the two cities. Basel has a cultural tradition that dates from the middle ages, and the Balois have a genuine pride in it. They prefer a more 'baroque' style, and are the hosts to the Basel Art Fair, one of the best international art markets. Zurich is much more 'technology-financial', with a different tradition.

One attraction of Switzerland to me is this 'international' aspect, of which Basel Art Fair is the prime example. It attracts people from next door France and Germany, as well as those further afield. Though be warned one cannot just turn up with examples under the arm (or even photographs of work in a folder) and get into the show to do the rounds of the most influential galleries in Europe. You won't be allowed to. Try to make appointments, or contact them in more devious ways. Some galleries are interested but many aren't – they are there to sell. Note that the core of big galleries are the same ones that are on the committees of all the big European Art Fairs, they are the ones which control the market. Actually they seem to prefer to get rid of a lot of old stock (Dali, Picasso, Stella, etc) before they want to risk newcomers.

Switzerland has an impressive number of galleries and each village, newly colonised by urban ecologists, has its own, often run by an 'arty' person of quality. It is rare that sales cover even their basics, such as rent, and unfortunately the artist is also unlikely to sell enough to live on and the artist doesn't usually have the same private income. It is quite possible to have an exhibition, but you will probably have to pay rent, up to Sfr 3000 (£750) and a sales commission of 30%.

A second category of gallery owners usually rely on an unrelated source of income from sale of books, cafés, teaching, etc. They have the advantage for the artist of being quite open minded. They also enable the work of more or less unknowns to be appreciated by the public.

A third category are the professionals, who know what they want, and they usually want established artists who can guarantee a certain quantity of sales. Commissions vary from 50% to a reputed 70% paid by one well-known artist in Basel. It is very difficult to get accepted by these galleries, and they usually take work on a contract basis – but until recently they were the best commercial proposition.

Normally the artist pays the gallery to exhibit, whatever the category. For the gallery to pay a fee is rare. Add in cost of the publicity and a 'vernissage' and it can be a costly experience. So what are the advantages of the Swiss market? High prices when you can get them, but for someone living in Switzerland they are not high enough, overheads, costs and rents will take a large bite out of what you can earn. For someone outside it could be worth the effort. Notice the conditional – I've never had to try to get into the Swiss market from outside – it should be possible but....

As well as galleries, there are various other ways of reaching the art world. In Yverdon there is an information centre which has information and photography about artists living in Switzerland, organised by a lively art critic, Bernadette Pillaud. She promotes exchanges between artists and galleries. Some magazines also give useful information. In French *Voir, magazine des arts*, published in Lausanne, and as well as the end of the week magazine published in *Neue Zurcher Zeitung* (NZZ), Zurich. Other newspapers have art supplements, but these are mainly full of jewellery and watches.

Motivated curators offer possibilities of showing works through local museums. Exhibitions can be based on styles or themes but these shows have little impact. There are unfortunately very few 'open' exhibitions

Switzerland

Service des Expositions, Hôtel de Ville, Place Pestalozzi, 1400 Yverdon. Houses an information centre run by Bernadette Pillaud

VOIR: Magazine des arts, 6 bis, Ch August-Pidou, Case postale 1494, 1001 Lausanne

Beue Zunrcher Zeitung und Schweizerisches Handelsblatt (NZZ), Postfach, 8021 Zurich.

Connaissance des Arts (French monthly art magazine with a Swiss supplement), 254 rue Ponthieu, 75008 Paris

as in England. Banks and restaurants also show limited amounts of work. In the latter, works tend to lose their value, and if there are sales in the former it is a 'secret bancaire'.

Don't assume that because Switzerland is in the middle of the European map, that it is part of the Common Market. To live and work here you will need some sort of permit – 'A', 'B' or 'C' – or cash. You may be lucky enough to find some sort of 'gainful employment', in which case the company can ask for the permit, but these are limited by quotas in each canton. Cantons further from the borders may still have unfilled quotas, while others are screaming for more.

Teaching? Always assuming that you know the appropriate language, it is possible to find 'supply' teaching posts. Fixed posts are jealously guarded. Freelance illustration and publicity? Oddly enough, there are very few illustrators but there are plenty of 'graphists'. They used to command high fees, but I think that recently there has been a slimming down of the field. The ones that do work tend to be technically good, with few regular clients. Subsidies and grants are simply not available in practice for non-Swiss.

Whatever job you may get, the hours are 40-42 hours per week basic – be warned.

The Swiss 'art mentality' is one of straight lines. For instance, to become a jeweller through the Art School of La Chaux-de-Fonds, the first six months are spent just in polishing and preparing metal. This discipline may provide excellent jewellers, but the imagination is not solicited. Don't imagine the Swiss lack imagination, it is only the policy of the art schools – to produce perfect technicians – that has a tendency to dampen it. If you wish to sell something to the Swiss then it should be technically sound, and perfectly finished and presented. Even if you wish to sell illustrations or designs, the finish should be extremely correct.

To live off one's production in Switzerland is nearly impossible. In this hyper-organised, conservative country it is rare to be well enough known to expect your 'name' to sell your work. Expenses can be heavy and the financial possibilities to earn 'enough to round off the month' are small. Switzerland already has a big problem with the 'financial refugees' who would like to live here, so do not expect to be welcomed with open arms. If you do persist, then you will almost certainly have to get a job of some sort. However, you can expect to sell some paintings , a few at a time. You won't make your name here, but the rest of Europe is probably more accessible than from England.

United Kingdom

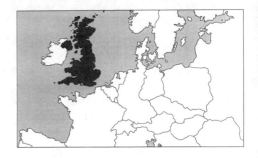

Member of the Council of Europe and the EC

LANGUAGE
Official: English – with strong regional accents
Others spoken: Irish, Welsh, Gaelic and wide range of language groups from around the world

CURRENCY
Official: 100 pence = 1 Pound Sterling
Others used: Northern Irish and Scottish notes may be accepted throughout the country at the discretion of the receiver (they are not legal tender in England and Wales but any high street bank will change the notes for you).
Convertible or not: yes
Travellers cheques/Eurocheques/credit cards: extensive use, tends to be less so in more remote areas

DOCUMENTS YOU NEED
For details on visa, etc contact the British Embassy/Consulate in your country

BANKS
Average opening Monday to Friday 9.30-15.30 with some longer hours, some banks open Saturday morning (There is also an extensive Building Society and Post Office banking system)

POST OFFICES
Usually open Monday to Friday 9.00-17.30 (The branch in Trafalgar Square, London open to 20.00), Saturday morning with shorter hours outside centres

BUSINESS HOURS
Average opening Monday to Saturday 9.00-17.30 – wide rage of variations, especially between city and rural areas. Most larger centres have a late night, look out for half-day closing mid-week, very few centres still have lunch-time closing.

ART GALLERIES/MUSEUMS
Many closed Monday, the majority do not charge for entry but when they do it is high

PUBLIC HOLIDAYS
Jan 1, Jan 2, Easter weekend, May Day, May Bank Holiday, Aug Bank Holiday, Dec 25/26 (with Scottish variations)

DISABILITY
Arts information & advice service for disabled people, London based but able to signpost to further information nationally & internationally Artsline 5 Crowndale Road, London NW1 1TU tel 071 388 2227

CONTACT IN THE UK
British Tourist Authority, Thames Tower, Blacks Road, London W6 9EL tel 081 846 9000
Minister for the Arts, Timothy Renton, Minister of State, Privy Council Office, Whitehall, London SW1 tel 071 270 3000
Embassy/Consulates:
See Diplomatic Yearbook or Europa World Guide in most good reference libraries
Chambers of Commerce:
Association of British Chambers of Commerce, Sovereign House, 212a Shaftesbury Ave, London WC2H 8EW tel 071 240 5831
Artists Association:
National Artists Association, (Membership) 17 Shakespeare Terrace, Sunderland SR2 7JG
Copyright/moral rights:
Design & Artists Copyright Society (DACS), St.Mary's Clergy House, 2 Whitechurch Lane,

Nina Edge

The United Kingdom is a union of four once independent nations, three of which have experienced domination by the other. A level of animosity remains. The four parts administer arts activity as separate operations. United as a single kingdom it is a small and often cosy one and-a-bit islands, the sea providing a crucial isolation barrier which might deter travellers. Goodwill toward the 'foreign' varies wildly, with few adults speaking European languages, although they are taught in schools. Young people will often be able to translate basic needs for you. A particular form of the English language is important here, and all access to all education pivots on your ability to speak and write it. Reactions to the accent of people who speak English as their second, third or fourth language can range from impatience to abusive. Accents from outside the 'Western World' are regarded with added suspicion, as are skins, hairstyles and clothes from 'outside'. This outsider role can be inherited, by those descended from non-Europeans, who as a result are often to be found working together. The kingdom is small, but that doesn't make it easy to cross. Allow a wide margin (like two hours) for train travel to important appointments. The rail service is as unreliable as it is fascinating. Be prepared. If you plan to use galleries, promoters or agents contact them well ahead of arrival. There is no single agency through which the industry facilitates communication with itself but many small units divided by geography and media and on occasions by race and gender. The divergent priorities of these small units enables a certain range of practices to co-exist.

So you arrive. The ground rules are not always logical and they are not always written down. It is as well to know something of these rules, whether or not you decide to play by them. Those who stand to lose much, and gain not at all should these rules be ignored or amended, attempt to uphold them. They include ideologies about who makes 'real art' who is eligible to teach or learn it, write about it, or own it. They include constants about who will be paid, and how much, where they will be allowed to produce or show art works.

For example be prepared if you approach an art school to find the permanent full-time staff almost exclusively male in its make-up. This should give you a reasonable pointer as to the likelihood of this becoming a source of income; check your gender. Women are allowed to teach art at 'lower' levels. Lower paid that is. Adult, youth, child or special needs classes are open to women. Very open to women, being lower paid, less secure and of lower status.

The effect of such restrictive practice is some women have to work many more hours in order to support studio practice should sales

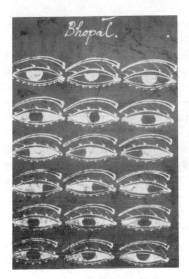

Bhopal, Nina Edge, batik on cotton

alone not suffice. The market is about the size of the country at present although 'looking to Europe' will doubtless be big, and hopefully lead to the formation of a national communication process for the arts here. Many artists sell some work and support themselves with additional work. The taxation system does not encourage art purchasing, neither is there national policy for all new public buildings to have 1% for art sewn into their budgets. Despite this a buying market does exist and although centred in London, is in existence all over England and Wales.

Likewise provision of exhibition spaces is not vastly different geographically although the way in which they are staffed and programmed, and the audiences they attract is extreme in its range.

The British are very interested indeed in being British and have evolved a culture and education system which has at its base an expression of innate superiority over all else. This results in very particular icons being awarded space on the gallery walls particularly in the permanent collection. They all have more in the cellar. For example many galleries own substantial collections of notable women artists, particularly painters and this is accessible if a permission is sought and granted prior to your arrival. Be prepared.

In perpetuating a particular view of Britain, Black practitioners have been marginalised by mainstream cultural institutions. The bias of educators does not allow many to tread too close to some subjects. This does not stop people from eventually studying what they will, but it has an effect on the expectations brought to bear on works produced by Black practitioners. The mainstream has a range of acceptable concepts with which it will consort. Ideas of considerable power to Black consumers and producers of culture may not be considered appropriate material for 'art'. There is also a hierarchy of media at play which pays 'craftworkers' less than it pays 'artworkers', if at all.

My work is requested for exhibitions faster than I can make it, accessing exhibition space has not been difficult although receiving hanging fees, administration or other expenses continues to be. This relates to my use of media associated by the mainstream with 'craft' practice. It also arises from the practice of showing women and Black artists in large groups while commissioning works, or supporting solo shows by the others. Likewise teaching and arts administration work has been available to me in the tightly delineated area to which I am allowed access.

The mainstream critical discourse around my work and the work of my contemporaries has usually centred around the fact that we produce at all, what materials we use for production, what we take as subject and who might be empowered by it. The more positive discourse being available as we meet – making, showing, writing and eating together – rather than published in books or magazines. Although a largely tokenistic approach has been developed towards the Black producers, it hasn't stopped the sector from successfully curating itself over the last decade. So, looking forward to Europe will further diversify and excite cultural interplay. One would hope.

Gianni Piacentini

Pepiniéres
Set up by Eurocreation. Contact in the UK, The Princes Trust, 8 Bedford Row, London WC1R 4BA tel 071 4055 799 The main office is 3 rue Debelleyme, 75003 Paris tel 48047879

In 1990 I took part in the European competition 'Pepinières' published by Eurocreation, the French office of young innovators in Europe. The competitors could to propose a project in fields ranging from music to scenography, from videos to environmental art, and including 'visual arts'. Out of the ten European cities involved, I felt particularly interested in considering Glasgow for a series of reasons, not least its being the 'Culture Capital' of 1990. I felt this would make way for meetings and exchanges of experiences, thanks to the fact many artists and events had been drawn here. I was, in any case, aware of the fertility of the local artistic environment. Having trained in the study of art history, and aquired a conceptual approach, I was interested in the possibilities of figurative art (which I feel I would be able to undertake) and was hoping to find some reason for considering these forms. In Rome, where I was born and where I live, the figurative image applies to some very innovative artists today.

I am interested in working with people and Glaswegians are well-known for being helpful and cordial. Also, this industrial port, with all that it entails, was absent from my 'memory scenario', so I particularly wished to go there.

After the national selection, and then the European selection in Paris, I moved from the role of candidate to artist. This was quite a step for me I must confess. I am a hotel porter and if I deal with art, it is is an underground activity, to which I can only dedicate a limited amount of time. I use art basically to meet potential objects of desire – all other people's works of art (always more interesting than my own) or people – art is just an excuse. For a six-month stay in Glasgow, my staus as an

Scale 1:1, Gianni Piancentini, silhouette from the Ceiling of the 'Living Room' installation, Glascow 1991. The ceiling had plastic silhouettes glued to it, mirroring, on a 1:1 scale, real objects below – in this case the edge of a door.

artist was a privileged one. I was able to rely on a monthly salary as well as a private apartment, the expenses of which were also covered.

A spacious, but not heated, studio though was turning me into an 'action painter'. Because I donn't use large dimensions for my work, and don't want to do gymnastics, I left this ex-industrial kitchen studio for better purposes. I started to work at home, as I in fact do in my native city, on a modest desk without painting materials, since I do not know about them. I make notes of projects or do small works which, alas, no one wants to sell or buy. In Glasgow I did do some physically heavy work, but then I was unable to cope with the transport costs, and so abandoned this heavy work.

For the first three months I concentrated on getting on with my work, particularly gathering experiences, visiting studios and galleries, and generally getting to know the city. But it became gradually more and more necessary to work hand in glove with some of the artists I met. I became great friends with a few artists invited to Glasgow for exchanges in the framework of the 'Capital of Culture', in particular with Vincent Vasseur, and Elise Perré and Charlotte Moerker, who also had a grant from Eurocreation. If it became clear at a certain point that the projects for which we had been selected could not be completed, due to lack of sponsors, but there was not much else to complain about. My main aim was being present in the place, and operating in reciprocal recognition with the artistic environment of Glasgow which I was getting to know.

In this sense, I wanted to use my apartment to the best of its potential, with its well-lit lounge. The 'Living Room' project (it literally was a living room) was created thanks to the work of 23 invited artists, whom I asked to propose an installation, painting or intervention for the household interior. Having made available my living room (just advising a degree of precaution in its use) we launched various meetings of all the artists present, while others, now abroad, sent us their projects, getting in touch by telephone and letter. Some artists who were difficult to contact had entrusted their work to me for the time being.

The artists involved, from all over Europe, were Boris Achour, David Allan, Claire Barclay, Alfio Bonanno, Christine Borland, Martin Boyce, Roderick Buchanan, Panos Charlambous, Kenny Davison, Jacqueline Donachie, Douglas Gordon, Harvey Jackson, Dan Mihaltianu,

Charlotte Moerker, Jonathan Monk, Elise Parré, Craig Richardson, Alex Rigg, Julie Roberts, Ross Sinclair, Marios Spiliopoulos, Vincent Vasseur, Kieren Vaughan and George Wylie. All 23 artists looked at the entire strategy of each intervention, and it was finally decided to propose five multiple installations (of several artists) for one week each. Each installation used the re-vitalised living room, which was adapted to become an environment where, on first impression, an average of five simultaneous interventions could take place. We arrived at this solution, on the exclusive basis of the specific qualities of the individual jobs and their compatibility with others. The group established a nominative programme for the five occasions, which was not necessarily binding, leaving open the possibility of new agreements at other times. For example, Jonathan Mark and David Allen proposed 'surprise' interventions over the five week period.

While remaining a dwelling place, the 'Living Room' was now open to outsiders. People were sent printed invitations. /pening times were divided into three different phases from 5-8pm, Friday to Sunday. The invitations were distributed thanks to the collaboration of the Transmission Gallery which had its mail-out at the same time. But, to gain a wider audience, I contacted various newspapers, especially those not specialising in art, who all responded.

The guests, that is what they were, had the possibility of sitting down together for tea, meeting artists and enjoying the works which acquired meaning thanks to the happy mixture of 'household privacy', a friendly meeting, and a reciprocal stimulation in reading them. Whoever came to the 'Living Room' came to speak, taking part in a meeting of artists and others. The 'Living Room' is set in a rich tradition of artist's initiatives in Glasgow, such as 'Windfall '91'.

While the 'Living Room' is in no way aimed at being an alternative denial of consolidated systems, it obviously has something new to propose. Gallery schedules are planned well in advance (in most cases it cannot be otherwise), so works with a sense of timing and works which concern a certain topical reality, can only be seen a long time afterwards. A work connected to a given historic or environmental crisis deserves to be enjoyed at the time.

Examples of this are the installation of Craig Richardson on the theme of political treaties, and of Rodderick Buckannan on 'carpet bombing' at the time of the 'theatre' of Gulf war broadcasts on TV.

The 'Living Room' is a model of the use of the home as a vital place in which interventions can take place. But, at the outset, I was quite discouraged in carrying on with the project merely for safety reasons (emergency exits, fire-fighting equipment etc) and bureaucracy (apartment for private use etc). In this sense, I resolved to reduce access to the apartment with the invitations, in such a way that the numbers of people present would be similar to those of a party. The artists saw their 'colleagues' working in various phases, in my opinion a great opportunity to get oneself known via work. The perishability of most of the materials used, far from being a limiting factor, showed the precious spontaneity of the project, and the value of the individual experiments. Personally, I am grateful for the experience, the conversations, the friendships born between a work and a performance, a tea and then later an evening together. I hope it will be possible to develop more complex interventions – different and in other places.

In February 1992 I returned to Glasgow for an exhibition at the Transmission gallery called 'Outta Here'. While there I wrote a letter to the Lady Provost of Glasgow requesting honorary citizenship of the city. This wasn't motivated by excessive self esteem but by the pleasure I derive from my welcome each time I visit Glasgow. On my return to Rome I received a letter from the Lady Provost granting my request. I am pleased to be recognised as a member of a community with which, and for which, I have worked as an artist.

Yugoslavia

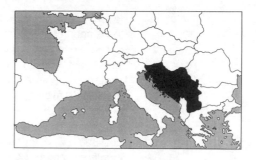

All the below is subject to alteration, this piece was researched in January 1992 and was correct at that time. At time of research the Foreign Office advise against travel to Bosnia Hercegovnia and Croatia, and recommend caution in Slovenia; there is no UK government representation in Slovenia and the mission in Croatia had been closed. For up to date information call the Foreign Office Central Europe Enquiry Desk tel 071 270 3459 or the Foreign Office Travel Desk tel 071 270 4179.

LANGUAGE
Official: Serbo-Croat and Slovene in the north and Macedonian in the south
Others spoken: German, Albanian and Italian in border areas
English spoken: main foreign language taught in schools, extensive in tourist areas

CURRENCY
Official: 100 para = 1 new dinar
Others used: dollar and Deutschmark
Convertible or not: very weak economy with hyper inflation
Travellers cheques/Eurocheques/credit cards: quite widely usable

DOCUMENTS YOU NEED
For information on visa, work permit and residence permit contact: Yugoslav Consulate General, 7 Lexham Gardens, London W8 5JJ tel 071 370 6100, Office of Croatian Information tel 071 434 2946, Office of Information Slovenia tel 071 436 0676

YUGOSLAV DTI DESK
OT 3/5B Room 335 tel 071 215 5267/5152

BANKS
7.00-19.00 Monday to Friday; Saturday 7.00-13.00; varies outside centres

POST OFFICES
7.00-19.00 Monday to Saturday; some Sunday hours in larger cities

BUSINESS HOURS
Open 8.00-20.00 Monday to Friday, 8.00-15.00 Saturday in centres; elsewhere, especially the South, 7.00-12.00 to 17.00-20.00

ART GALLERIES/MUSEUMS
Closed on Mondays and often on Sundays; open 9.00/10.00-12.00/13.00 and some afternoons

PUBLIC HOLIDAYS
Jan 2, May 1/2, Jul 4, Nov 29/30, Dec 25 plus dates for each Republic

CONTACT IN THE UK
Yugoslav National Tourist Office, 143 Regent Street, London W1R 8AE tel 071 734 5243 or the Slovene & Croatian offices listed above

CONTACT ABROAD
British Council, Generala Zdanova 34-Mezanin, PO Box 248, 11001 Belgrade tel 332441 and Ilica 12/1, PO Box 55, 41001 Zagreb tel 273491
Ministry of Culture, Chamber of Commerce, Terazije 23, POB 1003, 11000 Belgrade tel 339461
Embassy/Consulate:
British Embassy, Generala Zdanova 46, 11000 Belgrade tel 645053.Consulates in Dubrovnik, Split, Zagreb (check with Foreign Office above)
Copyright/moral rights:
No Yugoslav organisation noted, try Design & Artists Copyright Society (DACS), St. Mary's Clergy House, 2 Whitechurch Lane, London E1 7QR tel 071 247 1650

Rajko Radovanovic

I was born in a country which does not exist any longer and I also hope to die in a non-existing one.

Regardless of the present-day political and national distinction (separatism) and hatred among the people of what was Yugoslavia, the common attitudes and events on the artistic scene during the sixties, the seventies and the eighties – in Belgrade SKC (The Student's Cultural Center), in Zagreb the Basement Group and in Ljubljana the Laibach Group – cannot and must not be forgotten. At this very moment it is necessary to point out the existence of artists whose art was always in advance of politics – an art that by its iconography anticipated the decay of the ideology that had preached up the idea of 'The Great Collective Happiness'. By their attitudes, behaviour and work they gave notice of danger from totalitarianism and repetition of history, which is happening right now in the Balkans.

They used the language of the leading ideology and party against that same ideology and party. A radical subjectivism in relation to the ideas which had been accepted by society (community) as their own ideas, was one of the characteristics of such art. That ideology was in a way a reason for the existence and motifs of such art. The artists often came into conflict with that ideology through its institutions and its uniformed protectors.

My conflict with them has lasted, so to speak, since my birth, thanks to the happy circumstances that my father was a Yugoslav People's Army (JNA) officer. In 1976, after one year of obligatory military service in the JNA, for the first time I exhibited one of my works in the gallery 'The Window into Art', run by artist Zeljko Jerman. The official decision of the military (JNA) authorities about my punishment in custody – due to non-discipline – was a part of my work too. After the reporting by an unknown but conscientious citizen about my use of a military document in a public place, the military police removed and confiscated my work. Then the Home Office and the military police investigated the owner of the gallery and me. That event determined in a certain way my further engagement with art.

In May of 1978, twenty of us, artists from Zagreb (the capital of the Republic of Croatia), decided to work and act together in response to inert cultural institutions. Till then we had worked, as one might say, illegally (underground), being ignored by official cultural institutions and by official art critics. We exhibited our works of art in a rather small basement room, called 'The Basement'. As a group, we had neither a common programme nor a similar opinion about art. The principle of exhibiting the works and the question of criteria were based upon the

attitude that every artist stands behind his/her work. The decision about a mutual work and action was conditioned by the character of our works, which were analytical with reference to medium, and subversively critical, regarding the social context in which those works were appearing. Such a subversively critical opinion was most clearly expressed through the form of slogans and quotations of Dadaistic, anarchistic contents: Vlado Martek, 'Death to the State, Freedom to the Art!', 'Sand is more precious than the Party', 'Go and tell lies to the State!' Mladen Stilinovic, 'The conditions for my work are not in my hands, but fortunately, not in yours too!', 'Work is illness!' Sven Stilinovic, 'When using arms, a man becomes a murderer or a suicide; when using a paint brush, he becomes an artist or decorator!' Darko Simicic, 'The dead can never be our friends!' Marijan Molnar, 'For democratization of Art!'

New Altars of Tempel of Happiness, Rajko Radovanovic, **1989, acrylic on canvas, 90x90cm**

Our works continued in the experience of the artistic movements of the sixties and the seventies (Fluxus, happenings, conceptualism, etc). In the meantime, other artists joined us, and in 1981, *Hrvatsko Drustvo Likovnih Umjetnika* (the Croatian Association of Fine Artists) accepted us as members with equal rights. We were given a showroom within the building of the association, which, from that time, acted under the name *Galerija prosirenih medija* (the Gallery of Expanded Media), where artists from Canada, Austria, Netherlands, Germany and France have exhibited.

The Basement gallery was also a place for artists to meet, discuss, hold lectures, slide projections and a place for parties. Each artist combined its own (central) medium such as painting, sculpture, photography, film and poetry with other means of expression, which involved wider concepts of art.

'Some artists use photography in order to formulate certain pre-conceived ideas, and what is designated by the term photography as an art work. Others use it to document a work performance. When

Sindicatradnika delatnosti vaspitanja, obrazoranja, nauke i kulture (Cultural Workers Union), trg. Marksa i Engelsa 5 (Dom Sindika), 11000 Belgrade tel 330481

Artists Union Macedonia, Orce Nikolov 79, 91000 Skopje tel 230273

Artists Union Croatia, Lapadska obala 9, 50000 Dubrovnik tel 26879

Artists Union Yugoslavia, Terazije 26, 1000 Belgrade tel 687486

Artists Union Montenegro, Vuka Karadzica 1, 81335 Sutomore

Artists Union Kosovo, Istarka 16, 38000 Pristina tel 20356

Artists Union Serbia, Baba Visnijina 19, 11000 Belgrade tel 28356

Artists Union Bosnia-Hercegovnia, Skenderija, Mice Sokolovica bb, 7100 Sarajevo tel 518756

Artists Union Slovenia, Lj. Komenskega 8, 61000 Ljubliana tel 321886

photography functions wholly as the realisation of an artist's idea, or when no other information about a kind of work exists or is necessary, the artist considers photography the work. However, when photography records a performance, behaviour at certain points of the performance and its duration in time and space, the artist will speak of photography as a document. Thus, depending on the content, meaning and character of the work, the author attaches two significantly different functions to photography. The difference between these two functions often depend on the attitude of the author rather than on the appearance of the work.... Some of the artists use photography to analyse the medium itself, beginning with the basic elements: the sensitivity of the photographic paper, light, chemicals....' (Branka Stipancic from the catalogue 'Nova fotografija 3', 1980, Zagreb).

One of the other characteristics of the group was showing works of art in public spaces which were centres of daily activity such as squares, streets and parks. With these manifestations in open spaces we did not want just to 'decorate' the space. We passively accepted the historical and architectural characteristics of these places and used the particular qualities of our individual media in this location. In most cases works of art were made by using minimal materials such as paper and photography. We used accepted gallery materials in non-gallery spaces to find the connections between each media and the new context (urban space). The emphasis was on collective exhibitions-actions and performance.

Today when recent political events behind the former 'iron curtain' try to stop history and revive the past, there is a possibility of re-kindling 'non-arts' which existed in Germany and USSR in the 30s and 40s.

The characteristic of the Zagreb avant-garde artistic scene was and has been its concern with the margin of social events, which is especially true today, in a time of mythomaniac aggression on the Republic of Croatia. For instance, the rooms of the Croatian Association of Fine Artists have been, since September 1991, the headquarters of the militant Croatian Party of Rights. So there is no more senseless and dangerous profession than that of an artist in a nationally frustrated society. I think that all artists of what was Yugoslavia feel like that, and therefore I send a message to them, paraphrasing a Bolshevist slogan: 'Artists from all countries, do not give up!'

Today artists of Croatia from all disciplines work together on a mutual (common) project known as 'Croatian Art Forces', which has been patronised by the Ministry of Culture of the Republic of Croatia. Some of them are now on the front with arms in their hands, and others are working in the restoration of cultural monuments damaged in this

Yugoslavia

UK Action Art Committee for Peace in Croatia, I intend to organise and perform, under this title, artistic actions and projects, to promote the ideas of civil society and critical thought, against any sort of mental or army aggression on an individual or nation. Action has already started – sticking A4 posters up in Brighton and London, with the following 'Stop the aggression on Croatia'. Everyone ready to co-operate is welcomed to contact me: Rajko Radovanovic, 95 Addison Road, Hove

war, amounting already to 500 sites. Some of the monuments, such as Dubrovnik, have been a part of world cultural heritage, under the patronage of UNICEF. If Dubrovnik were a part of Africa, the OAU (Organisation of African Unity) would have reacted long ago and much faster than Europe has for a town and country which has belonged to it for about 1000 years.

It must be said that this war, which has taken place only on the territory of the Republic of Croatia, is not a conflict between two tribes. It is not a conflict caused by hatred from World War II, as some journalists in Great Britain have tried to represent. It is not a war between Serbs and Croats; none of these nations wanted that war. It is a conflict between two entirely different political concepts. One of them is a parliamentary democracy, for which the majority of the population in Croatia and Slovenia voted on the first post-war multi-party elections in 1990. The other is dogmatic communism that was built into all the leading structures and institutions of post-war Yugoslavia. Unfortunately, the majority in those structures and institutions were Serbian. Inventing foreign and home enemies to deceive, a dogmatically-communistic totalitarian consciousness has succeeded in securing power and authority by exercising full control of the media and by manipulating public opinion on Greater Serbia long before historical changes in the former Soviet Union. Serbian generals today protect their positions, because there is no place for them in a civil society, where peace rules. Serbian politicians fight for the nation and leader, and they need an army for that. They are all happy and content and, being deceived by the totalitarianism, they do not notice that they have pushed their own nation into fascism. The same totalitarian consciousness tried to do that to the Croatian people against their will in 1941. The fact that Tito, who was a Croat, was at that time one of the leaders of those forces in Europe, which resisted the fascist invasion, is being forgotten today.

Before I die in a non-existing country, I will tell my descendants the following story: 'Once upon a time Zeljko Jerman (he is one of two who invented a photography; he invented a black photography, and Man Ray invented a white one) and I travelled by train from Zagreb to Belgrade and drank beer. Somewhere near Sid, Jerman slapped me in a friendly way on my back and said: 'Swallow from the East, this is a border.' 'Of what?', I asked, not being informed. 'Of Croatia and Serbia', he answered well informed as a teacher of geography. He opened the door and, looking at each other, we urinated on the border, feeling religiously an alleviation. Then, for the first time in my life, I understood the real meaning of the word comrade. Comrade is a cold bottle of beer. Rasa Todosijevic welcomed us in Belgrade. 'Let's go for a drink', says

Jerman. We entered the café 'Dalmatinac' and ordered a drink. A local policeman is not surprised that Jerman was the only guest with a cousin in Premantura, nor when he hears the waiter, a Chinese, speaking Siberian with strong Bavarian accent. It was about five o'clock in the morning. Look how we travelled once in the 20th century in Yugoslavia, and we did it very often'.

And for the end a message to a friend: 'Dear Vlado in Nationalism, Rajko from Capitalism salutes you.'

Kerry Morrison

I went to Yugoslavia, funded by the Prince's Trust, to go and see young artists who work in a similar way to myself, and see if from this visit greater communications could be made and exchange projects happen. My time in Yugoslavia was spent in Macedonia, the southern-most state, and it is this region that I can clearly refer to. Before travelling to the country I made contact with a curator of the Museum of Contemporary Art in Skopje, and through him I was able to make contact and meet artists from the region. Without his help I think I may have had problems as there are no artists' groups or group studios in the area. He, like most of the artists I met, spoke good English and I was surprised to find out most people learnt the language from the lyrics of English records.

I knew very little about Yugoslavian art before my visit, just enough for me to want to know more. I had no idea how strong and individual the work would be. Prior to the beginning of this century, art in Macedonia fell into two categories: church art, (fresco paintings, icon and altar-piece carvings), and crafts. The history of fine art actually began less than one hundred years ago, and what is happening there now is practically running parallel with contemporary art in Western Europe. I went there with an interest in site specific sculpture, which is still in its infancy in Macedonia.

Visiting artists in Yugoslavia was an eye-opening experience. There is so much creative activity happening there that we in the UK are not aware of and should be, especially now Europe is opening up. It is practically impossible to see and experience all of this as an artist without having an overwhelming urge to create as well. Whilst there I made a sculpture for the Biannual Exhibition at the Museum in Skopje. I worked at the home of Hadji Boskov, a well respected older generation artist who has worked and exhibited in many countries including the UK and America. He was the professor at the Academy of Art and I met him through one of his pupils. Without this contact and his help it would have been very hard for me to make anything because of the lack of

Twist, Kerry Morrison**, 1991, 4'x10"x6"**

resources, tools, and work spaces. Even with this help it was still one of the most difficult sculptures I have ever had to make. The heat was incredible and I shed buckets of sweat, and the tools were not the best. I tend to use only a chainsaw for carving my sculptures and was lucky enough to be lent a little electric saw. I was also offered the use of a petrol one with the initial idea being that I carved the sculpture in the grounds of the museum. I was so pleased when it would not start, because quite frankly I would have been scared to use it; it had no chain guard and no brake, in fact no safety devices whatsoever. I was limited in the choice of tools and basically used what was available to crate the best sculpture I could in the time I had. Working with such limited resources was a good experience and actually broadened my approach to making, but it was just another aspect that made me realise how difficult it is to be a sculptor in Macedonia, and how easy, in comparison, we have it in this country.

Before leaving the country I went up into the mountains to see a ceremonial wedding in Galichnik, a small village which is only occupied during the summer months, in winter it is completely covered in snow and the villagers move down the mountain to live in the next village. In July 1991, Galichnik formed the base for an artist colony. The day of the wedding many of the artists I had previously met went there to begin the first day of the colony. Basically what happens is a group of artists come together and spend a few weeks in a remote place dedicating all their time to their art. The colonies usually last for around four weeks, after which the artists go back to their normal working schedule; they nearly all have full-time jobs and children. Artists from any discipline are welcome to join the colony, however some stipulate only works on paper can be done. Next summer I intend to join the colony giving me the chance to work again in Yugoslavia. For me, having made friends over there, this will be a relatively cheap holiday. Yugoslavia is not the cheapest of places to visit. In Macedonia there are only a couple of bed and breakfasts, which cost around £12.50 a night. There are several hotels, but they are much more expensive, on average, £27.50 and I never became aware of any hostels in the area. The cheapest time to visit is in the winter, which is freezing. I was told it is possible to find accommodation out of the city for £7 a day which includes bed, breakfast, and evening meals. Food and eating out is cheap in Macedonia, along with the local wine, beer, and spirits. It is also a country for smokers with cigarettes costing 17p a pack.

I arrived in Yugoslavia just days after the situation there had erupted. It was a strange time to visit the country. However the feeling I had when I left was that whatever happens, and whether or not Yugoslavia remains, becomes a fractured country, or several new countries, the artists that remain will still essentially be artists.

Possibly a new way of creating and expressing may emerge and unless it becomes life threatening to visit and work over there I will still return, and encourage other artists interested in finding out about more of this country to go there and experience it as I did. It's a great place with truly exciting and creative artistic things happening that can offer us so much, and we should not let communications cease, and I will continue to write to the artists I met and visit and work over there as often as I can.

Further Information

PASSPORTS/VISAS

All UK post offices carry forms for full and temporary UK passports. For details of visas, work permits and residence permits contact the embassy/consulate of the appropriate country well before your travel date – see chapter introductions for addresses or 'Diplomatic Yearbook', 'Europa World Guide' for detailed lists.

EUROPEAN COMMUNITY

Visas: EC citizens can enter any other member state and remain for up to three months quite easily, though many countries have a registration system.

Work permit: for an EC citizen working in another EC country will be even easier after 1.1.93. If you are an EC resident or a non-EC citizen keep in touch with changes as they may restrict your movement or access to opportunities.

Residence permit: easier in EC countries for EC citizens, but contact the appropriate consulate/ embassy before you travel as it is often not possible to make arrangements when already in a country, especially non-EC.

EC Commission, DG XXIII, rue de la Loi, 200 (ARLN), B-1049 Brussels, Belgium. Information for small/medium businesses and the crafts.

European Documentation Centres 45 UK regional centres providing wide-ranging information on the EC. See telephone directory for you local EDC or contact Ian Thompson, Chair of European Information Association, University of Wales, College of Cardiff, PO Box 430, Cardiff CF1 3XT

IMPORT/EXPORT INFORMATION

Customs & Excise, New Kings Beam House, 22 Upper Ground, London SE1 9PJ tel 071 620 1313. See also the telephone directory for your local office. For EC countries ask for Notice 756 (Community Carnets). For non-EC ask for Notice 501 (Import Procedures) and 502 (Export Procedures).

Centre for European Business Information, Small Firms Service, 11 Belgrave Road, London S1V 1RB tel 071 828 6201 for copy of free information pack and details of other centres.

Department of Trade & Industry Hotline for free publications on the European Single Market tel 081 200 1992. The DTI also have an information desk for each country regarding trading regulations, standards etc, for those who are trading in general – do not expect specific information for artists. The room and telephone number for each country are listed in the appropriate chapter. See also the telephone directory for your local office.

Export Market Information Centre, DTI, Ashdown House, 123 Victoria St, London SW1 tel 071 215 5444

EXBO Export Buying Offices Association, 74 Great Titichfield Street, London W1. Association of London Buying Offices formed to encourage and promote exports of consumer goods made in the UK and Ireland

Association of British Chambers of Commerce, Sovereign House, 212a Shaftesbury Ave, London WC2H 8EW tel 071 240 5831. Will have details of all the Chambers in the UK and of National Chambers with representation in the UK. To benefit from the system you need to be accepted as a member, most Chambers may have some designer members, but artist members less likely. If you are involved in public art, looking for local support (financial and otherwise), or exporting your work it will be worth looking at what services are on offer.

Rural Development Commission, 11 Cowley Street, London SW1P 3NA 071-276-6969. Offers advice and support to businesses and the self-employed. See telephone directory for local office.

TECS Training & Enterprise Councils offer training, business advice and support. They have a brief to respond to the needs of small businesses and the self-employed. See telephone directory for your local TEC.

HEALTH

'Health Advice for Travellers' (**T2**/EC countries and **T3**/non-EC countries) produced by the Department of Health is free from any UK Post Office. T2 includes an E111 form (ensures emergency treatment) to fill in and both clearly state your healthcare rights in each country and the preparations you need to make before travelling. Essential, reciprocal agreements and E111 forms only cover basic/emergency care, which may have to be paid for on the spot and claims for refund made on return to your own country – receipts and notes of treatment must be kept. Accidents, serious illness and more than basic dental care will not be covered other than by personal travel insurance.

Innoculations: unnecessary in general see T2/T3 and talk to your doctor, diarrhoea can be a problem in Southern Europe. PRESTEL page 50063 gives daily updates

HIV test certificate requirements: National Aids Helpline Freefone 0800 567123 for information and advice.

Documents needed to get medical treatment: any combination of NHS medical card/ valid passport/ driving licence/endorsed E111/ travel insurance certificate; in non-EC countries you may need further certification contact DSS Overseas Branch, Newcastle-upon-Tyne, NE98 1YX. Contact them if you intend living/working abroad.

Department of Health, General Enquiries, Richmond House, 79 Whitehall, London SW1 tel 071 210 5983. International Relations Unit, Hannibal House, Elephant and Castle, London SE1 6TE tel 071 972 2000 or see T2/T3.

For non-UK details contact the national health agency of your own country.

TRAVEL

Rail: InterRail pass now available to both under and over 26 year olds. Contact BR Europe, Victoria Station, London SW1 tel 071 834 2345 for details of train times throughout Europe.

Driving/hiring cars: contact AA or RAC for details of International Drivers Permit, Green Card insurance,

vehicle registration documents, insurance etc. RAC European Motoring Guide give details of national driving regulations and general information. Automobile Association(AA) tel 0256 20123. Royal Automobile Club(RAC) tel 081 686 0088

Air travel: many airlines will not permit the carriage of certain goods used regularly by artists (eg combustible materials). If anything is found before you travel it and/or you may be refused carriage; if discovered on arrival you and/or the airline may be fined. Contact Civil Aviation Authority, Dangerous Goods Unit, Aviation House, South Area, Gatwick Airport, West Sussex RH6 0YR tel 071 379 7311

Coach: Eurolines, 52 Grosvenor Gardens, London SW1 tel 071 730 0202

Maps: National Tourist Office/Stanford's, 12-14 Long Acre, London WC2 tel 071 836 1321

UK ARTS BODIES

The following should be able to give information on Europe, direct you to other sources or offer financial assistance. In practice this varies widely, the RABs in particular often being unable to offer good information resources. Nevertheless these facilities are developing and all these bodies should be approached for what assistance they can give.

Arts Council of Great Britain, International Information Unit, 14 Great Peter St, London SW1 tel 071 333 0100

Arts Council of Northern Ireland, 181a Stranmillis Road, Belfast, Northern Ireland BT9 5DU tel 0232 381591

Scottish Arts Council, 19 Charlotte Street, Edinburgh, Scotland EH2 4DF tel 031 226 6051

Welsh Arts Council/Cyngor y Celfyddydau, Museum Place, Cardiff, Wales CF1 3NX tel 0222-394711

Crafts Council, 44a Pentonville Road, London N1 9BY tel 071 278 7700. Very good information section, which deals with Europe, also ask for Sales Development. UK contact for World Crafts Council.

The British Council, Visual Arts Department, 11 Portland Place, London W1N 4EJ tel 071 398 3043. Offers assistance for travel and for exhibiting outside the UK but this often has to be through their office in the country concerned. Ask for details of overseas offices. Specialist Tours, 65 Davies Street, London W1Y 2AA tel 071 389 7737 information on other schemes for travel, research and study tours .

Further information

Visiting Arts, 11 Portland Place, London W1N 4EJ tel 071 389 3018. Supports visits from artists of other countries to the UK, doesn't fund individuals.

Eastern Arts Board, Cherry Hinton Hall, Cherry Hinton Road, Cambridge CB1 4DW tel 0223 215355. (covers Bedfordshire, Cambridge, Essex, Hertfordshire, Lincolnshire, Norfolk, Sussex)

East Midlands Arts Board, Mountfields House, Forest Road, Loughborough LE11 3HU tel 0509 218292. (covers Leicestershire, Nottinghamshire, Northamptonshire and part of Derbyshire, not the High Peak District)

London Arts Board, Coriander Building, 20 Gainsford Street, London, SE1 2NE tel 071 403 9013. (covers Greater London area)

Northern Arts Board, 10 Osborne Terrace, Newcastle-upon-Tyne NE2 1NZ tel 091 281 6334. (covers Cleveland, Cumbria, Durham, Northumberland, Tyne & Wear)

Arts Board North West, 4th Floor, 12 Harter Street, Manchester M1 6HY tel 061 228 3062. (covers Cheshire, Greater Manchester, Lancashire, Merseyside, and the High Peak area of Derbyshire)

Southern Arts Board, 13 St Clements Street, Winchester SO23 9UQ tel 0962 55099. (covers Berkshire, Buckinghamshire, Hampshire, Isle of Wight, Oxfordshire, Wiltshire and the Poole, Bournemouth and Christchurch areas of Dorset)

South East Arts Board, 10 Mount Ephraim, Tunbridge Wells TN4 8AS tel 0892 515210. (covers Kent, Surrey and Sussex, excluding Greater London Areas)

South West Arts Board, Bradninch Place, Gandy Street, Exeter EX4 3LS tel 0392 218188. (covers Avon, Cornwall, Devon and Dorset, except Bournemouth, Christchurch and Poole, Gloucestershire and Somerset)

West Midlands Arts Board, 82 Granville Street, Birmingham B1 2LH tel 021 631 3121. (covers Hereford &Worcester, Shropshire, Staffordshire, Warwickshire & West Midlands)

Yorkshire and Humberside Arts Board, Glyde House, Glydegate, Bradford BD5 0BQ tel 0274 723051. (covers Humberside and North, South and West Yorkshire)

Artsline, 5 Crowndale Road, London NW1 1TU tel 071 388 2227. Arts information & advice service for disabled people, London-based but able to signpost to further information nationally & internationally

Arts and Entertainment Training Council, 3 St Peter's Street, Leeds LS9 8AJ

National Association for Fine Art Education, Visual and Performing Arts, Newcastle upon Tyne Polytechnic, Squires Building, Sandyford Road, Newcastle NE1 8ST

Central Bureau for Educational Visits & Exchanges, Seymour Mews, London W1H 9PE tel 071 486 5101 oversee exchange programmes for higher education colleges.

DACS Design & Artists Copyright Society, St. Mary's Clergy House, 2 Whitechurch Lane, London E1 7QR 071-247-1650 have reciprocal and unilateral agreements worldwide ask for details.

LOCAL GOVERNMENT

Local Government International Office, 35 Great Smith Street, London SW1 – information on any local authority twinning initiative from city to parish councils. Local authority departments that could be useful for European links include arts, economic planning, publicity and tourism.

INTERNATIONAL ORGANISATIONS

International Association of Art, Maison de l'UNESCO, 1 rue Miollis, 75015 Paris, France tel 45682655

World Crafts Council, POB 2045. 1012 Copenhagen K, Denmark tel 461060

European Society of Culture, Dorsoduro 909 (Zattere ai Gesuati/Campo Sant'Agnese, 30123 Venice, Italy tel 5230210

Euroform (European Culture and Arts Exchange), Projekt fur Europaischen Kulturaustausch Kunstverein, Alt/Buch 64-66, 0-1115 Berlin, Germany tel 3497179. Aims to give 'impetus to international cultural actions in Europe'

SPECIALIST LIBRARIES

Foreign Office Library, telephone enquiries 071 270 3022 (personal visits by appointment only)

National Art Library, Victoria and Albert Museum, Cromwell Road, London SW7 2RL tel 071 938 8315

DTI Library and Information Centre, 123 Victoria St, London SW1E 6RB tel 071 215 4245

Contact your local central library for information on European resources in you area. You may find these in public, college and business libraries.

Further reading

BOOKS FROM AN PUBLICATIONS

AN Publications specialises in publishing and distributing practical information and advice for all working in the visual arts. Listed below are a selection of books which will be helpful for people thinking of travelling and working in Europe. All prices are inclusive of postage and are available by mail order from AN Publications, FREEPOST, PO Box 23, Sunderland SR1 1BR or by credit card on 091 514 3600. For a comprehensive listing of all our titles please see the order form at the end of this book.

Artists Newsletter, AN Publications, UK Subscription £15, Eire/Europe £22.50. Monthly magazine listing awards and opportunities in the UK and internationally for artists, craftspeople and photographers. Will include coverage of countries not dealt with in 'Across Europe'.

Directory of Exhibition Spaces (2nd edition), ed Susan Jones, AN Publications, £12.50 ISBN 0 90773 005 1; 3rd edition available October 1992, £13.99, ISBN 0 90773 017 5. Comprehensive listing of over 2000 galleries in the UK and Ireland.

Making Connections: the craftspersons guide to Europe, Judith Staines, South West Arts, £4.95 ISBN 0 95069 919 5. Award winning sourcebook for makers guiding you through the maze of 'Europaperwork'. Includes selective listings of contacts and organisations in 15 European countries and includes the World Crafts Council's Europe Directory.

Travellers Survival Kit – Europe, David Woodworth, Vacation Work, £7.95, ISBN 1 85458 033 7. Covers over 20 countries, detailed information on travel, language, money, law, insurance, communications, religion, people, health, accomodation etc.

Live and Work in France, Mark Hempshell, Vacation Work, £7.95, ISBN 1 85458 050 7. Substantial information on job hunting and employment, pus masses of invaluable background information.

Live and Work in Spain and Portugal, Vacation Work, Victoria Pybus & Rachael Robinson, £8.95, ISBN 1 85458 061 2

Live and Work in Italy, Vacation Work, Victoria Pybus & Rachael Robinson, £7.95, ISBN 1 85458 067 1

Europe: a manual, The Prince's Trust. Directory of European contacts in art, craft and design and other fields. Primarily for under 25s, but an excellent resource for all in the visual arts. £5.95

The Handbook of Grants, Museum Development Company, £16.45 ISBN 1 873114 00 1. Grants from public sources for visual arts organisations. Information on pupose of grant, special conditions, recent recipients.

The Arts Funding Guide, Directory of Social Change, £16.45 ISBN 0 907164 72 2. Practical advice and ideas on raising money from the Arts Council, RABs and othe bodies, plus details of local authority funding, grant making trusts and business sponsorship.

Craft Fairs, Kathryn Saloman, AN Publications, £1.85. Fact Pack with selected list and details of UK and international fairs.

Postgraduate Courses, Debbie Duffin, AN Publications, £1.85. Fact Pack listing with details courses in the UK.

Travelling, Selling & Working in the EC, Emma Lister, AN Publications, £1.85. Fact Pack with current regulations, sources of funding and lists of contacts.

Further reading

INFORMATION BOOKS

US Foundation Grants in Europe, ed Kerry Robinson, Directory of Social Change, £12.50 ISBN 0 907164 52 8. Details the grants policies of around 100 major US foundations which make substantial grants in Europe.

European Company Giving, ed Brian Dabson, Directory of Social Change, £12.50, ISBN 0 907164 74 9. Survey of the company giving practices in 11 of the 12 member states (excludes Luxembourg).

Grants from Europe, Ann Davison & Bill Seary, Bedford Square Press, £7.95, ISBN 0 71991 304 7. Lists grants from the EC, advice on raising money and influencing policy, practical tips for when visiting Brussels. Not an arts specific book.

European Tax and Giving, Directory of Social Change, £5.95, ISBN 0 907164 79 X. Details for each EC member state of tax relief on donations to non-profit bodies.

The Single Market, tel DTI Hotline 081 200 1992 for set of free publications offering advice on the single market. Includes "TheFacts' 'Guide to Sorces of Advice', 'Europe Open for Professionals',

The Guide to Art & Craft Workshops, ShawGuides, £12.95 ISBN 0 945834 11 X. Workshops, travel programmes, residencies and retreats throughout Europe and the rest of the world.

Who Does What in Europe, Rod Fisher, Arts Council of Great Britain, £7.50, 0 7287 0630 X. Gives information on the EC, Council of Europe, UNESCO, various foundations and other organisations.

Networking in Europe, Arts Council of Great Britain, £10. information and addresses on over 150 networks, institutionalised and informal in the cultural sector.

Briefing Notes on The Administration and Support of Culture in Europe, Arts Council of Great Britain, £5. Features 29 countries with summary of administrative structure, listings of organisations, basic cultural statistics and sources of further information.

Handbook for Plastic Arts, ed Raymonde Moulin, EC, ISBN 92 825 7107 6. Survey of EC members covering art markets, artists associations, legal issues, funding, taxation, exhibiting, contacts.

Help!? Guidelines on international youth exchanges, Youth Exchange Centre, £10. Practical information with discussion of overall aims of undertaking an international project.

Women in the Arts – Networking Internationally, Women in Arts & Women Artists Slide Library, £3. Information and articles on international travel, exchange and opportunities.

An Introductory Guide to Travel Opportunities for Black Arts Practitioners, Susan Okokon, Arts Council of Great Britain. Good list of funding opportunities internationally.

TRAVEL BOOKS

Art Guides, A&C Black. Guides to Paris, London, Glasgow, Amsterdam, Madrid and Berlin with information on galleries, art fairs, magazines, art schools, art materials suppliers, and general travel information on restaurants, cinemas, theatres, hotels etc.

Europe A Manual for Hitch-hikers, ed Simon Calder, Vacation Work, £3.95, ISBN 0 907638 28 7. Advice on fast, free travel in 30 countries. Includes maps of over 50 motorways showing the best place to stand and directions out of 135 towns and cities.

Guide books. Look for those with detailed information supplied and updated by people who have actually stayed in the hotels, eaten in the restaurants, used the buses etc. Good ones are Rough Guides (from Harrap Columbus), Fodors, Let's Go (from Harvard Student Agencies).

Paupers Paris, Miles Turner, Pan, £5.99, ISBN 0 330 32421 7. Lives up to its title with plenty of detail.

Researching European Opportunities

Find out for yourself at the new national centre for the crafts

Reference Library

Books, catalogues, directories and reference works on crafts in Europe and around the world

Information Services

Summaries of export bulletins; DTI information; facts and figures about sales and selling at home and abroad

Exhibitions

'The European Influence' - a survey of continental influences on British crafts over the last 100 years - 16 April - 14 June 1992

National Register of Makers

All those on the Register receive free copies of 'Makers News' which regularly includes details of opportunities and new facts about the European market

Crafts Council
44a Pentonville Road
Islington London N1 9BY
Telephone 071 278 7700
Fax 071 837 6891

Tuesday - Saturday 11 am - 6 pm
Sunday 2 pm - 6 pm
Monday closed

Other AN Publications

AN Publications is the only publisher to specialise in information for visual artists, photographers, time-based artists and craftspeople. So if you need to know:

> **what** awards, competitions and opportunities are in the offing
> **which** galleries are worth approaching to show your work
> **how** to make the most of your skills
> **who** supplies environmentally safe art materials
> **where** to find help, information and advice
> **when** to apply for grants

and any other practical information, we can help you through our directories, handbooks, fact packs and monthly magazine, *Artists Newsletter.*

Artists Newsletter	The essential monthly magazine packed with up-to-the-minute information on residencies, awards, commissions, jobs, competitions, etc. The visual artist's 'lifeline'.
Making Ways	*The visual artist's guide to surviving and thriving.* Written by artists for artists, with first-hand advice on all aspects 'business' practice. 368 pages.
Directory of Exhibition Spaces	A comprehensive listing of over 2000 exhibition spaces in the UK and Eire to help you find the ideal space for your work. 500 pages.
Residencies in Education:	*setting them up and making them work.* Explores the strengths and weaknesses of six residencies, to help you get the best out of placements of all kinds.124 pages.
Health & Safety:	*making art & avoiding dangers.* Advice on health and safety across all art and craft forms. Plus help on preparing COSHH assessments. 128 pages.
Money Matters:	*the artist's financial guide.* User-friendly advice on: tax, national insurance, keeping accounts, pricing work and much more. Features an accounting system devised for artists. 128 pages.
Copyright:	*protection, use & responsibilities.* Essential advice on negotiating copyright agreements, exploiting earning and promotional potential, and dealing with infringements. 128 pages.
Organising your Exhibition:	*the self-help guide.* Excellent advice on all aspects of organising exhibitions, from dealing with printers to buying wine. 128 pages.

AN Publications, PO Box 23, Sunderland SR4 6DG. Tel 091 567 3589. Fax 091 564 1600

Live Art	For everyone who wants to develop, earn from or promote live art. Gives practical advice as well as comments from and experiences of artists. 178 pages.
Independent Photography Directory	Listing of over 250 organisations involved with photography plus awards, fellowships, funding bodies, press lists, etc. 224 pages.
Code of Practice for Independent Photography	Guidelines for successful negotiations with advice on employment, copyright, exhibiting, commissions... plus sample fees and rates of pay. 32 pages.
FACT PACKS	Indispensible factsheets for artists, makers and administrators.
Rates of Pay	Information on current pay rates for artists.
Slide Indexes	Includes a national listing of artists' registers and slide indexes.
Mailing the Press	Includes a press list of national dailies, weeklies, and magazines.
Getting TV & Radio Coverage	Includes a contact list of TV and radio stations.
Craft Fairs	Includes a selected list of national and international fairs with details.
Insurance	Advice on types of insurance artists need and why.
Post-graduate Courses	A detailed listing of post-graduate courses in the UK.
Green Art Materials	A listing of 'green' art products and suppliers.
Clay	Ceramics materials and equipment, a comprehensive listing of suppliers and manufacturers in the UK.
Basic Survival Facts	Essential practical information for all new artists on getting started.
OTHER BOOKS	We also supply books produced by other publishers covering areas such as fundraising, crafts and illustration. Please ask for our brochure.

AN Publications, PO Box 23, Sunderland SR4 6DG. Tel 091 567 3589. Fax 091 564 1600

If you found this book useful...

...help us stay in touch with your needs and interests by filling in and returning this freepost form. Your opinions are important, and will help us to continue to publish the kinds of books you need, when you need them. To thank you for your help, we will send you a discount voucher for use when purchasing other books from AN Publications.

Title of book _____

Where did you buy it? _____

Why did you choose it?
- ☐ Best coverage of the subject
- ☐ Recognised the author
- ☐ Recognised the publisher
- ☐ The price was right
- ☐ Other (please specify)_____

Where did you hear about this book?
- ☐ Book review in _____
- ☐ Leaflet in _____
- ☐ Advertisement in_____
- ☐ Browsing in _____bookshop
- ☐ Personal recommendation
- ☐ Other (please specify)_____

Have you any comments on the content of this book?

_____
_____
_____
_____
_____

Thank you for taking the time to fill in this form. Where shall we send your discount voucher?

Name _____

Address _____

_____ Postcode _____

SEND TO: Lynn Evans
AN Publications, Freepost, PO Box 23, Sunderland SR1 1BR

Europe Update Sheet

The detail, accuracy and usefulness of AN Publications books and information depends on greatly on your help. If you have any information, advice or comments on working and travelling in any European country, eg accommodation, contacts, events, etc do share your experiences with us. Write your comments on this sheet or if you prefer on a separate paper and send this to the Freepost address (no stamp needed) to

'Europe'
AN Publications, Freepost, PO Box 23, Sunderland, England SR1 1BR

ORDER FORM

Only UK prices given, phone for overseas prices

	Qty	£
A Code of Practice for Independent Photography £3.25		
Copyright £7.25		
Directory of Exhibition Spaces £12.50		
Health & Safety £7.25		
Independent Photography Directory £5.00		
Organising Your Exhibition £7.25		
Live Art £9.95		
Making Ways £11.99		
Money Matters £7.25		
Residencies in Education £7.25		
Artists Newsletter £15.00 UK individual, £25.00 UK Institute Annual subscription beginning with _____ issue		
Fact Pack 1: Rates of Pay £1.50		
Fact Pack 2: Slide Indexes £1.50		
Fact Pack 3: Mailing the Press £1.50		
Fact Pack 4: Getting TV & Radio Coverage £1.50		
Fact Pack 5: Craft Fairs £1.50		
Fact Pack 6: Insurance £1.50		
Fact Pack 7: Post-graduate Courses £1.50		
Fact Pack 8: Green Art Materials £1.50		
Fact Pack 9: Ceramics Materials £1.50		
Basic Survival Facts £1.50		
TOTAL		

Name/Address

Name

Address

Postcode   Telephone

Payment by cheque/postal order

Send cheque/postal order made payable to AN Publications

Return to: AN Publications, FREEPOST, PO Box 23, Sunderland SR1 1BR

Payment by credit card   NB Visa/MasterCard only

Card number

Expiry date

Return to: AN Publications, FREEPOST, PO Box 23, Sunderland SR1 1BR

Telephone orders 091 514 3600 (Mon – Fri 9-5)

☐ Please send me a free sample issue of Artists Newsletter

AN Publications also distributes books for the visual arts produced by other publishers, ask for our full publication list.